CHRISTIANITY
&
LIBERALISM

LEGACY EDITION

J. GRESHAM MACHEN

Includes New Essays by the Faculty of
Westminster Theological Seminary

WESTMINSTER
SEMINARY PRESS
Philadelphia, Pennsylvania

To My Mother

Contents

Christianity and Liberalism

The Legacy of Christianity and Liberalism: Essays by the Faculty of Westminster Theological Seminary

Foreword

A fitting way for Westminster Theological Seminary to celebrate our 90th anniversary is to hark back to the work that firmly placed our founder, and former Princeton Theological Seminary professor, J. Gresham Machen, on the turbulent path to becoming the leading biblically minded reformer of the liberalizing Presbyterian church in the early twentieth century.

Machen's rigorous thinking, lucid communication, and trenchant criticism of liberalism endow his work with timeless character. Indeed, *Christianity and Liberalism* has become the seminal work that distinguishes historic Christianity from the subtly but utterly distinct and divergent theology of the modernizing church. For Machen, although Christianity and liberalism sounded much alike, they were, in essence, two different religions. The first was the revealed religion of the Lord Jesus Christ; the second was a manmade reconstruction of the former that intended to make that religion palatable to minds that had imbibed the tenets of autonomous reason trumpeted by post-Enlightenment theologians. The steps from the appearance of Machen's groundbreaking work to the birth of Westminster Theological Seminary in Philadelphia can be traced with unbroken historical clarity.

As this new edition of Machen's revolutionary work appears, a word of explanation may be appropriate. After all, the volume has remained in print longer than most books of its vintage, and new translations continue to appear abroad. There are three primary reasons that Westminster has chosen to issue this new publication: (1) a new milestone; (2) a declaration of theological fidelity; (3) a unanimous theological consensus from faculty members.

This new publication by Westminster faculty marks both the milestone of our 90th anniversary and the fact that, as of 2019, Machen's classic work is now in the public domain and no longer protected by copyright. It is fitting to celebrate this second milestone and the volume's new, unfettered stage with the anticipation that it will continue to offer its clarion witness to the historic truths of biblical Christianity.

The faculty reissues this book with a desire to do more than honor Machen in the 90th year of the seminary that he launched. The members of the Westminster faculty are keenly aware that the seminary was named for the Presbyterian Confession that most celebrates the inspiration and truthfulness of Holy Scripture. Indeed, the Confession begins by affirming that the Scriptures are the only sure foundation for theological truth. Thus we intend, by the new release of *Christianity and Liberalism*, to communicate collectively the vital significance that this work, as well as the Confession of Faith, has on our ministries and academic endeavors. We are proclaiming again Machen's vision to establish a seminary with a faculty that consciously subscribe *ex animo* to the Confession, with a full commitment to the "whole counsel of God." What Machen passionately pursued—namely, to bring a full, biblical reformation to the theology of the church— is what our faculty strive to do today. With this founding vision in mind—through rigorous, pastoral instruction based upon the inspired, infallible, and inerrant Word of God—the faculty daily train the next generations of leaders for Christ's global church.

The essays included here, one contributed by each member of the full-time faculty, reveal that Machen's visionary theological commitments remain a shared and unanimous concern among our faculty. We believe this is critical to communicate openly and broadly, given the substantial theological testing the seminary experienced and addressed in the not-too-distant past. The unity of the Westminster faculty in its commitment to biblical theology and to the clarity, certainty, and authority of the Word of God, is herein unmistakably heralded by an integrated witness to Scripture in the tradition of Machen.

Please welcome the publication of these new essays along with this historic and magisterial work. We encourage you to share this new edition with many. In so doing, you join us in fulfilling the founding vision of Westminster, for Westminster exists for nothing less than to train specialists in the Bible to proclaim the whole counsel of God for Christ and his global church. Could there be any greater mission for a seminary today or in the coming generations until the King of glory returns?

Sincerely on behalf of the faculty,
Dr. Peter A. Lillback, President
January 3, 2019

Introduction to the Legacy Edition

The Theological Leadership of J. Gresham Machen

David B. Garner

For I delivered to you as of first importance what I also received: that Christ died for our sins in accordance with the Scriptures, that he was buried, that he was raised on the third day in accordance with the Scriptures, (1 Cor. 15:3–4)

But even if we or an angel from heaven should preach to you a gospel contrary to the one we preached to you, let him be accursed. As we have said before, so now I say again: If anyone is preaching to you a gospel contrary to the one you received, let him be accursed. (Gal. 1:8–9)

Those who lead well discern precisely, believe passionately, and communicate clearly. Though leadership traits are shared across various spheres, some orbits of leadership matter more than others. Abraham Lincoln surely deserves greater admiration than Tom Brady. Yet, as transforming as Lincoln's leadership was, his political impact pales in significance when compared to effective leadership in the church of Jesus Christ. Such leadership impacts things ultimate and eternal.

Gospel truth well-spoken delivers the words of life. Hearers reckon with eternal life and death *literally.* So then, 20/20 spiritual vision, cloudless theological conviction, and compelling communication bear ultimate *gravitas* for the souls of mankind. To be sure, the founder of Westminster Theological Seminary and the author of *Christianity and Liberalism* bore these leadership marks, even as he grasped the soul-stakes of biblical truth.

In the early years of the twentieth century, J. Gresham Machen and a group of other luminaries at Princeton Theological Seminary perceived that their seminary's glory had departed. Belief in biblical truth and in the glorious gospel of Jesus Christ were in serious peril. Forced out by the tyranny within that institution, they took a great risk. They left pay, pensions, and prestige at Princeton to launch a new seminary built upon the sure and unchanging foundation of Scripture's supreme authority. Following Machen's lead, this small group of biblical scholars founded Westminster Theological Seminary in the fall of 1929.

Understanding the times and the stakes, Machen stood up and spoke resolutely. When Machen rang the bell for the start of the seminary's inaugural classes at the first convocation on September 25, 1929, he sounded an alarm as well:

Our new institution is devoted to an unpopular cause; it is devoted to the service of One who is despised and rejected by the world and increasingly belittled by the visible church, the majestic Lord and Savior who is presented to us in the Word of God. From him men are turning away one by one. His sayings are too hard, his deeds of power too strange, his atoning death too great an offense to human pride. But to him, despite all, we hold.[1]

Relinquishing comforts and sureties of this world for themselves and their families, Machen and his cohorts marched forward with conviction while they humbly held fast to the Christ of Scripture.

Just nine months earlier, Machen, already a proven Princeton New Testament scholar, articulately addressed the board of directors at that esteemed seminary. Having served in his professorship for thirteen years (appointed in May 1915), Machen read the board of directors' plan of December 13, 1928, with a heavy heart. He could not ignore the forces of unbelief sucking the soul out of Princeton orthodoxy. Like any good leader, Machen saw the need for bold and open action, and he took it. He reflected carefully for two weeks on the matter and penned a respectful yet unambiguous letter to the board of directors, saying, "I cannot do what seems to me to be contrary to the cause of truth."[2] Machen could not sit idly. A gospel leader never saunters past theological problems.

The kind of courage it took to launch the new seminary was becoming a pattern in this young leader. Six years earlier, when the winds of Harry Emerson Fosdick's famed sermon, "Shall the Fundamentalists Win?," whipped across the American ecclesial landscape, Machen penned his classic, lucid expression of the Christian faith: *Christianity and Liberalism*. In it, he delivered

---

1. J. Gresham Machen, "Inaugural Lecture," Westminster Theological Seminary, 1929.

2. Letter from J. Gresham Machen to the Princeton Theological Seminary board of directors, December 27, 1928. Princeton Theological Seminary Archives (accessed September 24, 2018).

a decisive blow and a stern warning: "Shall we accept the Jesus of the New Testament as our Saviour, or shall we reject Him with the liberal Church?"[3] Machen's question was provocative and perceptive. Liberalism, he contended, offered no alternative version of Christianity but a religion of an entirely different species. "The plain fact is that liberalism, whether it be true or false, is no mere 'heresy'—no mere divergence at isolated points from Christian teaching. On the contrary it proceeds from a totally different root, and it constitutes, in essentials, a unitary system of its own."[4] Liberal "Christianity" was not Christianity at all.

All around him, Machen witnessed the deterioration of orthodox Christian theology. Liberal forces had imposed elastic redefinitions and stretched the sacred faith beyond its breaking point. Yet here was the rub: Liberalism was (and is) attractive. It appeared friendly because it refused narrowness. It brought compelling breadth to combat ostensibly unfriendly and bigoted Christian theology. It brought desirable warmth to combat allegedly cold Christian dogma. It offered a plausible platform, complete with a universalist parachute to provide a soft spiritual landing for all men everywhere.

Machen was no stranger to the potent magnetism of liberalism's version of love. Once tempted by the plausible arguments (Col. 2:4) of liberal scholarship, Machen himself had tasted unbelief. For a season, he flirted with its compelling compromises, yet by the grace of God, he resisted its inebriating effects, discerning that any attempted *synthesis* of liberalism with Christian orthodoxy remained pure liberalism. Liberal leaven spoiled

---

3. Page 113 of this present volume.
4. Pages 176–77 of this present volume.

the whole loaf. To abandon biblical authority was to dive into a stewpot that cooks out the life-giving and life-transforming power of the gospel.

Having escaped the alluring cauldron, Machen was never the same. He could not help but speak; he could not help but lead. He proclaimed the pure, biblical gospel of Christ Jesus—in its exclusivity and theological brilliance—as that which alone changes lives. Indeed, it changed his. Armed with a clear vision of gospel power and a conviction of the anemic effects of liberalism, Machen went into the trenches of theological warfare clutching an uncompromising claim: Liberalism's changing theology changes no one. Scripture's unchanging theology, in stark contrast, changes lives eternally.

To counter liberalism's attractiveness and seeming plausibility, Machen offered an unvarnished rendering of its desperate and dark soul: "Modern liberalism, placing Jesus alongside other benefactors of mankind, is perfectly inoffensive in the modern world. All men speak well of it. It is entirely inoffensive. But it is also entirely futile. The offence of the Cross is done away, but so is the glory and the power."[5] However compelling and attractive it might be, liberalism is un-Christian. As such, it is powerless. In fact, it is anti-Christian and intrinsically damning.

No wonder the book created—and continues to create— such a stir! Such spiritually discerning leadership jolts people from their sleepy delusions. It warns of flimsy scaffolding and broken foundations. It boldly tells the man in his burning mansion that he will die if he does not depart. It denies a soft spiritual landing for all men everywhere. Theological leaders tell the

---

5. Page 128 of this present volume.

truth—they advance the gospel of Jesus Christ and the authority of God's Word, they combat every gospel nemesis.

To the contention that Christianity is not about doctrine but about life, Machen exposed the doctrinal foundation beneath Christian morality. "The Christian movement at its inception was not just a way of life in the modern sense, but a way of life founded upon a message. It was based, not upon mere feeling, not upon a mere program of work, but upon an account of facts. In other words it was based upon doctrine."[6] To the contention that Christianity is about love, not dogma, Machen similarly exposed a blinding fallacy. "Human affection, apparently so simple, is really just bristling with dogma."[7] To the contention that Jesus was merely an ethical leader, Machen evidenced not an ounce of theological *or evangelical* sympathy: "Let us not deceive ourselves. A Jewish teacher of the first century can never satisfy the longing of our souls. Clothe Him with all the art of modern research, throw upon Him the warm, deceptive calcium-light of modern sentimentality; and despite it all common sense will come to its rights again, and for our brief hour of self-deception—as though we had been with Jesus—will wreak havoc upon us the revenge of hopeless disillusionment."[8]

In *Christianity and Liberalism*, Machen leads. And for that leadership, the warring Machen endured much criticism in his life. Such denunciation has not ceased with his death. But his undaunted leadership prevails, because his words continue to expose and to address the *gravitas* of divine grace. Machen's voice

---

6. Page 21 of this present volume.
7. Page 55–56 of this present volume.
8. Page 41 of this present volume.

still speaks clearly of what really matters. His concern remains as much missional as it is theological: "If we really love our fellowmen we shall never be content with binding up their wounds or pouring on oil and wine or rendering them any such lesser service. We shall indeed do such things for them. But the main business of our lives will be to bring them to the Saviour of their souls."[9]

Machen's 20/20 vision, undaunted conviction, and verbal precision deliver clarity concerning truth and error, life and death, freedom and bondage. Truth, life, and freedom come *only in the gospel of Jesus Christ,* the historic Son of God, born, crucified, and raised from the dead according to the Scriptures (1 Cor. 15:1–3). Liberalism's flawed recipe concocts the sure formula for spiritual incarceration and eternal death. "Emancipation from the blessed will of God always involves bondage to some worse taskmaster."[10]

Christianity and Liberalism is, among other things, a leadership book. It leads us to see the Christian faith in its exclusive, life-giving, freedom-granting beauty. Machen profiles the gospel in its historical and redemptive contours, its doctrinal and ethical truth, and its power and warmth. He exposes the errors and consequences of unbelief and urges us to trust completely in the Word of God. *Christianity and Liberalism* will not tolerate reading for amusement or mere intellectual interest. Machen's words lead us, and those words expect—no, *demand*—a response. You will either follow Machen or you will fight him, but *Christianity and Liberalism* eliminates spiritual no-man's land. You must either embrace his thesis or reject it; you cannot merely dismiss it.

---

9. Page 162 of this present volume.
10. Page 149 of this present volume.

REV. DR. DAVID B. GARNER (PhD, Westminster Theological Seminary) is vice president of advancement and associate professor of systematic theology at Westminster Theological Seminary. An ordained teaching elder in the PCA, Dr. Garner previously served as pastor of teaching at Proclamation Presbyterian Church in Bryn Mawr, PA, and as a missionary to Bulgaria. He is the author of *Sons in the Son: The Riches and Reach of Adoption in Christ*.

Acknowledgments

This commemorative edition would not have been possible without the generous cooperation of so many in the Westminster Theological Seminary community. President Peter Lillback, whose excitement at seeing *Christianity and Liberalism* enter the public domain was matched only by his determination to ensure our seminary's continued association with the book, is owed a debt of gratitude for his leadership and vision. Special thanks go to Josh Currie of Westminster Seminary Press for guiding this project, and ensuring every detail enjoyed his meticulous care. Though he had many scattered sheep to gather, his skill in shepherding this volume to publication was coupled with commendable perseverance and patience.

Thanks are due to Pierce T. Hibbs and Rachel Stout for their competent editorial work. I am also grateful to Josh Brownfield, for culling the Westminster Theological Seminary and Orthodox Presbyterian Church archives for photographs, and to Michael Hunter, for his many hours correcting the index. Tom DeVries and the team at Eerdmans Publishing have kept this book in print for many years, and we are deeply appreciative of their permission to base the current typesetting on Eerdman's own 2009 edition.

For their varied and valuable contributions in seeing this edition through to publication, thanks go to James Baird, Lucy Baird, Jean Baker, Jennifer Chun, Alyssa Curtis, Ben Dahlvang, John Kim, Victor Kim, Hukmin Kwon, Chun Lai, Nate Morgan

Locke, Angie Messinger, Sheldon Nordhues, Danny Olinger, Josiah Pettit, and Jim Sweet. Jim Sweet deserves special note, as his vision for the publication of this current volume spans more than a decade.

Finally, let me express my gratitude to each of my colleagues who devoted precious time and energy to craft their essays for this special volume. The Westminster Theological Seminary faculty's shared appreciation for our theological legacy and our common commitment to perpetuate that legacy—to proclaim the whole counsel of God for Christ and his global church—give testimony to God's ongoing kindness upon our 90-year old institution. Through these essays and the republication of Machen's *Christianity and Liberalism*, we seek to extol Jesus Christ and to advance his pure and glorious gospel, as revealed in the Holy Scriptures. For the gift of common convictions and for God's grace in granting my colleagues skill to handle his Word so capably yet humbly, I give thanks to our Lord Jesus Christ. *Soli Deo Gloria.*

David B. Garner, Editor
February 4, 2019

Preface

On November 3, 1921, the author of the present book delivered before the Ruling Elders' Association of Chester Presbytery an address which was subsequently published in *The Princeton Theological Review*, vol. xx, 1922, pp. 93-117, under the title "Liberalism or Christianity." The interest with which the published address was received has encouraged the author to undertake a more extensive presentation of the same subject. By courtesy of *The Princeton Theological Review*, free use has been made of the address, which may be regarded as the nucleus of the present book. Grateful acknowledgment is also due to the editor of *The Presbyterian* for kind permission to use various brief articles which were published in that journal. The principal divisions of the subject were originally suggested to the author by a conversation which he held in 1921 with the Rev. Paul Martin of Princeton, who has not, however, been consulted as to the method of treatment.

1

Introduction

The purpose of this book is not to decide the religious issue of the present day, but merely to present the issue as sharply and clearly as possible, in order that the reader may be aided in deciding it for himself. Presenting an issue sharply is indeed by no means a popular business at the present time; there are many who prefer to fight their intellectual battles in what Dr. Francis L. Patton has aptly called a "condition of low visibility."[1] Clear-cut definition of terms in religious matters, bold facing of the logical implications of religious views, is by many persons regarded as an impious proceeding. May it not discourage contribution to mission boards? May it not hinder the progress of consolidation, and produce a poor showing in columns of Church statistics? But with such persons we cannot possibly bring ourselves to agree. Light may seem at times to be an impertinent intruder, but it is always beneficial in the end. The type of religion which rejoices in the pious sound of traditional phrases, regardless of their meanings, or shrinks from "controversial" matters, will never stand amid the shocks of life. In the sphere of religion, as in other spheres, the things about which men are agreed are apt to be the things that are least worth holding; the really important things are the things about which men will fight.

---

1. Francis L. Patton, in the introduction to William Hallock Johnson, *The Christian Faith Under Modern Searchlights*, [1916], p. 7.

In the sphere of religion, in particular, the present time is a time of conflict; the great redemptive religion which has always been known as Christianity is battling against a totally diverse type of religious belief, which is only the more destructive of the Christian faith because it makes use of traditional Christian terminology. This modern non-redemptive religion is called "modernism" or "liberalism." Both names are unsatisfactory; the latter, in particular, is question-begging. The movement designated as "liberalism" is regarded as "liberal" only by its friends; to its opponents it seems to involve a narrow ignoring of many relevant facts. And indeed the movement is so various in its manifestations that one may almost despair of finding any common name which will apply to all its forms. But manifold as are the forms in which the movement appears, the root of the movement is one; the many varieties of modern liberal religion are rooted in naturalism—that is, in the denial of any entrance of the creative power of God (as distinguished from the ordinary course of nature) in connection with the origin of Christianity. The word "naturalism" is here used in a sense somewhat different from its philosophical meaning. In this non-philosophical sense it describes with fair accuracy the real root of what is called, by what may turn out to be a degradation of an originally noble word, "liberal" religion.

The rise of this modern naturalistic liberalism has not come by chance, but has been occasioned by important changes which have recently taken place in the conditions of life. The past one hundred years have witnessed the beginning of a new era in human history, which may conceivably be regretted, but certainly cannot be ignored, by the most obstinate conservatism. The change is not something that lies beneath the surface and might be visible only to the discerning eye; on the contrary it forces itself upon the attention of the plain man at a hundred points. Modern inventions and the industrialism that has been built upon them have given us in many respects a new world to live in; we can no more remove ourselves from that world than we can escape from the atmosphere that we breathe.

But such changes in the material conditions of life do not stand alone; they have been produced by mighty changes in the human mind, as in their turn they themselves give rise to further spiritual changes. The industrial world of to-day has been produced not by blind forces of nature but by the conscious activity of the human spirit; it has been produced by the achievements of science. The outstanding feature of recent history is an enormous widening of human knowledge, which has gone hand in hand with such perfecting of the instrument of investigation that scarcely any limits can be assigned to future progress in the material realm.

The application of modern scientific methods is almost as broad as the universe in which we live. Though the most palpable achievements are in the sphere of physics and chemistry, the sphere of human life cannot be isolated from the rest, and with the other sciences there has appeared, for example, a modern science of history, which, with psychology and sociology and the like, claims, even if it does not deserve, full equality with its sister sciences. No department of knowledge can maintain its isolation from the modern lust of scientific conquest; treaties of inviolability, though hallowed by all the sanctions of age-long tradition, are being flung ruthlessly to the winds.

In such an age, it is obvious that every inheritance from the past must be subject to searching criticism; and as a matter of fact some convictions of the human race have crumbled to pieces in the test. Indeed, dependence of any institution upon the past is now sometimes even regarded as furnishing a presumption, not in favor of it, but against it. So many convictions have had to be abandoned that men have sometimes come to believe that all convictions must go.

If such an attitude be justifiable, then no institution is faced by a stronger hostile presumption than the institution of the Christian religion, for no institution has based itself more squarely upon the authority of a by-gone age. We are not now inquiring whether such policy is wise or historically justifiable; in any case the fact itself is plain, that Christianity during many centuries has consistently appealed for the truth of its claims, not merely and not even primarily to current experience, but to certain ancient books the most recent of which was written some nineteen hundred years ago. It is no wonder that that appeal is being criticized to-day; for the writers of the books in question were no doubt men of their own age, whose outlook upon the material world, judged by modern standards, must have been of the crudest and most elementary kind. Inevitably the question arises whether the opinions of such men can ever be normative for men of the present day; in other words, whether first-century religion can ever stand in company with twentieth-century science.

However the question may be answered, it presents a serious problem to the modern Church. Attempts are indeed sometimes made to make the answer easier than at first sight it appears to be. Religion, it is said, is so entirely separate from science, that the two, rightly defined, cannot possibly come into conflict. This attempt at separation, as it is hoped the following pages may show, is open to objections of the most serious kind. But what must now be observed is that even if the separation is justifiable it cannot be effected without effort; the removal of the problem of religion and science itself constitutes a problem. For, rightly or wrongly, religion during the centuries has as a matter of fact connected itself with a host of convictions, especially in the sphere of history, which may form the subject of scientific investigation; just as scientific investigators, on the other hand, have sometimes attached themselves, again rightly or wrongly, to conclusions which impinge upon the innermost domain of philosophy and of religion. For example, if any simple Christian of one hundred years ago, or even of to-day, were asked what would become of his religion if history should prove indubitably that no man called Jesus ever lived and died in the first century of our era, he would undoubtedly answer that his religion would fall away. Yet the investigation of events in the first century in Judæa, just as much as in Italy or in Greece, belongs to the sphere of scientific history. In other words, our simple Christian, whether rightly or wrongly, whether wisely or unwisely, has as a matter of fact connected his religion, in a way that to him seems indissoluble, with convictions about which science also has a right to speak. If, then, those convictions, ostensibly religious, which belong to the sphere of science, are not really religious at all, the demonstration of that fact is itself no trifling task. Even if the problem of science and religion reduces itself to the problem of disentangling religion from pseudo-scientific accretions, the seriousness of the problem is not thereby diminished. From every point of view, therefore, the problem in question is the most serious concern of the Church. What is the relation between Christianity and modern culture; may Christianity be maintained in a scientific age?

It is this problem which modern liberalism attempts to solve. Admitting that scientific objections may arise against the particularities of the Christian religion—against the Christian doctrines of the person of Christ, and of redemption through His death and resurrection—the liberal theologian seeks to rescue certain of the general principles of religion, of which these particularities are thought to be mere temporary symbols, and these general principles he regards as constituting "the essence of Christianity."

It may well be questioned, however, whether this method of defence will really prove to be efficacious; for after the apologist has abandoned his outer defences to the enemy and withdrawn into some inner citadel, he will probably discover that the enemy pursues him even there. Modern materialism, especially in the realm of psychology, is not content with occupying the lower quarters of the Christian city, but pushes its way into all the higher reaches of life; it is just as much opposed to the philosophical idealism of the liberal preacher as to the Biblical doctrines that the liberal preacher has abandoned in the interests of peace. Mere concessiveness, therefore, will never succeed in avoiding the intellectual conflict. In the intellectual battle of the present day there can be no "peace without victory"; one side or the other must win.

As a matter of fact, however, it may appear that the figure which has just been used is altogether misleading; it may appear that what the liberal theologian has retained after abandoning to the enemy one Christian doctrine after another is not Christianity at all, but a religion which is so entirely different from Christianity as to belong in a distinct category. It may appear further that the fears of the modern man as to Christianity were entirely ungrounded, and that in abandoning the embattled walls of the city of God he has fled in needless panic into the open plains of a vague natural religion only to fall an easy victim to the enemy who ever lies in ambush there.

Two lines of criticism, then, are possible with respect to the liberal attempt at reconciling science and Christianity. Modern liberalism may be criticized (1) on the ground that it is un-Christian and (2) on the ground that it is unscientific. We shall concern ourselves here chiefly with the former line of criticism; we shall be interested in showing that despite the liberal use of traditional phraseology modern liberalism not only is a different religion from Christianity but belongs in a totally different class of religions. But in showing that the liberal attempt at rescuing Christianity is false we are not showing that there is no way of rescuing Christianity at all; on the contrary, it may appear incidentally, even in the present little book, that it is not the Christianity of the New Testament which is in conflict with science, but the supposed Christianity of the modern liberal Church, and that the real city of God, and that city alone, has defences which are capable of warding off the assaults of modern unbelief. However, our immediate concern is with the other side of the problem; our principal concern just now is to show that the liberal attempt at reconciling Christianity with modern science has really relinquished everything distinctive of Christianity, so that what remains is in essentials only that same indefinite type of religious aspiration which was in the world before Christianity came upon the scene. In trying to remove from Christianity everything that could possibly be objected to in the name of science, in trying to bribe off the enemy by those concessions which the enemy most desires, the apologist has really abandoned what he started out to defend. Here as in many other departments of life it appears that the things that are sometimes thought to be hardest to defend are also the things that are most worth defending.

In maintaining that liberalism in the modern Church represents a return to an un-Christian and sub-Christian form of the religious life, we are particularly anxious not to be misunderstood. "Un-Christian" in such a connection is sometimes taken as a term of opprobrium. We do not mean it at all as such. Socrates was not a Christian, neither was Goethe; yet we share to the full the respect with which their names are regarded. They tower immeasurably above the common run of men; if he that is least in the Kingdom of Heaven is greater than they, he is certainly greater not by any inherent superiority, but by virtue of an undeserved privilege which ought to make him humble rather than contemptuous.

Such considerations, however, should not be allowed to obscure the vital importance of the question at issue. If a condition could be conceived in which all the preaching of the Church should be controlled by the liberalism which in many quarters has already become preponderant, then, we believe, Christianity would at last have perished from the earth and the gospel would have sounded forth for the last time. If so, it follows that the inquiry with which we are now concerned is immeasurably the most important of all those with which the Church has to deal. Vastly more important than all questions with regard to methods of preaching is the root question as to what it is that shall be preached.

Many, no doubt, will turn in impatience from the inquiry— all those, namely, who have settled the question in such a way that they cannot even conceive of its being reopened. Such, for example, are the pietists, of whom there are still many. "What," they say, "is the need of argument in defence of the Bible? Is it not the Word of God, and does it not carry with it an immediate certitude of its truth which could only be obscured by defence? If science comes into contradiction with the Bible so much the worse for science!" For these persons we have the highest respect, for we believe that they are right in the main point; they have arrived by a direct and easy road at a conviction which for other men is attained only through intellectual struggle. But we cannot reasonably expect them to be interested in what we have to say.

Another class of uninterested persons is much more numerous. It consists of those who have definitely settled the question in the opposite way. By them this little book, if it ever comes into their hands, will soon be flung aside as only another attempt at defence of a position already hopelessly lost. There are still individuals, they will say, who believe that the earth is flat; there are also individuals who defend the Christianity of the Church, miracles and atonement and all. In either case, it will be said, the phenomenon is interesting as a curious example of arrested development, but it is nothing more.

Such a closing of the question, however, whether it approve itself finally or no, is in its present form based upon a very imperfect view of the situation; it is based upon a grossly exaggerated estimate of the achievements of modern science. Scientific investigation, as has already been observed, has certainly accomplished much; it has in many respects produced a new world. But there is another aspect of the picture which should not be ignored. The modern world represents in some respects an enormous improvement over the world in which our ancestors lived; but in other respects it exhibits a lamentable decline. The improvement appears in the physical conditions of life, but in the spiritual realm there is a corresponding loss. The loss is clearest, perhaps, in the realm of art. Despite the mighty revolution which has been produced in the external conditions of life, no great poet is now living to celebrate the change; humanity has suddenly become dumb. Gone, too, are the great painters and the great musicians and the great sculptors. The art that still subsists is largely imitative, and where it is not imitative it is usually bizarre. Even the appreciation of the glories of the past is gradually being lost, under the influence of a utilitarian education that concerns itself only with the production of physical well-being. The "Outline of History" of Mr. H. G. Wells, with its contemptuous neglect of all the higher ranges of human life, is a thoroughly modern book.

This unprecedented decline in literature and art is only one manifestation of a more far-reaching phenomenon; it is only one instance of that narrowing of the range of personality which has been going on in the modern world. The whole development of modern society has tended mightily toward the limitation of the realm of freedom for the individual man. The tendency is most clearly seen in socialism; a socialistic state would mean the reduction to a minimum of the sphere of individual choice. Labor and recreation, under a socialistic government, would both be prescribed, and individual liberty would be gone. But the same tendency exhibits itself to-day even in those communities where the name of socialism is most abhorred. When once the majority has determined that a certain régime is beneficial, that régime without further hesitation is forced ruthlessly upon the individual man. It never seems to occur to modern legislatures that although "welfare" is good, forced welfare may be bad. In other words, utilitarianism is being carried out to its logical conclusions; in the interests of physical well-being the great principles of liberty are being thrown ruthlessly to the winds.

The result is an unparalleled impoverishment of human life. Personality can only be developed in the realm of individual choice. And that realm, in the modern state, is being slowly but steadily contracted. The tendency is making itself felt especially in the sphere of education. The object of education, it is now assumed, is the production of the greatest happiness for the greatest number. But the greatest happiness for the greatest number, it is assumed further, can be defined only by the will of the majority. Idiosyncrasies in education, therefore, it is said, must be avoided, and the choice of schools must be taken away from the individual parent and placed in the hands of the state. The state then exercises its authority through the instruments that are ready to hand, and at once, therefore, the child is placed under the control of psychological experts, themselves without the slightest acquaintance with the higher realms of human life, who proceed to prevent any such acquaintance being gained by those who come under their care. Such a result is being slightly delayed in America by the remnants of Anglo-Saxon individualism, but the signs of the times are all contrary to the maintenance of this half-way position; liberty is certainly held by but a precarious tenure when once its underlying principles have been lost. For a time it looked as though the utilitarianism which came into vogue in the middle of the nineteenth century would be a purely academic matter, without influence upon daily life. But such appearances have proved to be deceptive. The dominant tendency, even in a country like America, which formerly prided itself on its freedom from bureaucratic regulation of the details of life, is toward a drab utilitarianism in which all higher aspirations are to be lost.

Manifestations of such a tendency can easily be seen. In the state of Nebraska, for example, a law is now in force according to which no instruction in any school in the state, public or private, is to be given through the medium of a language other than English, and no language other than English is to be studied even as a language until the child has passed an examination before the county superintendent of education showing that the eighth grade has been passed.[2] In other words, no foreign language, apparently not even Latin or Greek, is to be studied until the child is too old to learn it well. It is in this way that modern collectivism deals with a kind of study which is absolutely essential to all genuine mental advance. The minds of the people of Nebraska, and of any other states where similar laws prevail,[3] are to be kept by the power of the state in a permanent condition of arrested development.

It might seem as though with such laws obscurantism had reached its lowest possible depths. But there are depths lower still. In the state of Oregon, on Election Day, 1922, a law was passed by a referendum vote in accordance with which all children in the state are required to attend the public schools. Christian schools and private schools, at least in the all-important lower grades, are thus wiped out of existence. Such laws, which if the present temper of the people prevails will probably soon be extended far beyond the bounds of one state,[4] mean of course the ultimate destruction of all real education. When one considers what the public schools of America in many places already

2. See *Laws, Resolutions* and *Memorials* passed by the Legislature of the State of Nebraska at the Thirty-Seventh Session, 1919, Chapter 249, p. 1019.

3. Compare, for example, *Legislative Acts* of the General Assembly of Ohio, Vol. cviii, 1919, pp. 614f.; and *Acts and Joint Resolutions* of the General Assembly of Iowa, 1919, Chapter 198, p. 219.

4. In Michigan, a bill similar to the one now passed in Oregon recently received an enormous vote at a referendum, and an agitation looking at least in the same general direction is said to be continuing.

are—their materialism, their discouragement of any sustained intellectual effort, their encouragement of the dangerous pseudo-scientific fads of experimental psychology—one can only be appalled by the thought of a commonwealth in which there is no escape from such a soul-killing system. But the principle of such laws and their ultimate tendency are far worse than the immediate results.[5] A public-school system, in itself, is indeed

---

5. The evil principle is seen with special clearness in the so-called "Lusk Laws" in the state of New York. One of these refers to teachers in the public schools. The other provides that "No person, firm, corporation or society shall conduct, maintain or operate any school, institute, class or course of instruction in any subjects whatever without making application for and being granted a license from the university of the state of New York to so conduct, maintain or operate such institute, school, class or course." It is further provided that "A school, institute, class or course licensed as provided in this section shall be subject to visitation by officers and employees of the university of the state of New York." See *Laws of the State of New York*, 1921, Vol. III, Chapter 667, pp. 2049–2051. This law is so broadly worded that it could not possibly be enforced, even by the whole German army in its pre-war efficiency or by all the espionage system of the Czar. The exact measure of enforcement is left to the discretion of officials, and the citizens are placed in constant danger of that intolerable interference with private life which a real enforcement of the provision about "courses of instruction in any subjects whatever" would mean. One of the exemptions is in principle particularly bad. "Nor shall such license be required," the law provides, "by schools now or hereafter established and maintained by a religious denomination or sect well recognized as such at the time this section takes effect." One can certainly rejoice that the existing churches are freed, for the time being, from the menace involved in the law. But in principle the limitation of the exemption to the existing churches really runs counter to the fundamental idea of religious liberty; for it sets up a distinction between established religions and those that are not established. There was always tolerance for established religious bodies, even in the Roman Empire; but religious liberty consists in equal rights for religious bodies that are new. The other exemptions do not remove in the slightest the oppressive character of the law. Bad as the law must be in its immediate effects, it is far more alarming in what it reveals about the temper of the people. A people which tolerates such preposterous legislation upon the statute books is a people that has wandered far away from the principles of American liberty. True patriotism will not conceal the menace, but will rather seek to recall the citizens to those great principles for which our fathers, in America and in England, were willing to bleed and die. There are some encouraging indications that the Lusk Laws may soon be repealed. If they are repealed, they will still serve as a warning that only by constant watchfulness can liberty be preserved.

of enormous benefit to the race. But it is of benefit only if it is kept healthy at every moment by the absolutely free possibility of the competition of private schools. A public-school system, if it means the providing of free education for those who desire it, is a noteworthy and beneficent achievement of modern times; but when once it becomes monopolistic it is the most perfect instrument of tyranny which has yet been devised. Freedom of thought in the middle ages was combated by the Inquisition, but the modern method is far more effective. Place the lives of children in their formative years, despite the convictions of their parents, under the intimate control of experts appointed by the state, force them then to attend schools where the higher aspirations of humanity are crushed out, and where the mind is filled with the materialism of the day, and it is difficult to see how even the remnants of liberty can subsist. Such a tyranny, supported as it is by a perverse technique used as the instrument in destroying human souls, is certainly far more dangerous than the crude tyrannies of the past, which despite their weapons of fire and sword permitted thought at least to be free.

The truth is that the materialistic paternalism of the present day, if allowed to go on unchecked, will rapidly make of America one huge "Main Street," where spiritual adventure will be discouraged and democracy will be regarded as consisting in the reduction of all mankind to the proportions of the narrowest and least gifted of the citizens. God grant that there may come a reaction, and that the great principles of Anglo-Saxon liberty may be rediscovered before it is too late! But whatever solution be found for the educational and social problems of our own country, a lamentable condition must be detected in the world at large. It

cannot be denied that great men are few or non-existent, and
that there has been a general contracting of the area of personal
life. Material betterment has gone hand in hand with spiritual
decline.

Such a condition of the world ought to cause the choice
between modernism and traditionalism, liberalism and conservatism, to be approached without any of the prejudice which is
too often displayed. In view of the lamentable defects of modern life, a type of religion certainly should not be commended
simply because it is modern or condemned simply because it
is old. On the contrary, the condition of mankind is such that
one may well ask what it is that made the men of past generations so great and the men of the present generation so small. In
the midst of all the material achievements of modern life, one
may well ask the question whether in gaining the whole world
we have not lost our own soul. Are we forever condemned to
live the sordid life of utilitarianism? Or is there some lost secret
which if rediscovered will restore to mankind something of the
glories of the past?

Such a secret the writer of this little book would discover in
the Christian religion. But the Christian religion which is meant
is certainly not the religion of the modern liberal Church, but
a message of divine grace, almost forgotten now, as it was in
the middle ages, but destined to burst forth once more in God's
good time, in a new Reformation, and bring light and freedom
to mankind. What that message is can be made clear, as is the
case with all definition, only by way of exclusion, by way of contrast. In setting forth the current liberalism, now almost dominant in the Church, over against Christianity, we are animated,

therefore, by no merely negative or polemic purpose; on the contrary, by showing what Christianity is not we hope to be able to show what Christianity is, in order that men may be led to turn from the weak and beggarly elements and have recourse again to the grace of God.

2

Doctrine

Modern liberalism in the Church, whatever judgment may be passed upon it, is at any rate no longer merely an academic matter. It is no longer a matter merely of theological seminaries or universities. On the contrary its attack upon the fundamentals of the Christian faith is being carried on vigorously by Sunday-School "lesson-helps," by the pulpit, and by the religious press. If such an attack be unjustified, the remedy is not to be found, as some devout persons have suggested, in the abolition of theological seminaries, or the abandonment of scientific theology, but rather in a more earnest search after truth and a more loyal devotion to it when once it is found.

At the theological seminaries and universities, however, the roots of the great issue are more clearly seen than in the world at large; among students the reassuring employment of traditional phrases is often abandoned, and the advocates of a new religion are not at pains, as they are in the Church at large, to maintain an appearance of conformity with the past. But such frankness, we are convinced, ought to be extended to the people as a whole. Few desires on the part of religious teachers have been more harmfully exaggerated than the desire to "avoid giving offence." Only too often that desire has come perilously near dishonesty; the religious teacher, in his heart of hearts, is well aware of the radicalism of his views, but is unwilling to relinquish his place in

the hallowed atmosphere of the Church by speaking his whole
mind. Against all such policy of concealment or palliation, our
sympathies are altogether with those men, whether radicals or
conservatives, who have a passion for light.

What then, at bottom, when the traditional phrases have
all been stripped away, is the real meaning of the present revolt
against the fundamentals of the Christian faith? What, in brief,
are the teachings of modern liberalism as over against the teachings of Christianity?

At the outset, we are met with an objection. "Teachings,"
it is said, "are unimportant; the exposition of the teachings of
liberalism and the teachings of Christianity, therefore, can arouse
no interest at the present day; creeds are merely the changing
expression of a unitary Christian experience, and provided only
they express that experience they are all equally good. The teachings of liberalism, therefore, might be as far removed as possible from the teachings of historic Christianity, and yet the two
might be at bottom the same."

Such is the way in which expression is often given to the
modern hostility to "doctrine." But is it really doctrine as such
that is objected to, and not rather one particular doctrine in the
interests of another? Undoubtedly, in many forms of liberalism
it is the latter alternative which fits the case. There are doctrines
of modern liberalism, just as tenaciously and intolerantly upheld
as any doctrines that find a place in the historic creeds. Such
for example are the liberal doctrines of the universal fatherhood
of God and the universal brotherhood of man. These doctrines
are, as we shall see, contrary to the doctrines of the Christian
religion. But doctrines they are all the same, and as such they
require intellectual defence. In seeming to object to all theology,

the liberal preacher is often merely objecting to one system of theology in the interests of another. And the desired immunity from theological controversy has not yet been attained.

Sometimes, however, the modern objection to doctrine is more seriously meant. And whether the objection be well-founded or not, the real meaning of it should at least be faced.

That meaning is perfectly plain. The objection involves an out-and-out skepticism. If all creeds are equally true, then since they are contradictory to one another, they are all equally false, or at least equally uncertain. We are indulging, therefore, in a mere juggling with words. To say that all creeds are equally true, and that they are based upon experience, is merely to fall back upon that agnosticism which fifty years ago was regarded as the deadliest enemy of the Church. The enemy has not really been changed into a friend merely because he has been received within the camp. Very different is the Christian conception of a creed. According to the Christian conception, a creed is not a mere expression of Christian experience, but on the contrary it is a setting forth of those facts upon which experience is based.

But, it will be said, Christianity is a life, not a doctrine. The assertion is often made, and it has an appearance of godliness. But it is radically false, and to detect its falsity one does not even need to be a Christian. For to say that "Christianity is a life" is to make an assertion in the sphere of history. The assertion does not lie in the sphere of ideals; it is far different from saying that Christianity ought to be a life, or that the ideal religion is a life. The assertion that Christianity is a life is subject to historical investigation exactly as is the assertion that the Roman Empire under Nero was a free democracy. Possibly the Roman Empire under Nero would have been better if it had been a free democracy, but the historical question is simply whether as a matter of fact it was a free democracy or no. Christianity is an historical phenomenon, like the Roman Empire, or the Kingdom of Prussia, or the United States of America, And as an historical phenomenon it must be investigated on the basis of historical evidence.

Is it true, then, that Christianity is not a doctrine but a life? The question can be settled only by an examination of the beginnings of Christianity. Recognition of that fact does not involve any acceptance of Christian belief; it is merely a matter of common sense and common honesty. At the foundation of the life of every corporation is the incorporation paper, in which the objects of the corporation are set forth. Other objects may be vastly more desirable than those objects, but if the directors use the name and the resources of the corporation to pursue the other objects they are acting *ultra vires* of the corporation. So it is with Christianity. It is perfectly conceivable that the originators of the Christian movement had no right to legislate for subsequent generations; but at any rate they did have an inalienable right to legislate for all generations that should choose to bear the name of "Christian." It is conceivable that Christianity may now have to be abandoned, and another religion substituted for it; but at any rate the question what Christianity is can be determined only by an examination of the beginnings of Christianity.

The beginnings of Christianity constitute a fairly definite historical phenomenon. The Christian movement originated a few days after the death of Jesus of Nazareth. It is doubtful whether anything that preceded the death of Jesus can be called Christianity. At any rate, if Christianity existed before that event, it was Christianity only in a preliminary stage. The name originated after the death of Jesus, and the thing itself was also something new. Evidently there was an important new beginning among the disciples of Jesus in Jerusalem after the crucifixion. At that time is to be placed the beginning of the remarkable movement which spread out from Jerusalem into the Gentile world—the movement which is called Christianity.

About the early stages of this movement definite historical information has been preserved in the Epistles of Paul, which are regarded by all serious historians as genuine products of the first Christian generation. The writer of the Epistles had been in direct communication with those intimate friends of Jesus who had begun the Christian movement in Jerusalem, and in the Epistles he makes it abundantly plain what the fundamental character of the movement was.

But if any one fact is clear, on the basis of this evidence, it is that the Christian movement at its inception was not just a way of life in the modern sense, but a way of life founded upon a message. It was based, not upon mere feeling, not upon a mere program of work, but upon an account of facts. In other words it was based upon doctrine.

Certainly with regard to Paul himself there should be no debate; Paul certainly was not indifferent to doctrine; on the contrary, doctrine was the very basis of his life. His devotion to doctrine did not, it is true, make him incapable of a magnificent tolerance. One notable example of such tolerance is to be found during his imprisonment at Rome, as attested by the Epistle to the Philippians. Apparently certain Christian teachers at Rome had been jealous of Paul's greatness. As long as he had been at liberty they had been obliged to take a secondary place; but now that he was in prison, they seized the supremacy. They sought to raise up affliction for Paul in his bonds; they preached Christ even of envy and strife. In short, the rival preachers made of the preaching of the gospel a means to the gratification of low personal ambition; it seems to have been about as mean a piece of business as could well be conceived. But Paul was not disturbed. "Whether in pretence, or in truth," he said, "Christ is preached; and I therein do rejoice, yea, and will rejoice" (Phil. 1:18). The way in which the preaching was being carried on was wrong, but the message itself was true; and Paul was far more interested in the content of the message than in the manner of its presentation. It is impossible to conceive a finer piece of broad-minded tolerance.

But the tolerance of Paul was not indiscriminate. He displayed no tolerance, for example, in Galatia. There, too, there were rival preachers. But Paul had no tolerance for them. "But though we," he said, "or an angel from heaven, preach any other gospel unto you than that which we have preached unto you, let him be accursed" (Gal. 1:8). What is the reason for the difference in the apostle's attitude in the two cases? What is the reason for the broad tolerance in Rome, and the fierce anathemas in Galatia? The answer is perfectly plain. In Rome, Paul was tolerant, because there the content of the message that was being proclaimed by the rival teachers was true; in Galatia he was intolerant, because there the content of the rival message was false. In neither case did personalities have anything to do with Paul's attitude. No doubt the motives of the Judaizers in Galatia were far from pure, and in an incidental way Paul does point out their impurity. But that was not the ground of his opposition. The Judaizers no doubt were morally far from perfect, but Paul's opposition to them would have been exactly the same if they had all been angels from heaven. His opposition was based altogether

upon the falsity of their teaching; they were substituting for the
one true gospel a false gospel which was no gospel at all. It never
occurred to Paul that a gospel might be true for one man and
not for another; the blight of pragmatism had never fallen upon
his soul. Paul was convinced of the objective truth of the gospel
message, and devotion to that truth was the great passion of his
life. Christianity for Paul was not only a life, but also a doctrine,
and logically the doctrine came first.[1]

But what was the difference between the teaching of Paul
and the teaching of the Judaizers? What was it that gave rise to
the stupendous polemic of the Epistle to the Galatians? To the
modern Church the difference would have seemed to be a mere
theological subtlety. About many things the Judaizers were in
perfect agreement with Paul. The Judaizers believed that Jesus
was the Messiah; there is not a shadow of evidence that they
objected to Paul's lofty view of the person of Christ. Without the
slightest doubt, they believed that Jesus had really risen from the
dead. They believed, moreover, that faith in Christ was necessary
to salvation. But the trouble was, they believed that something
else was also necessary; they believed that what Christ had done
needed to be pieced out by the believer's own effort to keep the
Law. From the modern point of view the difference would have
seemed to be very slight. Paul as well as the Judaizers believed
that the keeping of the law of God, in its deepest import, is in-
separably connected with faith. The difference concerned only
the logical—not even, perhaps, the temporal—order of three

---

1. See *The Origin of Paul's Religion*, 1921, p. 168. It is not maintained that doctrine
for Paul comes *temporally* before life, but only that it comes *logically* first. Here is to be
found the answer to the objection which Dr. Lyman Abbott raised against the assertion in
The Origin of Paul's Religion. See *The Outlook*, vol. 132, 1922, pp. 104f.

steps. Paul said that a man (1) first believes on Christ, (2) then is justified before God, (3) then immediately proceeds to keep God's law. The Judaizers said that a man (1) believes on Christ and (2) keeps the law of God the best he can, and then (3) is justified. The difference would seem to modern "practical" Christians to be a highly subtle and intangible matter, hardly worthy of consideration at all in view of the large measure of agreement in the practical realm. What a splendid cleaning up of the Gentile cities it would have been if the Judaizers had succeeded in extending to those cities the observance of the Mosaic law, even including the unfortunate ceremonial observances! Surely Paul ought to have made common cause with teachers who were so nearly in agreement with him; surely he ought to have applied to them the great principle of Christian unity.

As a matter of fact, however, Paul did nothing of the kind; and only because he (and others) did nothing of the kind does the Christian Church exist to-day. Paul saw very clearly that the difference between the Judaizers and himself was the difference between two entirely distinct types of religion; it was the difference between a religion of merit and a religion of grace. If Christ provides only a part of our salvation, leaving us to provide the rest, then we are still hopeless under the load of sin. For no matter how small the gap which must be bridged before salvation can be attained, the awakened conscience sees clearly that our wretched attempt at goodness is insufficient even to bridge that gap. The guilty soul enters again into the hopeless reckoning with God, to determine whether we have really done our part. And thus we groan again under the old bondage of the law. Such an attempt to piece out the work of Christ by our own merit, Paul saw clearly, is the very essence of unbelief; Christ will do everything or nothing, and the only hope is to throw ourselves unreservedly on His mercy and trust Him for all.

Paul certainly was right. The difference which divided him from the Judaizers was no mere theological subtlety, but concerned the very heart and core of the religion of Christ. "Just as I am without one plea, But that Thy blood was shed for me"— that was what Paul was contending for in Galatia; that hymn would never have been written if the Judaizers had won. And without the thing which that hymn expresses there is no Christianity at all.

Certainly, then, Paul was no advocate of an undogmatic religion; he was interested above everything else in the objective and universal truth of his message. So much will probably be admitted by serious historians, no matter what their own personal attitude toward the religion of Paul may be. Sometimes, indeed, the modern liberal preacher seeks to produce an opposite impression by quoting out of their context words of Paul which he interprets in a way as far removed as possible from the original sense. The truth is, it is hard to give Paul up. The modern liberal desires to produce upon the minds of simple Christians (and upon his own mind) the impression of some sort of continuity between modern liberalism and the thought and life of the great Apostle. But such an impression is altogether misleading. Paul was not interested merely in the ethical principles of Jesus; he was not interested merely in general principles of religion or of ethics. On the contrary, he was interested in the redeeming work of Christ and its effect upon us. His primary interest was in Christian doctrine, and Christian doctrine not merely in its presuppositions but at its centre. If Christianity is to be made independent of doctrine, then Paulinism must be removed from Christianity root and branch.

But what of that? Some men are not afraid of the conclusion. If Paulinism must be removed, they say, we can get along without it. May it not turn out that in introducing a doctrinal element into the life of the Church Paul was only perverting a primitive Christianity which was as independent of doctrine as even the modern liberal preacher could desire?

This suggestion is clearly overruled by the historical evidence. The problem certainly cannot be solved in so easy a way. Many attempts have indeed been made to separate the religion of Paul sharply from that of the primitive Jerusalem Church; many attempts have been made to show that Paul introduced an entirely new principle into the Christian movement or even was the founder of a new religion.[2] But all such attempts have resulted in failure. The Pauline Epistles themselves attest a fundamental unity of principle between Paul and the original companions of Jesus, and the whole early history of the Church becomes unintelligible except on the basis of such unity. Certainly with regard to the fundamentally doctrinal character of Christianity Paul was no innovator. The fact appears in the whole character of Paul's relationship to the Jerusalem Church as it is attested by the Epistles, and it also appears with startling clearness in the precious passage in 1 Cor. 15:3–7, where Paul summarizes the tradition which he had received from the primitive Church. What is it that forms the content of that primitive teaching? Is it a general principle of the fatherliness of God or the brotherliness

---

2. Some account of these attempts has been given by the present writer in *The Origin of Paul's Religion*, 1921.

of man? Is it a vague admiration for the character of Jesus such as that which prevails in the modern Church? Nothing could be further from the fact. "Christ died for our sins," said the primitive disciples, "according to the Scriptures; he was buried; he has been raised on the third day according to the Scriptures." From the beginning, the Christian gospel, as indeed the name "gospel" or "good news" implies, consisted in an account of something that had happened. And from the beginning, the meaning of the happening was set forth; and when the meaning of the happening was set forth then there was Christian doctrine. "Christ died"—that is history; "Christ died for our sins"—that is doctrine. Without these two elements, joined in an absolutely indissoluble union, there is no Christianity.

It is perfectly clear, then, that the first Christian missionaries did not simply come forward with an exhortation; they did not say: "Jesus of Nazareth lived a wonderful life of filial piety, and we call upon you our hearers to yield yourselves, as we have done, to the spell of that life." Certainly that is what modern historians would have expected the first Christian missionaries to say, but it must be recognized that as a matter of fact they said nothing of the kind. Conceivably the first disciples of Jesus, after the catastrophe of His death, might have engaged in quiet meditation upon His teaching. They might have said to themselves that "Our Father which art in heaven" was a good way of addressing God even though the One who had taught them that prayer was dead. They might have clung to the ethical principles of Jesus and cherished the vague hope that the One who enunciated such principles had some personal existence beyond the grave. Such reflections might have seemed very natural to the modern man. But to Peter, James and John they certainly never occurred. Jesus had raised in them high hopes; those hopes were destroyed by the Cross; and reflections on the general principles of religion and ethics were quite powerless to revive the hopes again. The disciples of Jesus had evidently been far inferior to their Master in every possible way; they had not understood His lofty spiritual teaching, but even in the hour of solemn crisis had quarreled over great places in the approaching Kingdom. What hope was there that such men could succeed where their Master had failed? Even when He had been with them, they had been powerless; and now that He was taken from them, what little power they may have had was gone.[3]

Yet those same weak, discouraged men, within a few days after the death of their Master, instituted the most important spiritual movement that the world has ever seen. What had produced the astonishing change? What had transformed the weak and cowardly disciples into the spiritual conquerors of the world? Evidently it was not the mere memory of Jesus' life, for that was a source of sadness rather than of joy. Evidently the disciples of Jesus, within the few days between the crucifixion and the beginning of their work in Jerusalem, had received some new equipment for their task. What that new equipment was, at least the outstanding and external element in it (to say nothing of the endowment which Christian men believe to have been received at Pentecost), is perfectly plain. The great weapon with which the disciples of Jesus set out to conquer the world was not a mere comprehension of eternal principles; it was an historical

---

3. Compare *History and Faith*, 1915 (reprinted from *Princeton Theological Review* for July, 1915), pp. 10f.

message, an account of something that had recently happened, it was the message, "He is risen."[4]

But the message of the resurrection was not isolated. It was connected with the death of Jesus, seen now to be not a failure but a triumphant act of divine grace; it was connected with the entire appearance of Jesus upon earth. The coming of Jesus was understood now as an act of God by which sinful men were saved. The primitive Church was concerned not merely with what Jesus had said, but also, and primarily, with what Jesus had done. The world was to be redeemed through the proclamation of an event. And with the event went the meaning of the event; and the setting forth of the event with the meaning of the event was doctrine. These two elements are always combined in the Christian message. The narration of the facts is history; the narration of the facts with the meaning of the facts is doctrine. "Suffered under Pontius Pilate, was crucified, dead and buried"—that is history. "He loved me and gave Himself for me"—that is doctrine. Such was the Christianity of the primitive Church.

"But," it may be said, "even if the Christianity of the primitive Church was dependent upon doctrine, we may still emancipate ourselves from such dependence; we may appeal from the primitive Church to Jesus Himself. It has already been admitted that if doctrine is to be abandoned Paul must be abandoned; it may now be admitted that if doctrine is to be abandoned, even the primitive Jerusalem Church, with its message of the resurrec-

---

4. Compare *A Rapid Survey of the Literature and History of New Testament Times*, published by the Presbyterian Board of Publication and Sabbath School Work, Student's Text Book, pp. 42f.

tion, must be abandoned. But possibly we can still find in Jesus Himself the simple, non-doctrinal religion that we desire." Such is the real meaning of the modern slogan, "Back to Christ."

Must we really take such a step as that? It would certainly be an extraordinary step. A great religion derived its power from the message of the redeeming work of Christ; without that message Jesus and His disciples would soon have been forgotten. The same message, with its implications, has been the very heart and soul of the Christian movement throughout the centuries. Yet we are now asked to believe that the thing that has given Christianity its power all through the centuries was a blunder, that the originators of the movement misunderstood radically the meaning of their Master's life and work, and that it has been left to us moderns to get the first inkling of the initial mistake. Even if this view of the case were correct, and even if Jesus Himself taught a religion like that of modern liberalism, it would still be doubtful whether such a religion could rightly be called Christianity; for the name Christian was first applied only after the supposed decisive change had taken place, and it is very doubtful whether a name which through nineteen centuries has been so firmly attached to one religion ought now suddenly to be applied to another. If the first disciples of Jesus really departed so radically from their Master, then the better terminology would probably lead us to say simply that Jesus was not the founder of Christianity, but of a simple, non-doctrinal religion, long forgotten, but now rediscovered by modern men. Even so, the contrast between liberalism and Christianity would still appear.

But as a matter of fact, such a strange state of affairs does not prevail at all. It is not true that in basing Christianity upon an event the disciples of Jesus were departing from the teaching of their Master. For certainly Jesus Himself did the same thing. Jesus did not content Himself with enunciating general principles of religion and ethics; the picture of Jesus as a sage similar to Confucius, uttering wise maxims about conduct, may satisfy Mr. H. G. Wells, as he trips along lightly over the problems of history, but it disappears so soon as one engages seriously in historical research. "Repent," said Jesus, "for the Kingdom of Heaven is at hand." The gospel which Jesus proclaimed in Galilee consisted in the proclamation of a coming Kingdom. But clearly Jesus regarded the coming of the Kingdom as an event, or as a series of events. No doubt He also regarded the Kingdom as a present reality in the souls of men; no doubt He represented the Kingdom in one sense as already present. We shall not really succeed in getting along without this aspect of the matter in our interpretation of Jesus' words. But we shall also not get along without the other aspect, according to which the coming of the Kingdom depended upon definite and catastrophic events. But if Jesus regarded the coming of the Kingdom as dependent upon a definite event, then His teaching was similar at the decisive point to that of the primitive Church; neither He nor the primitive Church enunciated merely general and permanent principles of religion; both of them, on the contrary, made the message depend upon something that happened. Only, in the teaching of Jesus the happening was represented as being still in the future, while in that of the Jerusalem Church the first act of it at least lay already in the past. Jesus proclaimed the event as coming; the disciples proclaimed part of it at least as already past; but the important thing is that both Jesus and the disciples did proclaim an event. Jesus was certainly not a mere enunciator of permanent truths, like the modern liberal preacher; on the contrary He was conscious of standing at the turning-point of the ages, when what had never been was now to come to be.

But Jesus announced not only an event; He announced also the meaning of the event. It is natural, indeed, that the full meaning could be made clear only after the event had taken place. If Jesus really came, then, to announce, and to bring about, an event, the disciples were not departing from His purpose, if they set forth the meaning of the event more fully than it could be set forth during the preliminary period constituted by the earthly ministry of their Master. But Jesus Himself, though by way of prophecy, did set forth the meaning of the great happening that was to be at the basis of the new era.

Certainly He did so, and grandly, if the words attributed to Him in all of the Gospels are really His. But even if the Fourth Gospel be rejected, and even if the most radical criticism be applied to the other three, it will still be impossible to get rid of this element in Jesus' teaching. The significant words attributed to Jesus at the Last Supper with regard to His approaching death, and the utterance of Jesus in Mk. 10:45 ("The Son of Man came not to be ministered unto but to minister, and to give His life a ransom for many"), have indeed been the subject of vigorous debate. It is difficult to accept such words as authentic and yet maintain the modern view of Jesus at all. Yet it is also difficult to get rid of them on any critical theory. What we are now concerned with, however, is something more general than the authenticity even of these precious words. What we are now concerned to observe is that Jesus certainly did not content Himself with the enunciation of permanent moral principles; He certainly did announce an approaching event; and He certainly did not announce the event without giving some account of its meaning. But when He gave an account of the meaning of the event, no matter how brief that account may have been, He was overstepping the line that separates an undogmatic religion, or even a dogmatic religion that teaches only eternal principles, from one that is rooted in the significance of definite historical facts; He was placing a great gulf between Himself and the philosophic modern liberalism which today incorrectly bears His name.

In another way also the teaching of Jesus was rooted in doctrine. It was rooted in doctrine because it depended upon a stupendous presentation of Jesus' own Person. The assertion is often made, indeed, that Jesus kept His own Person out of His gospel, and came forward merely as the supreme prophet of God. That assertion lies at the very root of the modern liberal conception of the life of Christ. But common as it is, it is radically false. And it is interesting to observe how the liberal historians themselves, so soon as they begin to deal seriously with the sources, are obliged to admit that the real Jesus was not all that they could have liked Jesus to be. A Houston Stewart Chamberlain,[5] indeed, can construct a Jesus who was the advocate of a pure, "formless," non-doctrinal religion; but trained historians, despite their own desires, are obliged to admit that there was an element in the real Jesus which refuses to be pressed into any such mould. There is to the liberal historians, as Heitmüller has significantly said, "something almost uncanny" about Jesus.[6]

This "uncanny" element in Jesus is found in His Messianic consciousness. The strange fact is that this pure teacher of righteousness appealed to by modern liberalism, this classical

---

5. *Mensch und Gott*, 1921. Compare the review in *Princeton Theological Review*, xx, 1922, pp. 327–329.
6. Heitmüller, *Jesus*, 1913, p. 71. See *The Origin of Paul's Religion*, 1921, p. 157.

exponent of the non-doctrinal religion which is supposed to underlie all the historical religions as the irreducible truth remaining after the doctrinal accretions have been removed—the strange fact is that this supreme revealer of eternal truth supposed that He was to be the chief actor in a world catastrophe and was to sit in judgment upon the whole earth. Such is the stupendous form in which Jesus applied to Himself the category of Messiahship.

It is interesting to observe how modern men have dealt with the Messianic consciousness of Jesus. Some, like Mr. H. G. Wells, have practically ignored it. Without discussing the question whether it be historical or not they have practically treated it as though it did not exist, and have not allowed it to disturb them at all in their construction of the sage of Nazareth. The Jesus thus reconstructed may be useful as investing modern programs with the sanctity of His hallowed name; Mr. Wells may find it edifying to associate Jesus with Confucius in a brotherhood of beneficent vagueness. But what ought to be clearly understood is that such a Jesus has nothing to do with history. He is a purely imaginary figure, a symbol and not a fact.

Others, more seriously, have recognized the existence of the problem, but have sought to avoid it by denying that Jesus ever thought that He was the Messiah, and by supporting their denial, not by mere assertions, but by a critical examination of the sources. Such was the effort, for example, of W. Wrede,[7] and a brilliant effort it was. But it has resulted in failure. The Messianic consciousness of Jesus is not merely rooted in the sources considered as documents, but it lies at the very basis of the whole

7. *Das Messiasgeheimnis in den Evangelien,* 1901.

edifice of the Church. If, as J. Weiss has pertinently said, the disciples before the crucifixion had merely been told that the Kingdom of God was coming, if Jesus had really kept altogether in the background His own part in the Kingdom, then why when despair finally gave place to joy did the disciples not merely say, "Despite Jesus' death, the Kingdom that He foretold will truly come"? Why did they say rather, "Despite His death, He is the Messiah"?[8] From no point of view, then, can the fact be denied that Jesus did claim to be the Messiah—neither from the point of view of acceptance of the Gospel witness as a whole, nor from the point of view of modern naturalism.

And when the Gospel account of Jesus is considered closely, it is found to involve the Messianic consciousness throughout. Even those parts of the Gospels which have been regarded as most purely ethical are found to be based altogether upon Jesus' lofty claims. The Sermon on the Mount is a striking example. It is the fashion now to place the Sermon on the Mount in contrast with the rest of the New Testament. "We will have nothing to do with theology," men say in effect, "we will have nothing to do with miracles, with atonement, or with heaven or with hell. For us the Golden Rule is a sufficient guide of life; in the simple principles of the Sermon on the Mount we discover a solution of all the problems of society." It is indeed rather strange that men can speak in this way. Certainly it is rather derogatory to Jesus to assert that never except in one brief part of His recorded words did He say anything that is worth while. But even in the Sermon on the Mount there is far more than some men suppose. Men say that it contains no theology; in reality it contains

---

8. J. Weiss, "Das Problem der Entstehung des Christentums," in *Archiv für Religionswissenschaft*, xvi, 1913, p. 456. See *The Origin of Paul's Religion*, 1921, p. 156.

theology of the most stupendous kind. In particular, it contains the loftiest possible presentation of Jesus' own Person. That presentation appears in the strange note of authority which pervades the whole discourse; it appears in the recurrent words, "But I say unto you." Jesus plainly puts His own words on an equality with what He certainly regarded as the divine words of Scripture; He claimed the right to legislate for the Kingdom of God. Let it not be objected that this note of authority involves merely a prophetic consciousness in Jesus, a mere right to speak in God's name as God's Spirit might lead. For what prophet ever spoke in this way? The prophets said, "Thus saith the Lord," but Jesus said, "I say." We have no mere prophet here, no mere humble exponent of the will of God; but a stupendous Person speaking in a manner which for any other person would be abominable and absurd. The same thing appears in the passage Matt. 7:21–23: "Not everyone who says to me Lord, Lord, shall enter into the Kingdom of Heaven, but he who does the will of my Father who is in heaven. Many shall say to me in that day: Lord, Lord, have we not prophesied in thy name, and in thy name cast out demons, and in thy name done many mighty works? And then I shall confess to them, 'I never knew you; depart from me, ye that work lawlessness.' " This passage is in some respects a favorite with modern liberal teachers; for it is interpreted—falsely, it is true, yet plausibly—as meaning that all that a man needs to attain standing with God is an approximately right performance of his duties to his fellow-men, and not any assent to a creed or even any direct relation to Jesus. But have those who quote the passage so triumphantly in this way ever stopped to reflect upon the other side of the picture—upon the stupendous fact that in this same passage the eternal destinies of men are made dependent upon the word of Jesus? Jesus here represents Himself as seated on the judgment-seat of all the earth, separating whom He will forever from the bliss that is involved in being present with Him. Could anything be further removed than such a Jesus from the humble teacher of righteousness appealed to by modern liberalism? Clearly it is impossible to escape from theology, even in the chosen precincts of the Sermon on the Mount. A stupendous theology, with Jesus' own Person at the centre of it, is the presupposition of the whole teaching.

But may not that theology still be removed? May we not get rid of the bizarre, theological element which has intruded itself even into the Sermon on the Mount, and content ourselves merely with the ethical portion of the discourse? The question, from the point of view of modern liberalism, is natural. But it must be answered with an emphatic negative. For the fact is that the ethic of the discourse, taken by itself, will not work at all. The Golden Rule furnishes an example. "Do unto others as you would have others do unto you"—is that rule a rule of universal application, will it really solve all the problems of society? A little experience shows that such is not the case. Help a drunkard to get rid of his evil habit, and you will soon come to distrust the modern interpretation of the Golden Rule. The trouble is that the drunkard's companions apply the rule only too well; they do unto him exactly what they would have him do unto them—by buying him a drink. The Golden Rule becomes a powerful obstacle in the way of moral advance. But the trouble does not lie in the rule itself; it lies in the modern interpretation of the rule. The error consists in supposing that the Golden Rule, with the rest of the Sermon on the Mount, is addressed to the whole world. As a matter of fact the whole discourse is expressly addressed to Jesus' disciples; and from them the great world outside is distinguished in the plainest possible way. The persons to whom the Golden Rule is addressed are persons in whom a great change has been wrought—a change which fits them for entrance into the Kingdom of God. Such persons will have pure desires; they, and they only, can safely do unto others as they would have others do unto them, for the things that they would have others do unto them are high and pure.

So it is with the whole of the discourse. The new law of the Sermon on the Mount, in itself, can only produce despair. Strange indeed is the complacency with which modern men can say that the Golden Rule and the high ethical principles of Jesus are all that they need. In reality, if the requirements for entrance into the Kingdom of God are what Jesus declares them to be, we are all undone; we have not even attained to the external righteousness of the scribes and Pharisees, and how shall we attain to that righteousness of the heart which Jesus demands? The Sermon on the Mount, rightly interpreted, then, makes man a seeker after some divine means of salvation by which entrance into the Kingdom can be obtained. Even Moses was too high for us; but before this higher law of Jesus who shall stand without being condemned? The Sermon on the Mount, like all the rest of the New Testament, really leads a man straight to the foot of the Cross.

Even the disciples, to whom the teaching of Jesus was first addressed, knew well that they needed more than guidance in the way that they should go. It is only a superficial reading of the Gospels that can find in the relation which the disciples sustained to Jesus a mere relation of pupil to Master. When Jesus said, "Come unto me, all ye that labour and are heavy laden, and I will give you rest," he was speaking not as a philosopher calling pupils to his school; but as One who was in possession of rich stores of divine grace. And this much at least the disciples knew. They knew well in their heart of hearts that they had no right to stand in the Kingdom; they knew that only Jesus could win them entrance there. They did not yet know fully how Jesus could make them children of God; but they did know that He could do it and He alone. And in that trust all the theology of the great Christian creeds was in expectation contained.

At this point, an objection may arise. May we not—the modern liberal will say—may we not now return to that simple trust of the disciples? May we not cease to ask *how* Jesus saves; may we not simply leave the way to Him? What need is there, then, of defining "effectual calling," what need of enumerating "justification, adoption and sanctification and the several benefits which in this life do either accompany or flow from them"? What need even of rehearsing the steps in the saving work of Christ as they were rehearsed by the Jerusalem Church; what need of saying that "Christ died for our sins according to the Scriptures, that he was buried, that he has been raised on the third day according to the Scriptures"? Should not our trust be in a Person rather than in a message; in Jesus, rather than in what Jesus did; in Jesus' character rather than in Jesus' death?

Plausible words these are—plausible, and pitifully vain. Can we really return to Galilee; are we really in the same situation as those who came to Jesus when He was on earth? Can we hear Him say to us, "Thy sins are forgiven thee"? These are serious questions, and they cannot possibly be ignored. The plain fact is that Jesus of Nazareth died these nineteen hundred years ago. It was possible for the men of Galilee in the first century to trust Him for to them He extended His aid. For them, life's problem was easy. They needed only to push in through the crowd or be lowered through some Capernaum roof, and the long search was over. But we are separated by nineteen centuries from the One who alone could give us aid. How can we bridge the gulf of time that separates us from Jesus?

Some persons would bridge the gulf by the mere use of the historical imagination. "Jesus is not dead," we are told, "but lives on through His recorded words and deeds; we do not need even to believe it all; even a part is sufficient; the wonderful personality of Jesus shines out clear from the Gospel story. Jesus, in other words, may still be known; let us simply—without theology, without controversy, without inquiry about miracles—abandon ourselves to His spell, and He will heal us."

There is a certain plausibility about that. It may readily be admitted that Jesus lives on in the Gospel record. In that narrative we see not merely a lifeless picture, but receive the impression of a living Person. We can still, as we read, share the astonishment of those who listened to the new teaching in the synagogue at Capernaum. We can sympathize with the faith and devotion of the little band of disciples who would not leave Him when others were offended at the hard saying. We feel a sympathetic thrill of joy at the blessed relief which was given to those who were ill in body and in mind. We can appreciate the wonderful love and compassion of Him who was sent to seek and to save that which was lost. A wonderful story it is indeed—not dead, but pulsating with life at every turn.

Certainly the Jesus of the Gospels is a real, a living Person. But that is not the only question. We are going forward far too fast. Jesus lives in the Gospels—so much may freely be admitted—but we of the twentieth century, how may we come into vital relation to Him? He died nineteen hundred years ago. The life which He now lives in the Gospels is simply the old life lived over and over again. And in that life we have no place; in that life we are spectators, not actors. The life which Jesus lives in the Gospels is after all for us but the spurious life of the stage. We sit silent in the playhouse and watch the absorbing Gospel drama of forgiveness and healing and love and courage and high endeavor; in rapt attention we follow the fortunes of those who came to Jesus laboring and heavy laden and found rest. For a time our own troubles are forgotten. But suddenly the curtain falls, with the closing of the book, and out we go again into the cold hum-drum of our own lives. Gone are the warmth and gladness of an ideal world, and "in their stead a sense of real things comes doubly strong." We are no longer living over again the lives of Peter and James and John. Alas, we are living our own lives once more, with our own problems and our own misery and our own sin. And still we are seeking our own Saviour.

Let us not deceive ourselves. A Jewish teacher of the first century can never satisfy the longing of our souls. Clothe Him with all the art of modern research, throw upon Him the warm, deceptive calcium-light of modern sentimentality; and despite it all common sense will come to its rights again, and for our brief hour of self-deception—as though we had been with Jesus—will wreak upon us the revenge of hopeless disillusionment.

But, says the modern preacher, are we not, in being satisfied with the "historical" Jesus, the great teacher who proclaimed the Kingdom of God, merely restoring the simplicity of the primi-tive gospel? No, we answer, you are not, but, temporally at least, you are not so very far wrong. You are really returning to a very primitive stage in the life of the Church. Only, that stage is not the Galilean springtime. For in Galilee men had a living Saviour. There was one time and one time only when the disciples lived, like you, merely on the memory of Jesus. When was it? It was a gloomy, desperate time. It was the three sad days after the crucifixion. Then and then only did Jesus' disciples regard Him merely as a blessed memory. "We trusted," they said, "that it had been he which should have redeemed Israel." "We trusted"—but now our trust is gone. Shall we remain, with modern liberalism, forever in the gloom of those sad days? Or shall we pass out from it to the warmth and joy of Pentecost?

Certainly we shall remain forever in the gloom if we attend merely to the character of Jesus and neglect the thing that He has done, if we try to attend to the Person and neglect the message. We may have joy for sadness and power for weakness; but not by easy half-way measures, not by avoidance of controversy, not by trying to hold on to Jesus and yet reject the gospel. What was it that within a few days transformed a band of mourners into the spiritual conquerors of the world? It was not the memory of Jesus' life; it was not the inspiration which came from past contact with Him. But it was the message, "He is risen." That message alone gave to the disciples a living Saviour; and it alone can give to us a living Saviour to-day. We shall never have vital contact with Jesus if we attend to His person and neglect the message; for it is the message which makes Him ours.

But the Christian message contains more than the fact of the resurrection.[9] It is not enough to know that Jesus is alive; it is not enough to know that a wonderful Person lived in the

9. For what follows compare *A Rapid Survey of the History and Literature of New Testament Times*, published by the Presbyterian Board of Publication and Sabbath School Work, Teacher's Manual, pp. 44f.

first century of the Christian era and that that Person still lives, somewhere and somehow, to-day. Jesus lives, and that is well; but what good is it to us? We are like the inhabitants of far-off Syria or Phœnicia in the days of His flesh. There is a wonderful Person who can heal every ill of body and mind. But, alas, we are not with Him, and the way is far. How shall we come into His presence? How shall contact be established between us and Him? For the people of ancient Galilee contact was established by a touch of Jesus' hand or a word from His lips. But for us the problem is not so easy. We cannot find Him by the lake shore or in crowded houses; we cannot be lowered into any room where He sits amid scribes and Pharisees. If we employ only our own methods of search, we shall find ourselves on a fruitless pilgrimage. Surely we need guidance, if we are to find our Saviour.

And in the New Testament we find guidance full and free— guidance so complete as to remove all doubt, yet so simple that a child can understand. Contact with Jesus according to the New Testament is established by what Jesus does, not for others, but for us. The account of what Jesus did for others is indeed necessary. By reading how He went about doing good, how He healed the sick and raised the dead and forgave sins, we learn that He is a Person who is worthy of trust. But such knowledge is to the Christian man not an end in itself, but a means to an end. It is not enough to know that Jesus is a Person worthy of trust; it is also necessary to know that He is willing to have *us* trust Him. It is not enough that He saved others; we need to know also that He has saved us.

That knowledge is given in the story of the Cross. For us Jesus does not merely place His fingers in the ears and say, "Be opened"; for us He does not merely say, "Arise and walk." For us He has done a greater thing—for us He died. Our dreadful guilt, the condemnation of God's law—it was wiped out by an act of grace. That is the message which brings Jesus near to us, and makes Him not merely the Saviour of the men of Galilee long ago, but the Saviour of you and me.

It is vain, then, to speak of reposing trust in the Person without believing the message. For trust involves a personal relation between the one who trusts and him in whom the trust is reposed. And in this case the personal relation is set up by the blessed theology of the Cross. Without the eighth chapter of Romans, the mere story of the earthly life of Jesus would be remote and dead; for it is through the eighth chapter of Romans, or the message which that chapter contains, that Jesus becomes our Saviour to-day.

The truth is that when men speak of trust in Jesus' Person, as being possible without acceptance of the message of His death and resurrection, they do not really mean trust at all. What they designate as trust is really admiration or reverence. They reverence Jesus as the supreme Person of all history and the supreme revealer of God. But trust can come only when the supreme Person extends His saving power *to us.* "He went about doing good," "He spake words such as never man spake," "He is the express image of God"—that is reverence; "He loved me and gave Himself for me"—that is faith.

But the words "He loved me and gave Himself for me" are in historical form; they constitute an account of something that happened. And they add to the fact the meaning of the fact; they contain in essence the whole profound theology of redemption through the blood of Christ. Christian doctrine lies at the very roots of faith.

It must be admitted, then, that if we are to have a non-doctrinal religion, or a doctrinal religion founded merely on general truth, we must give up not only Paul, not only the primitive Jerusalem Church, but also Jesus Himself. But what is meant by doctrine? It has been interpreted here as meaning any presentation of the facts which lie at the basis of the Christian religion with the true meaning of the facts. But is that the only sense of the word? May the word not also be taken in a narrower sense? May it not also mean a systematic and minute and one-sidedly scientific presentation of the facts? And if the word is taken in this narrower sense, may not the modern objection to doctrine involve merely an objection to the excessive subtlety of controversial theology, and not at all an objection to the glowing words of the New Testament, an objection to the sixteenth and seventeenth centuries and not at all to the first century? Undoubtedly the word is so taken by many occupants of the pews when they listen to the modern exaltation of "life" at the expense of "doctrine." The pious hearer labors under the impression that he is merely being asked to return to the simplicity of the New Testament, instead of attending to the subtleties of the theologians. Since it has never occurred to him to attend to the subtleties of the theologians, he has that comfortable feeling which always comes to the churchgoer when some one else's sins are being attacked. It is no wonder that the modern invectives against doctrine constitute a popular type of preaching. At any rate, an attack upon Calvin or Turrettin or the Westminster divines does not seem to the modern churchgoer to be a very dangerous thing. In point of fact, however, the attack upon doctrine is not nearly so innocent a matter as our simple churchgoer supposes; for the things objected to in the theology of the Church are also at the very heart of the New Testament. Ultimately the attack is not against the seventeenth century, but against the Bible and against Jesus Himself.

Even if it were an attack not upon the Bible but only upon the great historic presentations of Biblical teaching, it would still be unfortunate. If the Church were led to wipe out of existence all products of the thinking of nineteen Christian centuries and start fresh, the loss, even if the Bible were retained, would be immense. When it is once admitted that a body of facts lies at the basis of the Christian religion, the efforts which past generations have made toward the classification of the facts will have to be treated with respect. In no branch of science would there be any real advance if every generation started fresh with no dependence upon what past generations have achieved. Yet in theology, vituperation of the past seems to be thought essential to progress. And upon what base slanders the vituperation is based! After listening to modern tirades against the great creeds of the Church, one receives rather a shock when one turns to the Westminster Confession, for example, or to that tenderest and most theological of books, the "Pilgrim's Progress" of John Bunyan, and discovers that in doing so one has turned from shallow modern phrases to a "dead orthodoxy" that is pulsating with life in every word. In such orthodoxy there is life enough to set the whole world aglow with Christian love.

As a matter of fact, however, in the modern vituperation of "doctrine," it is not merely the great theologians or the great creeds that are being attacked, but the New Testament and our Lord Himself. In rejecting doctrine, the liberal preacher is rejecting the simple words of Paul, "Who loved me and gave Himself for me," just as much as the *homoousion* of the Nicene Creed.

For the word "doctrine" is really used not in its narrowest, but in its broadest sense. The liberal preacher is really rejecting the whole basis of Christianity, which is a religion founded not on aspirations, but on facts. Here is found the most fundamental difference between liberalism and Christianity—liberalism is altogether in the imperative mood, while Christianity begins with a triumphant indicative; liberalism appeals to man's will, while Christianity announces, first, a gracious act of God.

In maintaining the doctrinal basis of Christianity, we are particularly anxious not to be misunderstood. There are certain things that we do not mean.

In the first place, we do not mean that if doctrine is sound it makes no difference about life. On the contrary, it makes all the difference in the world. From the beginning, Christianity was certainly a way of life; the salvation that it offered was a salvation from sin, and salvation from sin appeared not merely in a blessed hope but also in an immediate moral change. The early Christians, to the astonishment of their neighbors, lived a strange new kind of life—a life of honesty, of purity and of unselfishness. And from the Christian community all other types of life were excluded in the strictest way. From the beginning Christianity was certainly a life.

But how was the life produced? It might conceivably have been produced by exhortation. That method had often been tried in the ancient world; in the Hellenistic age there were many wandering preachers who told men how they ought to live. But such exhortation proved to be powerless. Although the ideals of the Cynic and Stoic preachers were high, these preachers never succeeded in transforming society. The strange thing about Christianity was that it adopted an entirely different method.

It transformed the lives of men not by appealing to the human will, but by telling a story; not by exhortation, but by the narration of an event. It is no wonder that such a method seemed strange. Could anything be more impractical than the attempt to influence conduct by rehearsing events concerning the death of a religious teacher? That is what Paul called "the foolishness of the message." It seemed foolish to the ancient world, and it seems foolish to liberal preachers to-day. But the strange thing is that it works. The effects of it appear even in this world. Where the most eloquent exhortation fails, the simple story of an event succeeds; the lives of men are transformed by a piece of news.

It is especially by such transformation of life, to-day as always, that the Christian message is commended to the attention of men. Certainly, then, it does make an enormous difference whether our lives be right. If our doctrine be true, and our lives be wrong, how terrible is our sin! For then we have brought despite upon the truth itself. On the other hand, however, it is also very sad when men use the social graces which God has given them, and the moral momentum of a godly ancestry, to commend a message which is false. Nothing in the world can take the place of truth.

In the second place, we do not mean, in insisting upon the doctrinal basis of Christianity, that all points of doctrine are equally important. It is perfectly possible for Christian fellowship to be maintained despite differences of opinion.

One such difference of opinion, which has been attaining increasing prominence in recent years, concerns the order of events in connection with the Lord's return. A large number of Christian people believe that when evil has reached its climax in the world, the Lord Jesus will return to this earth in bodily presence to bring about a reign of righteousness which will last a thousand years, and that only after that period the end of the world will come. That belief, in the opinion of the present writer, is an error, arrived at by a false interpretation of the Word of God; we do not think that the prophecies of the Bible permit so definite a mapping-out of future events. The Lord will come again, and it will be no mere "spiritual" coming in the modern sense—so much is clear—but that so little will be accomplished by the present dispensation of the Holy Spirit and so much will be left to be accomplished by the Lord in bodily presence—such a view we cannot find to be justified by the words of Scripture. What is our attitude, then, with regard to this debate? Certainly it cannot be an attitude of indifference. The recrudescence of "Chiliasm" or "premillennialism" in the modern Church causes us serious concern; it is coupled, we think, with a false method of interpreting Scripture which in the long run will be productive of harm. Yet how great is our agreement with those who hold the premillennial view! They share to the full our reverence for the authority of the Bible, and differ from us only in the interpretation of the Bible; they share our ascription of deity to the Lord Jesus, and our supernaturalistic conception both of the entrance of Jesus into the world and of the consummation when He shall come again. Certainly, then, from our point of view, their error, serious though it may be, is not deadly error; and Christian fellowship, with loyalty not only to the Bible but to the great creeds of the Church, can still unite us with them. It is therefore highly misleading when modern liberals represent the present issue in the Church, both in the mission field and at home, as being an issue between premillennialism and the opposite view. It is really an issue between Christianity, whether premillennial or not, on the one side, and a naturalistic negation of all Christianity on the other.

Another difference of opinion which can subsist in the midst of Christian fellowship is the difference of opinion about the mode of efficacy of the sacraments. That difference is indeed serious, and to deny its seriousness is a far greater error than to take the wrong side in the controversy itself. It is often said that the divided condition of Christendom is an evil, and so it is. But the evil consists in the existence of the errors which cause the divisions and not at all in the recognition of those errors when once they exist. It was a great calamity when at the "Marburg Conference" between Luther and the representatives of the Swiss Reformation, Luther wrote on the table with regard to the Lord's Supper, "This is my body," and said to Zwingli and Oecolampadius, "You have another spirit." That difference of opinion led to the breach between the Lutheran and the Reformed branches of the Church, and caused Protestantism to lose much of the ground that might otherwise have been gained. It was a great calamity indeed. But the calamity was due to the fact that Luther (as we believe) was wrong about the Lord's Supper; and it would have been a far greater calamity if being wrong about the Supper he had represented the whole question as a trifling affair. Luther was wrong about the Supper, but not nearly so wrong as he would have been if, being wrong, he had said to his opponents: "Brethren, this matter is a trifle; and it makes really very little difference what a man thinks about the table of the Lord." Such indifferentism would have been far more deadly than all the divisions between the branches of the Church. A Luther who would have compromised with regard to the Lord's Supper never would have said at the Diet of Worms, "Here I stand, I cannot

do otherwise, God help me, Amen." Indifferentism about doctrine makes no heroes of the faith.

Still another difference of opinion concerns the nature and
prerogatives of the Christian ministry. According to Anglican
doctrine, the bishops are in possession of an authority which has
been handed down to them, by successive ordination, from the
apostles of the Lord, and without such ordination there is no
valid priesthood. Other churches deny this doctrine of "apostolic succession," and hold a different view of the ministry. Here
again, the difference is no trifle, and we have little sympathy
with those who in the mere interests of Church efficiency try to
induce Anglicans to let down the barrier which their principles
have led them to erect. But despite the importance of this difference, it does not descend to the very roots. Even to the con-
scientious Anglican himself, though he regards the members of
other bodies as in schism, Christian fellowship with individuals
in those other bodies is still possible; and certainly those who
reject the Anglican view of the ministry can regard the Anglican
Church as a genuine and very noble member in the body of
Christ.

Another difference of opinion is that between the Calvinistic
or Reformed theology and the Arminianism which appears in
the Methodist Church. It is difficult to see how any one who has
really studied the question can regard that difference as an unimportant matter. On the contrary, it touches very closely some
of the profoundest things of the Christian faith. A Calvinist is
constrained to regard the Arminian theology as a serious impoverishment of the Scripture doctrine of divine grace; and equally
serious is the view which the Arminian must hold as to the doctrine of the Reformed Churches. Yet here again, true evangelical

fellowship is possible between those who hold, with regard to some exceedingly important matters, sharply opposing views.

Far more serious still is the division between the Church of Rome and evangelical Protestantism in all its forms. Yet how great is the common heritage which unites the Roman Catholic Church, with its maintenance of the authority of Holy Scripture and with its acceptance of the great early creeds, to devout Protestants today! We would not indeed obscure the difference which divides us from Rome. The gulf is indeed profound. But profound as it is, it seems almost trifling compared to the abyss which stands between us and many ministers of our own Church. The Church of Rome may represent a perversion of the Christian religion; but naturalistic liberalism is not Christianity at all.

That does not mean that conservatives and liberals must live in personal animosity. It does not involve any lack of sympathy on our part for those who have felt obliged by the current of the times to relinquish their confidence in the strange message of the Cross. Many ties—ties of blood, of citizenship, of ethical aims, of humanitarian endeavor—unite us to those who have abandoned the gospel. We trust that those ties may never be weakened, and that ultimately they may serve some purpose in the propagation of the Christian faith. But Christian service consists primarily in the propagation of a message, and specifically Christian fellowship exists only between those to whom the message has become the very basis of all life.

The character of Christianity as founded upon a message is summed up in the words of the eighth verse of the first chapter of Acts—"Ye shall be my witnesses both in Jerusalem, and in all Judea and Samaria, and unto the uttermost part of the earth." It is entirely unnecessary, for the present purpose, to argue about the historical value of the Book of Acts or to discuss the question whether Jesus really spoke the words just quoted. In any case the verse must be recognized as an adequate summary of what is known about primitive Christianity. From the beginning Christianity was a campaign of witnessing. And the witnessing did not concern merely what Jesus was doing within the recesses of the individual life. To take the words of Acts in that way is to do violence to the context and to all the evidence. On the contrary, the Epistles of Paul and all the sources make it abundantly plain that the testimony was primarily not to inner spiritual facts but to what Jesus had done once for all in His death and resurrection.

Christianity is based, then, upon an account of something that happened, and the Christian worker is primarily a witness. But if so, it is rather important that the Christian worker should tell the truth. When a man takes his seat upon the witness stand, it makes little difference what the cut of his coat is, or whether his sentences are nicely turned. The important thing is that he tell the truth, the whole truth, and nothing but the truth. If we are to be truly Christians, then, it does make a vast difference what our teachings are, and it is by no means aside from the point to set forth the teachings of Christianity in contrast with the teachings of the chief modern rival of Christianity.

The chief modern rival of Christianity is "liberalism." An examination of the teachings of liberalism in comparison with those of Christianity will show that at every point the two movements are in direct opposition. That examination will now be undertaken, though merely in a summary and cursory way.

3

God and Man

It has been observed in the last chapter that Christianity is based on an account of something that happened in the first century of our era. But before that account can be received, certain presuppositions must be accepted. The Christian gospel consists in an account of how God saved man, and before that gospel can be understood something must be known (1) about God and (2) about man. The doctrine of God and the doctrine of man are the two great presuppositions of the gospel. With regard to these presuppositions, as with regard to the gospel itself, modern liberalism is diametrically opposed to Christianity.

It is opposed to Christianity, in the first place, in its conception of God. But at this point we are met with a particularly insistent form of that objection to doctrinal matters which has already been considered. It is unnecessary, we are told, to have a "conception" of God; theology, or the knowledge of God, it is said, is the death of religion; we should not seek to know God, but should merely feel His presence.

With regard to this objection, it ought to be observed that if religion consists merely in feeling the presence of God, it is devoid of any moral quality whatever. Pure feeling, if there be such a thing, is non-moral. What makes affection for a human friend, for example, such an ennobling thing is the knowledge which we possess of the character of our friend. Human affection, apparently so simple, is really just bristling with dogma. It depends upon a host of observations treasured up in the mind with regard to the character of our friends. But if human affection is thus really dependent upon knowledge, why should it be otherwise with that supreme personal relationship which is at the basis of religion? Why should we be indignant about slanders directed against a human friend, while at the same time we are patient about the basest slanders directed against our God? Certainly it does make the greatest possible difference what we *think* about God; the knowledge of God is the very basis of religion.

How, then, shall God be known; how shall we become so acquainted with Him that personal fellowship may become possible? Some liberal preachers would say that we become acquainted with God only through Jesus. That assertion has an appearance of loyalty to our Lord, but in reality it is highly derogatory to Him. For Jesus Himself plainly recognized the validity of other ways of knowing God, and to reject those other ways is to reject the things that lay at the very centre of Jesus' life. Jesus plainly found God's hand in nature; the lilies of the field revealed to Him the weaving of God. He found God also in the moral law; the law written in the hearts of men was God's law, which revealed His righteousness. Finally Jesus plainly found God revealed in the Scriptures. How profound was our Lord's use of the words of prophets and psalmists! To say that such revelation of God was invalid, or is useless to us to-day, is to do despite to things that lay closest to Jesus' mind and heart.

But, as a matter of fact, when men say that we know God only as He is revealed in Jesus, they are denying all real knowledge of God whatever. For unless there be some idea of God independent of Jesus, the ascription of deity to Jesus has no meaning. To say, "Jesus is God," is meaningless unless the word "God" has an antecedent meaning attached to it. And the attaching of a meaning to the word "God" is accomplished by the means which have just been mentioned. We are not forgetting the words of Jesus in the Gospel of John, "He that hath seen me hath seen the Father." But these words do not mean that if a man had never known what the word "God" means, he could come to attach an idea to that word merely by his knowledge of Jesus' character. On the contrary, the disciples to whom Jesus was speaking had already a very definite conception of God; a knowledge of the one supreme Person was presupposed in all that Jesus said. But the disciples desired not only a knowledge of God but also intimate, personal contact. And that came through their intercourse with Jesus. Jesus revealed, in a wonderfully intimate way, the character of God, but such revelation obtained its true significance only on the basis both of the Old Testament heritage and of Jesus' own teaching. Rational theism, the knowledge of one Supreme Person, Maker and active Ruler of the world, is at the very root of Christianity.

But, the modern preacher will say, it is incongruous to attribute to Jesus an acceptance of "rational theism"; Jesus had a practical, not a theoretical, knowledge of God. There is a sense in which these words are true. Certainly no part of Jesus' knowledge of God was merely theoretical; everything that Jesus knew about God touched His heart and determined His actions. In that sense, Jesus' knowledge of God was "practical." But unfortunately that is not the sense in which the assertion of modern liberalism is meant. What is frequently meant by a "practical" knowledge of God in modern parlance is not a theoretical knowledge of God that is also practical, but a practical knowledge which is not theoretical—in other words, a knowledge which gives no information about objective reality, a knowledge which is no knowledge at all. And nothing could possibly be more unlike the religion of Jesus than that. The relation of Jesus to His heavenly Father was not a relation to a vague and impersonal goodness, it was not a relation which merely clothed itself in symbolic, personal form. On the contrary, it was a relation to a real Person, whose existence was just as definite and just as much a subject of theoretic knowledge as the existence of the lilies of the field that God had clothed. The very basis of the religion of Jesus was a triumphant belief in the real existence of a personal God.

And without that belief no type of religion can rightly appeal to Jesus to-day. Jesus was a theist, and rational theism is at the basis of Christianity. Jesus did not, indeed, support His theism by argument; He did not provide in advance answers to the Kantian attack upon the theistic proofs. But that means not that He was indifferent to the belief which is the logical result of those proofs, but that the belief stood so firm, both to Him and to His hearers, that in His teaching it is always presupposed. So to-day it is not necessary for all Christians to analyze the logical basis of their belief in God; the human mind has a wonderful faculty for the condensation of perfectly valid arguments, and what seems like an instinctive belief may turn out to be the result of many logical steps. Or, rather, it may be that the belief in a personal God is the result of a primitive revelation, and that the theistic proofs are only the logical confirmation of what was originally arrived at by a different means. At any rate, the logical confirmation of the belief in God is a vital concern to the Christian; at this point as at many others religion and philosophy are connected in the most intimate possible way. True religion can make no peace with a false philosophy, any more than with a science that is falsely so-called; a thing cannot possibly be true in religion and false in philosophy or in science. All methods of arriving at truth, if they be valid methods, will arrive at a harmonious result. Certainly the atheistic or agnostic Christianity which sometimes goes under the name of a "practical" religion is no Christianity at all. At the very root of Christianity is the belief in the real existence of a personal God.

Strangely enough, at the very time when modern liberalism is decrying the theistic proofs, and taking refuge in a "practical" knowledge which shall somehow be independent of scientifically or philosophically ascertained facts, the liberal preacher loves to use one designation of God which is nothing if not theistic; he loves to speak of God as "Father." The term certainly has the merit of ascribing personality to God. By some of those who use it, indeed, it is not seriously meant; by some it is employed because it is useful, not because it is true. But not all liberals are able to make the subtle distinction between theoretic judgments and judgments of value; some liberals, though perhaps a decreasing number, are true believers in a personal God. And such men are able to think of God truly as a Father.

The term presents a very lofty conception of God. It is not indeed exclusively Christian; the term "Father" has been applied to God outside of Christianity. It appears, for example, in the widespread belief in an "All-Father," which prevails among many races even in company with polytheism; it appears here and there in the Old Testament, and in pre-Christian Jewish writings subsequent to the Old Testament period. Such occurrences of the term are by no means devoid of significance. The Old Testament usage, in particular, is a worthy precursor of our Lord's teaching;

for although in the Old Testament the word "Father" ordinarily designates God in relation not to the individual, but to the nation or to the king, yet the individual Israelite, because of his part in the chosen people, felt himself to be in a peculiarly intimate relation to the covenant God. But despite this anticipation of the teaching of our Lord, Jesus brought such an incomparable enrichment of the usage of the term, that it is a correct instinct which regards the thought of God as Father as something characteristically Christian.

Modern men have been so much impressed with this element in Jesus' teaching that they have sometimes been inclined to regard it as the very sum and substance of our religion. We are not interested, they say, in many things for which men formerly gave their lives; we are not interested in the theology of the creeds; we are not interested in the doctrines of sin and salvation; we are not interested in atonement through the blood of Christ: enough for us is the simple truth of the fatherhood of God and its corollary, the brotherhood of man. We may not be very orthodox in the theological sense, they continue, but of course you will recognize us as Christians because we accept Jesus' teaching as to the Father God.

It is very strange how intelligent persons can speak in this way. It is very strange how those who accept only the universal fatherhood of God as the sum and substance of religion can regard themselves as Christians or can appeal to Jesus of Nazareth. For the plain fact is that this modern doctrine of the universal fatherhood of God formed no part whatever of Jesus' teaching. Where is it that Jesus may be supposed to have taught the universal fatherhood of God? Certainly it is not in the parable of the Prodigal Son. For in the first place, the publicans and sinners whose acceptance by Jesus formed the occasion both of the Pharisees' objection and of Jesus' answer to them by means of the parable, were not any men anywhere, but were members of the chosen people and as such might be designated as sons of God. In the second place, a parable is certainly not to be pressed in its details. So here because the joy of the father in the parable is like the joy of God when a sinner receives salvation at Jesus' hand, it does not follow that the relation which God sustains to still unrepentant sinners is that of a Father to his children. Where else, then, can the universal fatherhood of God be found? Surely not in the Sermon on the Mount; for throughout the Sermon on the Mount those who can call God Father are distinguished in the most emphatic way from the great world of the Gentiles outside. One passage in the discourse has indeed been urged in support of the modern doctrine: "But I say unto you, love your enemies and pray for them that persecute you; that ye may be sons of your Father who is in heaven; for He maketh His sun to rise on evil and good and sendeth rain on just and unjust" (Matt. 5:44, 45). But the passage certainly will not bear the weight which is hung upon it. God is indeed represented here as caring for all men whether evil or good, but He is certainly not called the Father of all. Indeed it might almost be said that the point of the passage depends on the fact that He is not the Father of all. He cares even for those who are not His children but His enemies; so His children, Jesus' disciples, ought to imitate Him by loving even those who are not their brethren but their persecutors. The modern doctrine of the universal fatherhood of God is not to be found in the teaching of Jesus.

And it is not to be found in the New Testament. The whole New Testament and Jesus Himself do indeed represent God as standing in a relation to all men, whether Christians or not, which is analogous to that in which a father stands to his children. He is the Author of the being of all, and as such might well be called the Father of all. He cares for all, and for that reason also might be called the Father of all. Here and there the figure of fatherhood seems to be used to designate this broader relationship which God sustains to all men or even to all created beings. So in an isolated passage in Hebrews, God is spoken of as the "Father of spirits" (Heb. 12:9). Here perhaps it is the relation of God, as creator, to the personal beings whom He has created which is in view. One of the clearest instances of the broader use of the figure of fatherhood is found in the speech of Paul at Athens, Acts 17:28: "For we are also His offspring." Here it is plainly the relation in which God stands to all men, whether Christians or not, which is in mind. But the words form part of an hexameter line and are taken from a pagan poet; they are not represented as part of the gospel, but merely as belonging to the common meeting-ground which Paul discovered in speaking to his pagan hearers. This passage is only typical of what appears, with respect to a universal fatherhood of God, in the New Testament as a whole. Something analogous to a universal fatherhood of God is taught in the New Testament. Here and there the terminology of fatherhood and sonship is even used to describe this general relationship. But such instances are extremely rare. Ordinarily the lofty term "Father" is used to describe a relationship of a far more intimate kind, the relationship in which God stands to the company of the redeemed.

The modern doctrine of the universal fatherhood of God, then, which is being celebrated as "the essence of Christianity," really belongs at best only to that vague natural religion which forms the presupposition which the Christian preacher can use when the gospel is to be proclaimed; and when it is regarded as a reassuring, all-sufficient thing, it comes into direct opposition to the New Testament. The gospel itself refers to something entirely different; the really distinctive New Testament teaching about the fatherhood of God concerns only those who have been brought into the household of faith.

There is nothing narrow about such teaching; for the door of the household of faith is open wide to all. That door is the "new and living way" which Jesus opened by His blood. And if we really love our fellowmen, we shall not go about the world, with the liberal preacher, trying to make men satisfied with the coldness of a vague natural religion. But by the preaching of the gospel we shall invite them into the warmth and joy of the house of God. Christianity offers men all that is offered by the modern liberal teaching about the universal fatherhood of God; but it is Christianity only because it offers also infinitely more.

But the liberal conception of God differs even more fundamentally from the Christian view than in the different circle of ideas connected with the terminology of fatherhood. The truth is that liberalism has lost sight of the very centre and core of the Christian teaching. In the Christian view of God as set forth in the Bible, there are many elements. But one attribute of God is absolutely fundamental in the Bible; one attribute is absolutely necessary in order to render intelligible all the rest. That attribute is the awful transcendence of God. From beginning to end the Bible is concerned to set forth the awful gulf that separates the creature from the Creator. It is true, indeed, that according to the Bible God is immanent in the world. Not a sparrow falls to the ground without Him. But he is immanent in the world not because He is identified with the world, but because He is the free Creator and Upholder of it. Between the creature and the Creator a great gulf is fixed.

In modern liberalism, on the other hand, this sharp distinction between God and the world is broken down, and the name "God" is applied to the mighty world process itself. We find ourselves in the midst of a mighty process, which manifests itself in the indefinitely small and in the indefinitely great—in the infinitesimal life which is revealed through the microscope and in the vast movements of the heavenly spheres. To this world-process, of which we ourselves form a part, we apply the dread name of "God." God, therefore, it is said in effect, is not a person distinct from ourselves; on the contrary our life is a part of His. Thus the Gospel story of the Incarnation, according to modern liberalism, is sometimes thought of as a symbol of the general truth that man at his best is one with God.

It is strange how such a representation can be regarded as anything new, for as a matter of fact, pantheism is a very ancient phenomenon. It has always been with us, to blight the religious life of man. And modern liberalism, even when it is not consistently pantheistic, is at any rate pantheizing. It tends everywhere to break down the separateness between God and the world, and the sharp personal distinction between God and man. Even the sin of man on this view ought logically to be regarded as part of the life of God. Very different is the living and holy God of the Bible and of Christian faith.

Christianity differs from liberalism, then, in the first place, in its conception of God. But it also differs in its conception of man.

Modern liberalism has lost all sense of the gulf that separates the creature from the Creator; its doctrine of man follows naturally from its doctrine of God. But it is not only the creature limitations of mankind which are denied. Even more important is another difference. According to the Bible, man is a sinner under the just condemnation of God; according to modern liberalism, there is really no such thing as sin. At the very root of the modern liberal movement is the loss of the consciousness of sin.[1]

The consciousness of sin was formerly the starting-point of all preaching; but to-day it is gone. Characteristic of the modern age, above all else, is a supreme confidence in human goodness; the religious literature of the day is redolent of that confidence. Get beneath the rough exterior of men, we are told, and we shall discover enough self-sacrifice to found upon it the hope of society; the world's evil, it is said, can be overcome with the world's good; no help is needed from outside the world.

What has produced this satisfaction with human goodness? What has become of the consciousness of sin? The consciousness of sin has certainly been lost. But what has removed it from the hearts of men?

In the first place, the war has perhaps had something to do with the change. In time of war, our attention is called so exclusively to the sins of other people that we are sometimes inclined to forget our own sins. Attention to the sins of other people is, indeed, sometimes necessary. It is quite right to be indignant against any oppression of the weak which is being carried on by the strong. But such a habit of mind, if made permanent, if carried over into the days of peace, has its dangers. It joins forces with the collectivism of the modern state to obscure the individual, personal character of guilt. If John Smith beats his wife

---

1. For what follows, see "The Church in the War," in *The Presbyterian*, for May 29, 1919, pp. 10f.

nowadays, no one is so old-fashioned as to blame John Smith for it. On the contrary, it is said, John Smith is evidently the victim of some more of that Bolshevistic propaganda; Congress ought to be called in extra session in order to take up the case of John Smith in an alien and sedition law.

But the loss of the consciousness of sin is far deeper than the war; it has its roots in a mighty spiritual process which has been active during the past seventy-five years. Like other great movements, that process has come silently—so silently that its results have been achieved before the plain man was even aware of what was taking place. Nevertheless, despite all superficial continuity, a remarkable change has come about within the last seventy-five years. The change is nothing less than the substitution of paganism for Christianity as the dominant view of life. Seventy-five years ago, Western civilization, despite inconsistencies, was still predominantly Christian; to-day it is predominantly pagan.

In speaking of "paganism," we are not using a term of reproach. Ancient Greece was pagan, but it was glorious, and the modern world has not even begun to equal its achievements. What, then, is paganism? The answer is not really difficult. Paganism is that view of life which finds the highest goal of human existence in the healthy and harmonious and joyous development of existing human faculties. Very different is the Christian ideal. Paganism is optimistic with regard to unaided human nature, whereas Christianity is the religion of the broken heart.

In saying that Christianity is the religion of the broken heart, we do not mean that Christianity ends with the broken heart; we do not mean that the characteristic Christian attitude is a continual beating on the breast or a continual crying of "Woe is me." Nothing could be further from the fact. On the contrary, Christianity means that sin is faced once for all, and then is cast, by the grace of God, forever into the depths of the sea. The trouble with the paganism of ancient Greece, as with the paganism of modern times, was not in the superstructure, which was glorious, but in the foundation, which was rotten. There was always something to be covered up; the enthusiasm of the architect was maintained only by ignoring the disturbing fact of sin. In Christianity, on the other hand, nothing needs to be covered up. The fact of sin is faced squarely once for all, and is dealt with by the grace of God. But then, after sin has been removed by the grace of God, the Christian can proceed to develop joyously every faculty that God has given him. Such is the higher Christian humanism—a humanism founded not upon human pride but upon divine grace.

But although Christianity does not end with the broken heart, it does begin with the broken heart; it begins with the consciousness of sin. Without the consciousness of sin, the whole of the gospel will seem to be an idle tale. But how can the consciousness of sin be revived? Something no doubt can be accomplished by the proclamation of the law of God, for the law reveals transgressions. The whole of the law, moreover, should be proclaimed. It will hardly be wise to adopt the suggestion (recently offered among many suggestions as to the ways in which we shall have to modify our message in order to retain the allegiance of the returning soldiers) that we must stop treating the little sins as though they were big sins. That suggestion means apparently that we must not worry too much about the little sins, but must let them remain unmolested. With regard to such an expedient, it may perhaps be suggested that in the moral battle we are fighting against a very resourceful enemy, who does not reveal the position of his guns by desultory artillery action when he plans a great attack. In the moral battle, as in the Great European War, the quiet sectors are usually the most dangerous. It is through the "little sins" that Satan gains an entrance into our lives. Probably, therefore, it will be prudent to watch all sectors of the front and lose no time about introducing the unity of command.

But if the consciousness of sin is to be produced, the law of God must be proclaimed in the lives of Christian people as well as in word. It is quite useless for the preacher to breathe out fire and brimstone from the pulpit, if at the same time the occupants of the pews go on taking sin very lightly and being content with the moral standards of the world. The rank and file of the Church must do their part in so proclaiming the law of God by their lives that the secrets of men's hearts shall be revealed.

All these things, however, are in themselves quite insufficient to produce the consciousness of sin. The more one observes the condition of the Church, the more one feels obliged to confess that the conviction of sin is a great mystery, which can be produced only by the Spirit of God. Proclamation of the law, in word and in deed, can prepare for the experience, but the experience itself comes from God. When a man has that experience, when a man comes under the conviction of sin, his whole attitude toward life is transformed; he wonders at his former blindness, and the message of the gospel, which formerly seemed to be an idle tale, becomes now instinct with light. But it is God alone who can produce the change.

Only, let us not try to do without the Spirit of God. The fundamental fault of the modern Church is that she is busily engaged in an absolutely impossible task—she is busily engaged in calling the righteous to repentance. Modern preachers are trying to bring men into the Church without requiring them to relinquish their pride; they are trying to help men avoid the conviction of sin. The preacher gets up into the pulpit, opens the Bible, and addresses the congregation somewhat as follows: "You people are very good," he says; "you respond to every appeal that looks toward the welfare of the community. Now we have in the Bible—especially in the life of Jesus—something so good that we believe it is good enough even for you good people." Such is modern preaching. It is heard every Sunday in thousands of pulpits. But it is entirely futile. Even our Lord did not call the righteous to repentance, and probably we shall be no more successful than He.

4

The Bible

Modern liberalism, it has been observed so far, has lost sight of the two great presuppositions of the Christian message—the living God, and the fact of sin. The liberal doctrine of God and the liberal doctrine of man are both diametrically opposite to the Christian view. But the divergence concerns not only the presuppositions of the message, but also the message itself.

The Christian message has come to us through the Bible. What shall we think about this Book in which the message is contained?

According to the Christian view, the Bible contains an account of a revelation from God to man, which is found nowhere else. It is true, the Bible also contains a confirmation and a wonderful enrichment of the revelations which are given also by the things that God has made and by the conscience of man. "The heavens declare the glory of God; and the firmament showeth his handywork"—these words are a confirmation of the revelation of God in nature; "all have sinned and fall short of the glory of God"—these words are a confirmation of what is attested by the conscience. But in addition to such reaffirmations of what might conceivably be learned elsewhere—as a matter of fact, because of men's blindness, even so much is learned elsewhere only in comparatively obscure fashion—the Bible also contains an account of a revelation which is absolutely new. That new revelation concerns the way by which sinful man can come into communion with the living God.

The way was opened, according to the Bible, by an act of God, when, almost nineteen hundred years ago, outside the walls of Jerusalem, the eternal Son was offered as a sacrifice for the sins of men. To that one great event the whole Old Testament looks forward, and in that one event the whole of the New Testament finds its centre and core. Salvation then, according to the Bible, is not something that was discovered, but something that happened. Hence appears the uniqueness of the Bible. All the ideas of Christianity might be discovered in some other religion, yet there would be in that other religion no Christianity. For Christianity depends, not upon a complex of ideas, but upon the narration of an event. Without that event, the world, in the Christian view, is altogether dark, and humanity is lost under the guilt of sin. There can be no salvation by the discovery of eternal truth, for eternal truth brings naught but despair, because of sin. But a new face has been put upon life by the blessed thing that God did when He offered up His only begotten Son.

An objection is sometimes offered against this view of the contents of the Bible.[1] Must we, it is said, depend upon what happened so long ago? Does salvation wait upon the examination of musty records? Is the trained student of Palestinian history the modern priest without whose gracious intervention no one can see God? Can we not find, instead, a salvation that is independent of history, a salvation that depends only on what is with us here and now?

---

1. For what follows compare *History and Faith*, 1915, pp. 13–15.

The objection is not devoid of weight. But it ignores one of the primary evidences for the truth of the gospel record. That evidence is found in Christian experience. Salvation does depend upon what happened long ago, but the event of long ago has effects that continue until today. We are told in the New Testament that Jesus offered Himself as a sacrifice for the sins of those who should believe on Him. That is a record of a past event. But we can make trial of it to-day, and making trial of it we find it to be true. We are told in the New Testament that on a certain morning long ago Jesus rose from the dead. That again is a record of a past event. But again we can make trial of it, and making trial of it we discover that Jesus is truly a living Saviour to-day.

But at this point a fatal error lies in wait. It is one of the root errors of modern liberalism. Christian experience, we have just said, is useful as confirming the gospel message. But because it is necessary, many men have jumped to the conclusion that it is all that is necessary. Having a present experience of Christ in the heart, may we not, it is said, hold that experience no matter what history may tell us as to the events of the first Easter morning? May we not make ourselves altogether independent of the results of Biblical criticism? No matter what sort of man history may tell us Jesus of Nazareth actually was, no matter what history may say about the real meaning of His death or about the story of His alleged resurrection, may we not continue to experience the presence of Christ in our souls?

The trouble is that the experience thus maintained is not Christian experience. Religious experience it may be, but Christian experience it certainly is not. For Christian experience depends absolutely upon an event. The Christian says to himself:

"I have meditated upon the problem of becoming right with God, I have tried to produce a righteousness that will stand in His sight; but when I heard the gospel message I learned that what I had weakly striven to accomplish had been accomplished by the Lord Jesus Christ when He died for me on the Cross and completed His redeeming work by the glorious resurrection. If the thing has not yet been done, if I merely have an idea of its accomplishment, then I am of all men most miserable, for I am still in my sins. My Christian life, then, depends altogether upon the truth of the New Testament record."

Christian experience is rightly used when it confirms the documentary evidence. But it can never possibly provide a substitute for the documentary evidence. We know that the gospel story is true partly because of the early date of the documents in which it appears, the evidence as to their authorship, the internal evidence of their truth, the impossibility of explaining them as being based upon deception or upon myth. This evidence is gloriously confirmed by present experience, which adds to the documentary evidence that wonderful directness and immediacy of conviction which delivers us from fear. Christian experience is rightly used when it helps to convince us that the events narrated in the New Testament actually did occur; but it can never enable us to be Christians whether the events occurred or not. It is a fair flower, and should be prized as a gift of God. But cut it from its root in the blessed Book, and it soon withers away and dies.

Thus the revelation of which an account is contained in the Bible embraces not only a reaffirmation of eternal truths—itself necessary because the truths have been obscured by the blinding effect of sin—but also a revelation which sets forth the meaning of an act of God.

The contents of the Bible, then, are unique. But another fact about the Bible is also important. The Bible might contain an account of a true revelation from God, and yet the account be full of error. Before the full authority of the Bible can be established, therefore, it is necessary to add to the Christian doctrine of revelation the Christian doctrine of inspiration. The latter doctrine means that the Bible not only is an account of important things, but that the account itself is true, the writers having been so preserved from error, despite a full maintenance of their habits of thought and expression, that the resulting Book is the "infallible rule of faith and practice."

This doctrine of "plenary inspiration" has been made the subject of persistent misrepresentation. Its opponents speak of it as though it involved a mechanical theory of the activity of the Holy Spirit. The Spirit, it is said, is represented in this doctrine as dictating the Bible to writers who were really little more than stenographers. But of course all such caricatures are without basis in fact, and it is rather surprising that intelligent men should be so blinded by prejudice about this matter as not even to examine for themselves the perfectly accessible treatises in which the doctrine of plenary inspiration is set forth. It is usually considered good practice to examine a thing for one's self before echoing the vulgar ridicule of it. But in connection with the Bible, such scholarly restraints are somehow regarded as out of place. It is so much easier to content one's self with a few opprobrious adjectives such as "mechanical," or the like. Why engage in serious criticism when the people prefer ridicule?

Why attack a real opponent when it is easier to knock down a man of straw?[2]

As a matter of fact, the doctrine of plenary inspiration does not deny the individuality of the Biblical writers; it does not ignore their use of ordinary means for acquiring information; it does not involve any lack of interest in the historical situations which gave rise to the Biblical books. What it does deny is the presence of error in the Bible. It supposes that the Holy Spirit so informed the minds of the Biblical writers that they were kept from falling into the errors that mar all other books. The Bible might contain an account of a genuine revelation of God, and yet not contain a true account. But according to the doctrine of inspiration, the account is as a matter of fact a true account; the Bible is an "infallible rule of faith and practice."

Certainly that is a stupendous claim, and it is no wonder that it has been attacked. But the trouble is that the attack is not always fair. If the liberal preacher objected to the doctrine of plenary inspiration on the ground that as a matter of fact there are errors in the Bible, he might be right and he might be wrong, but at any rate the discussion would be conducted on the proper ground. But too often the preacher desires to avoid the delicate question of errors in the Bible—a question which might give offence to the rank and file—and prefers to speak merely against "mechanical" theories of inspiration, the theory of "dictation," the "superstitious use of the Bible as a talisman," or the like. It all sounds to the plain man as though it were very harmless. Does

---

2. It is not denied that there are some persons in the modern Church who do neglect the context of Bible quotations and who do ignore the human characteristics of the Biblical writers. But in an entirely unwarrantable manner this defective way of using the Bible is attributed, by insinuation at least, to the great body of those who have held to the inspiration of Scripture.

not the liberal preacher say that the Bible is "divine"—indeed that it is the more divine because it is the more human? What could be more edifying than that? But of course such appearances are deceptive. A Bible that is full of error is certainly divine in the modern pantheizing sense of "divine," according to which God is just another name for the course of the world with all its imperfections and all its sin. But the God whom the Christian worships is a God of truth.

It must be admitted that there are many Christians who do not accept the doctrine of plenary inspiration. That doctrine is denied not only by liberal opponents of Christianity, but also by many true Christian men. There are many Christian men in the modern Church who find in the origin of Christianity no mere product of evolution but a real entrance of the creative power of God, who depend for their salvation, not at all upon their own efforts to lead the Christ life, but upon the atoning blood of Christ—there are many men in the modern Church who thus accept the central message of the Bible and yet believe that the message has come to us merely on the authority of trustworthy witnesses unaided in their literary work by any supernatural guidance of the Spirit of God. There are many who believe that the Bible is right at the central point, in its account of the redeeming work of Christ, and yet believe that it contains many errors. Such men are not really liberals, but Christians; because they have accepted as true the message upon which Christianity depends. A great gulf separates them from those who reject the supernatural act of God with which Christianity stands or falls.

It is another question, however, whether the mediating view of the Bible which is thus maintained is logically tenable, the trouble being that our Lord Himself seems to have held the high view of the Bible which is here being rejected. Certainly it is another question—and a question which the present writer would answer with an emphatic negative—whether the panic about the Bible, which gives rise to such concessions, is at all justified by the facts. If the Christian make full use of his Christian privileges, he finds the seat of authority in the whole Bible, which he regards as no mere word of man but as the very Word of God.

Very different is the view of modern liberalism. The modern liberal rejects not only the doctrine of plenary inspiration, but even such respect for the Bible as would be proper over against any ordinarily trustworthy book. But what is substituted for the Christian view of the Bible? What is the liberal view as to the seat of authority in religion?[3]

The impression is sometimes produced that the modern liberal substitutes for the authority of the Bible the authority of Christ. He cannot accept, he says, what he regards as the perverse moral teaching of the Old Testament or the sophistical arguments of Paul. But he regards himself as being the true Christian because, rejecting the rest of the Bible, he depends upon Jesus alone.

This impression, however, is utterly false. The modern liberal does not really hold to the authority of Jesus. Even if he did so, indeed, he would still be impoverishing greatly his knowledge of God and of the way of salvation. The words of Jesus, spoken during His earthly ministry, could hardly contain all that we need to know about God and about the way of salvation; for the meaning of Jesus' redeeming work could hardly be fully set forth before that work was done. It could be set forth indeed by

---

3. For what follows, compare "For Christ or Against Him," in *The Presbyterian*, for January 20, 1921, p. 9.

way of prophecy, and as a matter of fact it was so set forth by Jesus even in the days of His flesh. But the full explanation could naturally be given only after the work was done. And such was actually the divine method. It is doing despite, not only to the Spirit of God, but also to Jesus Himself, to regard the teaching of the Holy Spirit, given through the apostles, as at all inferior in authority to the teaching of Jesus.

As a matter of fact, however, the modern liberal does not hold fast even to the authority of Jesus. Certainly he does not accept the words of Jesus as they are recorded in the Gospels. For among the recorded words of Jesus are to be found just those things which are most abhorrent to the modern liberal Church, and in His recorded words Jesus also points forward to the fuller revelation which was afterwards to be given through His apostles. Evidently, therefore, those words of Jesus which are to be regarded as authoritative by modern liberalism must first be selected from the mass of the recorded words by a critical process. The critical process is certainly very difficult, and the suspicion often arises that the critic is retaining as genuine words of the historical Jesus only those words which conform to his own preconceived ideas. But even after the sifting process has been completed, the liberal scholar is still unable to accept as authoritative all the sayings of Jesus; he must finally admit that even the "historical" Jesus as reconstructed by modern historians said some things that are untrue.

So much is usually admitted. But, it is maintained, although not everything that Jesus said is true, His central "life-purpose" is still to be regarded as regulative for the Church. But what then was the life-purpose of Jesus? According to the shortest, and if modern criticism be accepted, the earliest of the Gospels, the Son of Man "came not to be ministered unto, but to minister, and to give his life a ransom for many" (Mk. 10:45). Here the vicarious death is put as the "life-purpose" of Jesus. Such an utterance must of course be pushed aside by the modern liberal Church. The truth is that the life-purpose of Jesus discovered by modern liberalism is not the life-purpose of the real Jesus, but merely represents those elements in the teaching of Jesus—isolated and misinterpreted—which happen to agree with the modern program. It is not Jesus, then, who is the real authority, but the modern principle by which the selection within Jesus' recorded teaching has been made. Certain isolated ethical principles of the Sermon on the Mount are accepted, not at all because they are teachings of Jesus, but because they agree with modern ideas.

It is not true at all, then, that modern liberalism is based upon the authority of Jesus. It is obliged to reject a vast deal that is absolutely essential in Jesus' example and teaching—notably His consciousness of being the heavenly Messiah. The real authority, for liberalism, can only be "the Christian consciousness" or "Christian experience." But how shall the findings of the Christian consciousness be established? Surely not by a majority vote of the organized Church. Such a method would obviously do away with all liberty of conscience. The only authority, then, can be individual experience; truth can only be that which "helps" the individual man. Such an authority is obviously no authority at all; for individual experience is endlessly diverse, and when once truth is regarded only as that which works at any particular time, it ceases to be truth. The result is an abysmal skepticism.

The Christian man, on the other hand, finds in the Bible the very Word of God. Let it not be said that dependence upon a book is a dead or an artificial thing. The Reformation of the sixteenth century was founded upon the authority of the Bible, yet it set the world aflame. Dependence upon a word of man would be slavish, but dependence upon God's word is life. Dark and gloomy would be the world, if we were left to our own devices, and had no blessed Word of God. The Bible, to the Christian is not a burdensome law, but the very Magna Charta of Christian liberty.

It is no wonder, then, that liberalism is totally different from Christianity, for the foundation is different. Christianity is founded upon the Bible. It bases upon the Bible both its thinking and its life. Liberalism on the other hand is founded upon the shifting emotions of sinful men.

5

Christian

Three points of difference between liberalism and Christianity have been noticed so far. The two religions are different with regard to the presuppositions of the Christian message, the view of God and the view of man; and they are also different with regard to their estimate of the Book in which the message is contained. It is not surprising, then, that they differ fundamentally with regard to the message itself. But before the message is considered, we must consider the Person upon whom the message is based. The Person is Jesus. And in their attitude toward Jesus, liberalism and Christianity are sharply opposed.

The Christian attitude toward Jesus appears in the whole New Testament. In examining the New Testament witness it has become customary in recent years to begin with the Epistles of Paul.[1] This custom is sometimes based upon error; it is sometimes based upon the view that the Epistles of Paul are "primary" sources of information, while the Gospels are considered to be only "secondary." As a matter of fact, the Gospels, as well as the Epistles, are primary sources of the highest possible value. But the custom of beginning with Paul is at least convenient. Its convenience is due to the large measure of agreement which prevails with regard to the Pauline Epistles. About the date and

---

1. This method of approach has been followed by the present writer in *The Origin of Paul's Religion*, 1921.

authorship of the Gospels there is debate; but with regard to
the authorship and approximate date of the principal epistles of
Paul all serious historians, whether Christian or non-Christian,
are agreed. It is universally admitted that the chief of the extant
epistles attributed to Paul were really written by a man of the first
Christian generation, who was himself a contemporary of Jesus
and had come into personal contact with certain of Jesus' intimate friends. What, then, was the attitude of this representative
of the first Christian generation toward Jesus of Nazareth?

The answer cannot be at all in doubt. The apostle Paul clearly
stood always toward Jesus in a truly religious relationship. Jesus
was not for Paul merely an example for faith; He was primarily
the object of faith. The religion of Paul did not consist in having
faith in God like the faith which Jesus had in God; it consisted
rather in having faith *in Jesus*. An appeal to the example of Jesus
is not indeed absent from the Pauline Epistles, and certainly it
was not absent from Paul's life. The example of Jesus was found
by Paul, moreover, not merely in the acts of incarnation and
atonement but even in the daily life of Jesus in Palestine. Exag-
geration with regard to this matter should be avoided. Plainly
Paul knew far more about the life of Jesus than in the Epistles he
has seen fit to tell; plainly the Epistles do not begin to contain
all the instruction which Paul had given to the Churches at the
commencement of their Christian life. But even after exaggerations have been avoided, the fact is significant enough. The plain
fact is that imitation of Jesus, important though it was for Paul,
was swallowed up by something far more important still. Not
the example of Jesus, but the redeeming work of Jesus, was the
primary thing for Paul. The religion of Paul was not primarily
faith in God like Jesus' faith; it was faith in Jesus; Paul commit-

ted to Jesus without reserve the eternal destinies of his soul. That is what we mean when we say that Paul stood in a truly religious relation to Jesus.

But Paul was not the first to stand in this religious relation to Jesus. Evidently, at this decisive point, he was only continuing an attitude toward Jesus which had already been assumed by those who had been Christians before him. Paul was not indeed led to assume that attitude by the persuasions of the earlier disciples; he was converted by the Lord Himself on the road to Damascus. But the faith so induced was in essentials like the faith which had already prevailed among the earlier disciples. Indeed, an account of the redeeming work of Christ is designated by Paul as something that he had "received"; and that account had evidently been accompanied already in the primitive Church by trust in the Redeemer. Paul was not the first who had faith in Jesus, as distinguished from faith in God like the faith which Jesus had; Paul was not the first to make Jesus the object of faith.

So much will no doubt be admitted by all. But who were the predecessors of Paul in making Jesus the object of faith? The obvious answer has always been that they were the primitive disciples in Jerusalem, and that answer really stands abundantly firm. A strange attempt has indeed been made in recent years, by Bousset and Heitmüller, to cast doubt upon it. What Paul "received," it has been suggested, was received, not from the primitive Jerusalem Church, but from such Christian communities as the one at Antioch. But this attempt at interposing an extra link between the Jerusalem Church and Paul has resulted in failure. The Epistles really provide abundant information as to Paul's relations to Jerusalem. Paul was deeply interested in the Jerusalem Church; in opposition to his Judaizing opponents, who had in certain matters appealed to the original apostles against him, he emphasizes his agreement with Peter and the rest. But even the Judaizers had had no objection to Paul's way of regarding Jesus as the object of faith; about that matter there is not in the Epistles the least suspicion of any debate. About the place of the Mosaic law in the Christian life there was discussion, though even with regard to that matter the Judaizers were entirely unjustified in appealing to the original apostles against Paul. But with regard to the attitude toward Jesus the original apostles had evidently given not even the slightest color for an appeal to them against the teaching of Paul. Evidently in making Jesus the object of religious faith—the thing that was the heart and soul of Paul's religion—Paul was in no disagreement with those who had been apostles before him. Had there been such disagreement, the "right hand of fellowship," which the pillars of the Jerusalem Church gave to Paul (Gal. 2:9), would have been impossible. The facts are really too plain. The whole of early Christian history is a hopeless riddle unless the Jerusalem Church, as well as Paul, made Jesus the object of religious faith. Primitive Christianity certainly did not consist in the mere imitation of Jesus.

But was this "faith in Jesus" justified by the teaching of Jesus Himself? The question has really been answered in Chapter II. It was there shown that Jesus most certainly did not keep His Person out of His gospel, but on the contrary presented Himself as the Saviour of men. The demonstration of that fact was the highest merit of the late James Penney. His work on "Jesus and the Gospel" is faulty in some respects; it is marred by an undue concessiveness toward some modern types of criticism. But just because of its concessiveness with regard to many important matters, its main thesis stands all the more firm. Penney has shown that no matter what view be taken of the sources underlying the Gospels, and no matter what elements in the Gospels be rejected as secondary, still even the supposed "historical Jesus," as He is left after the critical process is done, plainly presented Himself, not merely as an example for faith, but as the object of faith.

It may be added, moreover, that Jesus did not invite the confidence of men by minimizing the load which He offered to bear. He did not say: "Trust me to give you acceptance with God, because acceptance with God is not difficult; God does not regard sin so seriously after all." On the contrary Jesus presented the wrath of God in a more awful way than it was afterwards presented by His disciples; it was Jesus—Jesus whom modern liberals represent as a mild-mannered exponent of an indiscriminating love—it was Jesus who spoke of the outer darkness and the everlasting fire, of the sin that shall not be forgiven either in this world or in that which is to come. There is nothing in Jesus' teaching about the character of God which in itself can evoke trust. On the contrary the awful presentation can give rise, in the hearts of us sinners, only to despair. Trust arises only when we attend to God's way of salvation. And that way is found in Jesus. Jesus did not invite the confidence of men by a minimizing presentation of what was necessary in order that sinners might stand faultless before the awful throne of God. On the contrary, he invited confidence by the presentation of His own wondrous Person. Great was the guilt of sin, but Jesus was greater still. God, according to Jesus, was a loving Father; but He was a loving Father, not of the sinful world, but of those whom He Himself had brought into His Kingdom through the Son.

The truth is, the witness of the New Testament, with regard to Jesus as the object of faith, is an absolutely unitary witness.

The thing is rooted far too deep in the records of primitive Christianity ever to be removed by any critical process. The Jesus spoken of in the New Testament was no mere teacher of righteousness, no mere pioneer in a new type of religious life, but One who was regarded, and regarded Himself, as the Saviour whom men could trust.

But by modern liberalism He is regarded in a totally different way. Christians stand in a religious relation to Jesus; liberals do not stand in a religious relation to Jesus—what difference could be more profound than that? The modern liberal preacher reverences Jesus; he has the name of Jesus forever on his lips; he speaks of Jesus as the supreme revelation of God; he enters, or tries to enter, into the religious life of Jesus. But he does not stand in a religious relation to Jesus. Jesus for him is an example for faith, not the object of faith. The modern liberal tries to have faith in God like the faith which he supposes Jesus had in God; but he does not have faith in Jesus.

According to modern liberalism, in other words, Jesus was the Founder of Christianity because He was the first Christian, and Christianity consists in maintenance of the religious life which Jesus instituted.

But was Jesus really a Christian? Or, to put the same question in another way, are we able or ought we as Christians to enter in every respect into the experience of Jesus and make Him in every respect our example? Certain difficulties arise with regard to this question.

The first difficulty appears in the Messianic consciousness of Jesus. The Person whom we are asked to take as our example thought that He was the heavenly Son of Man who was to be the final Judge of all the earth. Can we imitate Him there? The trouble is not merely that Jesus undertook a special mission which can never be ours. That difficulty might conceivably be overcome; we might still take Jesus as our example by adapting to our station in life the kind of character which He displayed in His. But another difficulty is more serious. The real trouble is that the lofty claim of Jesus, if, as modern liberalism is constrained to believe, the claim was unjustified, places a moral stain upon Jesus' character. What shall be thought of a human being who lapsed so far from the path of humility and sanity as to believe that the eternal destinies of the world were committed into His hands? The truth is that if Jesus be merely an example, He is not a worthy example; for He claimed to be far more.

Against this objection modern liberalism has usually adopted a policy of palliation. The Messianic consciousness, it is said, arose late in the experience of Jesus, and was not really fundamental. What was really fundamental, the liberal historians continue, was the consciousness of sonship toward God—a consciousness which may be shared by every humble disciple. The Messianic consciousness, on this view, arose only as an afterthought. Jesus was conscious, it is said, of standing toward God in a relation of untroubled sonship. But He discovered that this relation was not shared by others. He became aware, therefore, of a mission to bring others into the place of privilege which He Himself already occupied. That mission made Him unique, and to give expression to His uniqueness He adopted, late in His life and almost against His will, the faulty category of Messiahship.

Many are the forms in which some such psychological reconstruction of the life of Jesus has been set forth in recent years. The modern world has devoted its very best literary efforts to this task. But the efforts have resulted in failure. In the first place, there is no real evidence that the reconstructed Jesus is historical. The sources know nothing of a Jesus who adopted the category of Messiahship late in life and against His will. On the contrary the only Jesus that they present is a Jesus who based the whole of His ministry upon His stupendous claim. In the second place, even if the modern reconstruction were historical it would not solve the problem at all. The problem is a moral and psychological problem. How can a human being who lapsed so far from the path of rectitude as to think Himself to be the judge of all the earth—how can such a human being be regarded as the supreme example for mankind? It is absolutely no answer to the objection to say that Jesus accepted the category of Messiahship reluctantly and late in life. No matter when He succumbed to temptation the outstanding fact is that, on this view, He did succumb; and that moral defeat places an indelible stain upon His character. No doubt it is possible to make excuses for Him, and many excuses are as a matter of fact made by the liberal historians. But what has become then of the claim of liberalism to be truly Christian? Can a man for whom excuses have to be made be regarded as standing to his modern critics in a relationship even remotely analogous to that in which the Jesus of the New Testament stands to the Christian Church?

But there is another difficulty in the way of regarding Jesus as simply the first Christian. This second difficulty concerns the attitude of Jesus toward sin. If Jesus is separated from us by his Messianic consciousness, He is separated from us even more fundamentally by the absence in Him of a sense of sin.

With respect to the sinlessness of Jesus modern liberal historians find themselves in a quandary. To affirm that He was sinless means to relinquish much of that ease of defending liberal religion which the liberal historians are anxious to preserve, and involves hazardous assumptions with regard to the nature of sin. For if sin is merely imperfection, how can an absolute negation of it be ventured upon within a process of nature which is supposed to be ever changing and ever advancing? The very idea of "sinlessness," much more the reality of it, requires us to conceive of sin as transgression of a fixed law or a fixed standard, and involves the conception of an absolute goodness. But to that conception of an *absolute* goodness the modern evolutionary view of the world properly speaking has no right. At any rate, if such absolute goodness is to be allowed to intrude at a definite point in the present world-process, we are involved in that supernaturalism which, as will be observed later, is the very thing that the modern reconstruction of Christianity is most anxious to avoid. Once affirm that Jesus was sinless and all other men sinful, and you have entered into irreconcilable conflict with the whole modern point of view. On the other hand, if there are scientific objections, from the liberal point of view, against an affirmation of the sinlessness of Jesus, there are also very obvious religious objections against an opposite affirmation of His sinfulness—difficulties for modern liberalism as well as for the theology of the historic Church. If Jesus was sinful like other men, the last remnant of his uniqueness would seem to have disappeared, and all continuity with the previous development of Christianity would seem to be destroyed.

In the face of this quandary the modern liberal historian is inclined to avoid rash assertions. He will not be sure that when Jesus taught His disciples to say, "Forgive us our debts," He did not pray that prayer with them; on the other hand he will not really face the results that logically follow from his doubt. In his

perplexity, he is apt to be content with the assertion that whether
Jesus was sinless or not He was at any rate immeasurably above
the rest of us. Whether Jesus was "sinless" is an academic question, we shall probably be told, that concerns the mysteries of
the absolute; what we need to do is to bow in simple reverence
before a holiness which compared with our impurity is as a white
light in a dark place.

That such avoidance of the difficulty is unsatisfactory hardly
requires proof; obviously the liberal theologian is trying to obtain the religious advantages of an affirmation of sinlessness in
Jesus at the same time that he obtains the supposed scientific
advantages of its denial. But just for the moment we are not
concerned with the question at all; we are not concerned to
determine whether as a matter of fact Jesus was sinless or no.
What we need to observe just now is that whether Jesus was
sinful or sinless at any rate in the record of His life which has
actually come into our hands He displays no consciousness of
sin. Even if the words "Why callest thou me good?" meant that
Jesus denied the attribute of goodness to Himself—which they
do not—it would still remain true that He never in His recorded
words deals in any intelligible way with sin in His own life. In
the account of the temptation we are told how He kept sin from
entering, but never how He dealt with it after its entrance had
been effected. The religious experience of Jesus, as it is recorded
in the Gospels, in other words, gives us no information about
the way in which sin shall be removed.

Yet in the Gospels Jesus is represented constantly as dealing
with the problem of sin. He always assumes that other men are
sinful; yet He never finds sin in Himself. A stupendous difference is found here between Jesus' experience and ours.

That difference prevents the religious experience of Jesus from serving as the sole basis of the Christian life. For clearly if Christianity is anything it is a way of getting rid of sin. At any rate, if it is not that it is useless; for all men have sinned. And as a matter of fact it was that from the very beginning. Whether the beginning of Christian preaching be put on the day of Pentecost or when Jesus first taught in Galilee, in either case one of its first words was "Repent." Throughout the whole New Testament the Christianity of the primitive Church is represented clearly as a way of getting rid of sin. But if Christianity is a way of getting rid of sin, then Jesus was not a Christian; for Jesus, so far as we can see, had no sin to get rid of.

Why then did the early Christians call themselves disciples of Jesus, why did they connect themselves with His name? The answer is not difficult. They connected themselves with His name not because He was their example in their ridding themselves of sin, but because their method of ridding themselves of sin was by means of Him. It was what Jesus did for them, and not primarily the example of His own life, which made them Christians. Such is the witness of all our primitive records. The record is fullest, as has already been observed, in the case of the Apostle Paul; clearly Paul regarded himself as saved from sin by what Jesus did for him on the cross. But Paul did not stand alone. "Christ died *for our sins*" was not something that Paul had originated; it was something he had "received." The benefits of that saving work of Christ, according to the primitive Church, were to be received by faith; even if the classic formulation of this conviction should prove to be due to Paul, the conviction itself clearly goes back to the very beginning. The primitive Christians felt themselves in need of salvation. How, they asked, should the load of sin be

removed? Their answer is perfectly plain. They simply trusted
Jesus to remove it. In other words they had "faith" in Him.

Here again we are brought face to face with the significant
fact which was noticed at the beginning of this chapter; the early
Christians regarded Jesus not merely as an example for faith but
primarily as the object of faith. Christianity from the beginning
was a means of getting rid of sin by trust in Jesus of Nazareth.
But if Jesus was thus the object of Christian faith, He Himself
was no more a Christian than God is a religious being. God is
the object of all religion, He is absolutely necessary to all religion; but He Himself is the only being in the universe who
can never in His own nature be religious. So it is with Jesus as
related to Christian faith. Christian faith is trust reposed in Him
for the removal of sin; He could not repose trust (in the sense
with which we are here concerned) in Himself; therefore He was
certainly not a Christian. If we are looking for a complete illustration of the Christian life we cannot find it in the religious
experience of Jesus.

This conclusion needs to be guarded against two objections.

In the first place, it will be said, are we not failing to do justice to the true humanity of Jesus, which is affirmed by the creeds
of the Church as well as by the modern theologians? When we
say that Jesus could not illustrate Christian faith any more than
God can be religious, are we not denying to Jesus that religious
experience which is a necessary element in true humanity? Must
not Jesus, if He be true man, have been more than the object
of religious faith; must He not have had a religion of His own?
The answer is not far to seek. Certainly Jesus had a religion of
His own; His prayer was real prayer, His faith was real religious
faith. His relation to His heavenly Father was not merely that

of a child to a father; it was that of a man to his God. Certainly Jesus had a religion; without it His humanity would indeed have been but incomplete. Without doubt Jesus had a religion; the fact is of the utmost importance. But it is equally important to observe that that religion which Jesus had was not Christianity. Christianity is a way of getting rid of sin, and Jesus was without sin. His religion was a religion of Paradise, not a religion of sinful humanity. It was a religion to which we may perhaps in some sort attain in heaven, when the process of our purification is complete (though even then the memory of redemption will never leave us); but certainly it is not a religion with which we can begin. The religion of Jesus was a religion of untroubled sonship; Christianity is a religion of the attainment of sonship by the redeeming work of Christ.

But if that be true, it may be objected, in the second place, that Jesus is being removed far from us, that on our view He is no longer our Brother and our Example. The objection is welcome, since it helps us to avoid misunderstandings and exaggerations.

Certainly if our zeal for the greatness and uniqueness of Jesus led us so to separate Him from us that He could no longer be touched with the feeling of our infirmities, the result would be disastrous; Jesus' coming would lose much of its significance. But it ought to be observed that likeness is not always necessary to nearness. The experience of a father in his personal relation to his son is quite different from that of the son in his relation to his father; but just that very difference binds father and son all the more closely together. The father cannot share the specifically filial affection of the son, and the son cannot share the specifically paternal affection of the father; yet no mere relationship of brotherhood, perhaps, could be quite so close. Fatherhood and sonship are complementary to each other; hence the dissimilarity, but hence also the closeness of the bond. It may be somewhat the same in the case of our relationship to Jesus. If He were exactly the same as ourselves, if He were merely our Brother, we should not be nearly so close to Him as we are when He stands to us in the relationship of a Saviour.

Nevertheless Jesus as a matter of fact is a Brother to us as well as a Saviour—an elder Brother whose steps we may follow. The imitation of Jesus has a fundamental place in Christian life; it is perfectly correct to represent Him as our supreme and only perfect example.

Certainly so far as the field of ethics is concerned, there can be no dispute. No matter what view may be taken of His origin and His higher nature, Jesus certainly led a true human life, and in it He came into those varied human relationships which provide opportunity for moral achievement. His life of perfect purity was led in no cold aloofness from the throng and press; His unselfish love was exercised not merely in mighty deeds, but in acts of kindness which the humblest of us has the power, if only we had the will, to imitate. More effective, too, than all detail is the indefinable impression of the whole; Jesus is felt to be far greater than any of His individual words or deeds. His calmness, unselfishness and strength have been the wonder of the ages; the world can never lose the inspiration of that radiant example.

Jesus is an example, moreover, not merely for the relations of man to man but also for the relation of man to God; imitation of Him may extend and must extend to the sphere of religion as well as to that of ethics. Indeed religion and ethics in Him were never separated; no single element in His life can be understood without reference to His heavenly Father. Jesus was the most religious man who ever lived; He did nothing and said nothing and thought nothing without the thought of God. If His example means anything at all it means that a human life without the conscious presence of God—even though it be a life of humanitarian service outwardly like the ministry of Jesus—is a monstrous perversion. If we would follow truly in Jesus' steps, we must obey the first commandment as well as the second that is like unto it; we must love the Lord our God with all our heart and soul and mind and strength. The difference between Jesus and ourselves serves only to enforce, certainly not to invalidate, the lesson. If the One to whom all power was given needed refreshment and strengthening in prayer, we more; if the One to whom the lilies of the field revealed the glory of God yet went into the sanctuary, surely we need such assistance even more than He; if the wise and holy One could say "Thy will be done," surely submission is yet more in place for us whose wisdom is as the foolishness of children.

Thus Jesus is the supreme example for men. But the Jesus who can serve as an example is not the Jesus of modern liberal reconstruction, but only the Jesus of the New Testament. The Jesus of modern liberalism advanced stupendous claims which were not founded upon fact—such conduct ought never to be made a norm. The Jesus of modern liberalism all through His ministry employed language which was extravagant and absurd—and it is only to be hoped that imitation of Him will not lead to an equal extravagance in His modern disciples. If the Jesus of naturalistic reconstruction were really taken as an example, disaster would soon follow. As a matter of fact, however, the modern liberal does not really take as his example the Jesus of the liberal historians; what he really does in practice is to manufacture as his example a simple exponent of a non-doctrinal religion whom the abler historians even of his own school know never to have existed except in the imagination of modern men.

Very different is the imitation of the real Jesus—the Jesus of the New Testament who actually lived in the first century of our era. That Jesus advanced lofty claims; but His claims, instead of being the extravagant dreams of an enthusiast, were sober truth. On His lips, therefore, language which in the reduced Jesus of modern reconstruction would be frenzied or absurd becomes fraught with blessing for mankind. Jesus demanded that those who followed Him should be willing to break even the holiest ties—He said, "If a man cometh to me and hateth not his father and mother ... he cannot be my disciple," and "Let the dead bury their dead." Coming from the mere prophet constructed by modern liberalism, those words would be monstrous; coming from the real Jesus, they are sublime. How great was the mission of mercy which justified such words! And how wonderful the condescension of the eternal Son! How matchless an example for the children of men! Well might Paul appeal to the example of the incarnate Saviour; well might he say, "Let the same mind be in you which was also in Christ Jesus." The imitation of the real Jesus will never lead a man astray.

But the example of Jesus is a perfect example only if He was justified in what He offered to men. And He offered, not primarily guidance, but salvation; He presented Himself as the object of men's faith. That offer is rejected by modern liberalism, but it is accepted by Christian men.

There is a profound difference, then, in the attitude assumed by modern liberalism and by Christianity toward Jesus the Lord. Liberalism regards Him as an Example and Guide; Christianity, as a Saviour: liberalism makes Him an example for faith; Christianity, the object of faith.

This difference in the attitude toward Jesus depends upon a profound difference as to the question who Jesus was. If Jesus was only what the liberal historians suppose that He was, then trust in Him would be out of place; our attitude toward Him could be that of pupils to a Master and nothing more. But if He was what the New Testament represents Him as being, then we can safely commit to Him the eternal destinies of our souls. What then is the difference between liberalism and Christianity with regard to the person of our Lord?

The answer might be difficult to set forth in detail. But the essential thing can be put almost in a word—liberalism regards Jesus as the fairest flower of humanity; Christianity regards Him as a supernatural Person.

The conception of Jesus as a supernatural Person runs all through the New Testament. In the Epistles of Paul, of course, it is quite clear. Without the slightest doubt Paul separated Jesus from ordinary humanity and placed Him on the side of God. The words in Gal. 1:1, "not from men nor through a man but through Jesus Christ and God the Father who raised Him from the dead," are only typical of what appears everywhere in the Epistles. The same contrast between Jesus Christ and ordinary humanity is everywhere presupposed. Paul does indeed call Jesus Christ a man. But the way in which he speaks of Jesus as a man only deepens the impression which has already been received. Paul speaks of the humanity of Jesus apparently as though the fact that Jesus was a man were something strange, something wonderful. At any rate, the really outstanding fact is that in the Epistles of Paul, Jesus is everywhere separated from ordinary humanity; the deity of Christ is everywhere presupposed. It is a matter of small consequence whether Paul ever applies to Jesus the Greek word which is translated "God" in the English Bible; certainly it is very difficult, in view of Rom. 9:5, to deny that he does. However that may be, the term "Lord," which is Paul's regular designation of Jesus, is really just as much a designation of deity as is the term "God." It was a designation of deity even in the pagan religions with which Paul's converts were familiar; and (what is far more important) in the Greek translation of the Old Testament which was current in Paul's day and was used by the Apostle himself, the term was used to translate the "Jahwe" of the Hebrew text. And Paul does not hesitate to apply to Jesus stupendous passages in the Greek Old Testament where the term Lord thus designates the God of Israel. But what is perhaps most significant of all for the establishment of the Pauline teaching about the Person of Christ is that Paul everywhere stands in a religious attitude toward Jesus. He who is thus the object of religious faith is surely no mere man, but a supernatural Person, and indeed a Person who was God.

Thus Paul regarded Jesus as a supernatural Person. The fact would be surprising if it stood alone. Paul was a contemporary of Jesus. What must this Jesus have been that He should be lifted thus quickly above the limits of ordinary humanity and placed upon the side of God?

But there is something far more surprising still. The truly surprising thing is that the view which Paul had of Jesus was also the view which was held by Jesus' intimate friends.[2] The fact ap-

2. Compare *The Origin of Paul's Religion*, 1921, pp. 118–127.

pears in the Pauline Epistles themselves, to say nothing of other evidence. Clearly the Epistles presuppose a fundamental unity between Paul and the original apostles with regard to the Person of Christ; for if there had been any controversy about this matter it would certainly have been mentioned. Even the Judaizers, the bitter opponents of Paul, seem to have had no objection to Paul's conception of Jesus as a supernatural Person. The really impressive thing about Paul's view of Christ is that it is not defended. Indeed it is hardly presented in the Epistles in any systematic way. Yet it is everywhere presupposed. The inference is perfectly plain—Paul's conception of the Person of Christ was a matter of course in the primitive Church. With regard to this matter Paul appears in perfect harmony with all Palestinian Christians. The men who had walked and talked with Jesus and had seen Him subject to the petty limitations of earthly life agreed with Paul fully in regarding Him as a supernatural Person, seated on the throne of all Being.

Exactly the same account of Jesus as that which is presupposed by the Pauline Epistles appears in the detailed narrative of the Gospels. The Gospels agree with Paul in presenting Jesus as a supernatural Person, and the agreement appears not in one or two of the Gospels, but in all four. The day is long past, if there ever was such a day, when the Gospel of John, as presenting a divine Jesus, could be contrasted with the Gospel of Mark, as presenting a human Jesus. On the contrary, all four Gospels clearly present a Person lifted far above the level of ordinary humanity; and the Gospel of Mark, the shortest and according to modern criticism the earliest of the Gospels, renders particularly prominent Jesus' superhuman works of power. In all four Gospels Jesus appears possessed of a sovereign power over the forces of nature; in all four Gospels, as in the whole New Testament, He appears clearly as a supernatural Person.[3]

But what is meant by a "supernatural Person"; what is meant by the supernatural?

The conception of the "supernatural" is closely connected with that of "miracle"; a miracle is the supernatural manifesting itself in the external world. But what is the supernatural? Many definitions have been proposed.

But only one definition is really correct. A supernatural event is one that takes place by the immediate, as distinguished from the mediate, power of God. The possibility of the supernatural, if supernatural be defined in this way, presupposes two things—it presupposes (1) the existence of a personal God, and (2) the existence of a real order of nature. Without the existence of a personal God, there could be no purposive entrance of God's power into the order of the world; and without the real existence of an order of nature there could be no distinction between natural events and those that are above nature—all events would be supernatural, or rather the word "supernatural" would have no meaning at all. The distinction between "natural" and "supernatural" does not mean, indeed, that nature is independent of God; it does not mean that while God brings to pass supernatural events, natural events are not brought to pass by Him. On the contrary, the believer in the supernatural regards everything that is done as being the work of God. Only, he believes that in the events called natural, God uses means, whereas in the events called supernatural He uses no means, but puts forth

---

3. Compare *History and Faith*, 1915, pp. 5f.

His creative power. The distinction between the natural and the supernatural, in other words, is simply the distinction between God's works of providence and God's work of creation; a miracle is a work of creation just as truly as the mysterious act which produced the world.

This conception of the supernatural depends absolutely upon a theistic view of God. Theism is to be distinguished (1) from deism and (2) from pantheism.

According to the deistic view, God set the world going like a machine and then left it independent of Himself. Such a view is inconsistent with the actuality of the supernatural; the miracles of the Bible presuppose a God who is constantly watching over and guiding the course of this world. The miracles of the Bible are not arbitrary intrusions of a Power that is without relation to the world, but are evidently intended to accomplish results within the order of nature. Indeed the natural and the supernatural are blended, in the miracles of the Bible, in a way entirely incongruous with the deistic conception of God. In the feeding of the five thousand, for example, who shall say what part the five loaves and two fishes had in the event; who shall say where the natural left off and the supernatural began? Yet that event, if any, surely transcended the order of nature. The miracles of the Bible, then, are not the work of a God who has no part in the course of nature; they are the work of a God who through His works of providence is "preserving and governing all His creatures and all their actions."

But the conception of the supernatural is inconsistent, not only with deism, but also with pantheism. Pantheism identifies God with the totality of nature. It is inconceivable, then, on the pantheistic view that anything should enter into the course of nature from outside. A similar incongruity with the supernatural appears also in certain forms of idealism, which deny real existence to the forces of nature. If what seems to be connected in nature is really only connected in the divine mind, then it is difficult to make any distinction between those operations of the divine mind which appear as miracles and those which appear as natural events. Again, it has often been said that all events are works of creation. On this view, it is only a concession to popular phraseology to say that one body is attracted toward another in accordance with a law of gravitation; what really ought to be said is that when two bodies are in proximity under certain conditions they come together. Certain phenomena in nature, on this view, are always followed by certain other phenomena, and it is really only this regularity of sequence which is indicated by the assertion that the former phenomena "cause" the latter; the only real cause is in all cases God. On the basis of this view, there can be no distinction between events wrought by the immediate power of God and those that are not; for on this view all events are so wrought. Against such a view, those who accept our definition of miracle will naturally accept the common-sense notion of cause. God is always the first cause, but there are truly second causes; and they are the means which God uses, in the ordinary course of the world, for the accomplishment of His ends. It is the exclusion of such second causes which makes an event a miracle.

It is sometimes said that the actuality of miracles would destroy the basis of science. Science, it is said, is founded upon the regularity of sequences; it assumes that if certain conditions within the course of nature are given, certain other conditions will always follow. But if there is to be any intrusion of events which by their very definition are independent of all previous conditions, then, it is said, the regularity of nature upon which science bases itself is broken up. Miracle, in other words, seems to introduce an element of arbitrariness and unaccountability into the course of the world.

The objection ignores what is really fundamental in the Christian conception of miracle. According to the Christian conception, a miracle is wrought by the immediate power of *God*. It is not wrought by an arbitrary and fantastic despot, but by the very God to whom the regularity of nature itself is due—by the God, moreover, whose character is known through the Bible. Such a God, we may be sure, will not do despite to the reason that He has given to His creatures; His interposition will introduce no disorder into the world that He has made. There is nothing arbitrary about a miracle, according to the Christian conception. It is not an uncaused event, but an event that is caused by the very source of all the order that is in the world. It is dependent altogether upon the least arbitrary and the most firmly fixed of all the things that are—namely upon the character of God.

The possibility of miracle, then, is indissolubly joined with "theism." Once admit the existence of a personal God, Maker and Ruler of the world, and no limits, temporal or otherwise, can be set to the creative power of such a God. Admit that God once created the world, and you cannot deny that He might engage in creation again. But it will be said, the actuality of miracles is different from the possibility of them. It may be admitted that miracles conceivably might occur. But have they actually occurred?

This question looms very large in the minds of modern men. The burden of the question seems to rest heavily even upon many who still accept the miracles of the New Testament. The miracles used to be regarded as an aid to faith, it is often said, but now they are a hindrance to faith; faith used to come on account of the miracles, but now it comes in despite of them; men used to believe in Jesus because He wrought miracles, but now we accept the miracles because on other grounds we have come to believe in Him.

A strange confusion underlies this common way of speaking. In one sense, certainly, miracles are a hindrance to faith—but who ever thought the contrary? It may certainly be admitted that if the New Testament narrative had no miracles in it, it would be far easier to believe. The more commonplace a story is, the easier it is to accept it as true. But commonplace narratives have little value. The New Testament without the miracles would be far easier to believe. But the trouble is, it would not be worth believing. Without the miracles the New Testament would contain an account of a holy man—not a perfect man, it is true, for He was led to make lofty claims to which He had no right—but a man at least far holier than the rest of men. But of what benefit would such a man, and the death which marked His failure, be to us? The loftier be the example which Jesus set, the greater becomes our sorrow at our failure to attain to it; and the greater our hopelessness under the burden of sin. The sage of Nazareth may satisfy those who have never faced the problem of evil in their own lives; but to talk about an ideal to those who are under the thralldom of sin is a cruel mockery. Yet if Jesus was merely a man like the rest of men, then an ideal is all that we have in Him. Far more is needed by a sinful world. It is small comfort to be told that there was goodness in the world, when what we need is goodness triumphant over sin. But goodness triumphant over sin involves an entrance of the creative power of God, and that creative power of God is manifested by the miracles. Without the miracles, the New Testament might be easier to believe. But the thing that would be believed would be entirely different from that which presents itself to us now. Without the miracles we should have a teacher; with the miracles we have a Saviour.

Certainly it is a mistake to isolate the miracles from the rest of the New Testament. It is a mistake to discuss the question of the resurrection of Jesus as though that which is to be proved were simply the resurrection of a certain man of the first century in Palestine. No doubt the existing evidence for such an event, strong as the evidence is, might be insufficient. The historian would indeed be obliged to say that no naturalistic explanation of the origin of the Church has yet been discovered, and that the evidence for the miracle is exceedingly strong; but miracles are, to say the least, extremely unusual events, and there is a tremendous hostile presumption against accepting the hypothesis of miracle in any given case. But as a matter of fact, the question in this case does not concern the resurrection of a man about whom we know nothing; it concerns the resurrection of Jesus. And Jesus was certainly a very extraordinary Person. The uniqueness of the character of Jesus removes the hostile presumption against miracle; it was extremely improbable that any ordinary man should rise from the dead, but Jesus was like no other man that ever lived.

But the evidence for the miracles of the New Testament is supported in yet another way; it is supported by the existence of an adequate occasion. It has been observed above that a miracle is an event produced by the immediate power of God, and that God is a God of order. The evidence of a miracle is therefore enormously strengthened when the purpose of the miracle can be detected. That does not mean that within a complex of miracles an exact reason must be assigned to every one; it does not mean that in the New Testament we should expect to see exactly why a miracle was wrought in one case and not in another. But it does mean that acceptance of a complex of miracles is made vastly easier when an adequate reason can be detected for the complex as a whole.

In the case of the New Testament miracles, such an adequate reason is not difficult to find. It is found in the conquest of sin. According to the Christian view, as set forth in the Bible, mankind is under the curse of God's holy law, and the dreadful penalty includes the corruption of our whole nature. Actual transgressions proceed from the sinful root, and serve to deepen every man's guilt in the sight of God. On the basis of that view, so profound, so true to the observed facts of life, it is obvious that nothing natural will meet our need. Nature transmits the dreadful taint; hope is to be sought only in a creative act of God.

And that creative act of God—so mysterious, so contrary to all expectation, yet so congruous with the character of the God who is revealed as the God of love—is found in the redeeming work of Christ. No product of sinful humanity could have redeemed humanity from the dreadful guilt or lifted a sinful race from the slough of sin. But a Saviour has come from God. There lies the very root of the Christian religion; there is the reason why the supernatural is the very ground and substance of the Christian faith.

But the acceptance of the supernatural depends upon a conviction of the reality of sin. Without the conviction of sin there can be no appreciation of the uniqueness of Jesus; it is only when we contrast our sinfulness with His holiness that we appreciate the gulf which separates Him from the rest of the children of men. And without the conviction of sin there can be no understanding of the occasion for the supernatural act of God; without the conviction of sin, the good news of redemption seems to be an idle tale. So fundamental is the conviction of sin in the Christian faith that it will not do to arrive at it merely by a process of reasoning; it will not do to say merely: All men (as I have been told) are sinners; I am a man; therefore I suppose I must be a sinner too. That is all the supposed conviction of sin amounts to sometimes. But the true conviction is far more immediate than that. It depends indeed upon information that comes from without; it depends upon the revelation of the law of God; it depends upon the awful verities set forth in the Bible as to the universal sinfulness of mankind. But it adds to the revelation that has come from without a conviction of the whole mind and heart, a profound understanding of one's own lost condition, an illumination of the deadened conscience which causes a Copernican revolution in one's attitude toward the world and toward God. When a man has passed through that experience, he wonders at his former blindness. And especially does he wonder at his former attitude toward the miracles of the New Testament, and toward the supernatural Person who is there revealed. The truly penitent man glories in the supernatural, for he knows that nothing natural would meet his need; the world has been shaken once in his downfall, and shaken again it must be if he is to be saved.

Yet an acceptance of the presuppositions of miracle does not render unnecessary the plain testimony to the miracles that have actually occurred. And that testimony is exceedingly strong.[4] The Jesus presented in the New Testament was clearly an historical Person—so much is admitted by all who have really come to grips with the historical problems at all. But just as clearly the Jesus presented in the New Testament was a supernatural Person. Yet for modern liberalism a supernatural person is never historical. A problem arises then for those who adopt the liberal point of view—the Jesus of the New Testament is historical, He is supernatural, and yet what is supernatural, on the liberal hypothesis, can never be historical. The problem could be solved only by the separation of the natural from the supernatural in the New Testament account of Jesus, in order that what is supernatural might be rejected and what is natural might be retained. But the process of separation has never been successfully carried out. Many have been the attempts—the modern liberal Church has put its very heart and soul into the effort, so that there is scarcely any more brilliant chapter in the history of the human spirit than this "quest of the historical Jesus"—but all the attempts have failed. The trouble is that the miracles are found not to be an excrescence in the New Testament account of Jesus, but belong to the very warp and woof. They are intimately connected with Jesus' lofty claims; they stand or fall with the undoubted purity of His character; they reveal the very nature of His mission in the world.

Yet miracles are rejected by the modern liberal Church, and with the miracles the entirety of the supernatural Person of our Lord. Not some miracles are rejected, but all. It is a matter of no importance whatever that some of the wonderful works of Jesus

---

4. Compare *History and Faith*, 1913, pp. 6–8.

are accepted by the liberal Church; it means absolutely nothing when some of the works of healing are regarded as historical. For those works are no longer regarded by modern liberalism as supernatural, but merely as faith-cures of an extraordinary kind. And it is the presence or absence of the true supernatural which is the really important thing. Such concessions as to faith-cures, moreover, carry us at best but a very short way—disbelievers in the supernatural must simply reject as legendary or mythical the great mass of the wonderful works.

The question, then, does not concern the historicity of this miracle or that; it concerns the historicity of all miracles. That fact is often obscured, and the obscuration of it often introduces an element of something like disingenuousness into the advocacy of the liberal cause. The liberal preacher singles out some one miracle and discusses that as though it were the only point at issue. The miracle which is usually singled out is the Virgin Birth. The liberal preacher insists on the possibility of believing in Christ no matter which view be adopted as to the manner of His entrance into the world. Is not the Person the same no matter how He was born? The impression is thus produced upon the plain man that the preacher is accepting the main outlines of the New Testament account of Jesus, but merely has difficulties with this particular element in the account. But such an impression is radically false. It is true that some men have denied the Virgin Birth and yet have accepted the New Testament account of Jesus as a supernatural Person. But such men are exceedingly few and far between. It might be difficult to find a single one of any prominence living to-day, so profoundly and so obviously congruous is the Virgin Birth with the whole New Testament presentation of Christ. The overwhelming majority of those who reject the Virgin Birth reject also the whole supernatural content of the New Testament, and make of the "resurrection" just what the word "resurrection" most emphatically did not mean—a permanence of the influence of Jesus or a mere spiritual existence of Jesus beyond the grave. Old words may here be used, but the thing that they designate is gone. The disciples believed in the continued personal existence of Jesus even during the three sad days after the crucifixion; they were not Sadducees; they believed that Jesus lived and would rise at the last day. But what enabled them to begin the work of the Christian Church was that they believed the body of Jesus already to have been raised from the tomb by the power of God. That belief involves the acceptance of the supernatural; and the acceptance of the supernatural is thus the very heart and soul of the religion that we profess.

Whatever decision is made, the issue should certainly not be obscured. The issue does not concern individual miracles, even so important a miracle as the Virgin Birth. It really concerns all miracles. And the question concerning all miracles is simply the question of the acceptance or rejection of the Saviour that the New Testament presents. Reject the miracles and you have in Jesus the fairest flower of humanity who made such an impression upon His followers that after His death they could not believe that He had perished but experienced hallucinations in which they thought they saw Him risen from the dead; accept the miracles, and you have a Saviour who came voluntarily into this world for our salvation, suffered for our sins upon the Cross, rose again from the dead by the power of God, and ever lives to make intercession for us. The difference between those two views is the difference between two totally diverse religions. It is high time that this issue should be faced; it is high time that the misleading use of traditional phrases should be abandoned and men should speak their full mind. Shall we accept the Jesus of the New Testament as our Saviour, or shall we reject Him with the liberal Church?

At this point an objection may be raised. The liberal preacher, it may be said, is often ready to speak of the "deity" of Christ; he is often ready to say that "Jesus is God." The plain man is much impressed. The preacher, he says, believes in the deity of our Lord; obviously then his unorthodoxy must concern only details; and those who object to his presence in the Church are narrow and uncharitable heresy-hunters.

But unfortunately language is valuable only as the expression of thought. The English word "God" has no particular virtue in itself; it is not more beautiful than other words. Its importance depends altogether upon the meaning which is attached to it. When, therefore, the liberal preacher says that "Jesus is God," the significance of the utterance depends altogether upon what is meant by "God."

And it has already been observed that when the liberal preacher uses the word "God," he means something entirely different from that which the Christian means by the same word. God, at least according to the logical trend of modern liberalism, is not a person separate from the world, but merely the unity that pervades the world. To say, therefore, that Jesus is God means merely that the life of God, which appears in all men, appears with special clearness or richness in Jesus. Such an assertion is diametrically opposed to the Christian belief in the deity of Christ.

Equally opposed to Christian belief is another meaning that is sometimes attached to the assertion that Jesus is God. The word "God" is sometimes used to denote simply the supreme object of men's desires, the highest thing that men know. We have given up the notion, it is said, that there is a Maker and Ruler of the universe; such notions belong to "metaphysics," and are rejected by the modern man. But the word "God," though it can no longer denote the Maker of the universe, is convenient as denoting the object of men's emotions and desires. Of some men, it can be said that their God is mammon—mammon is that for which they labor, and to which their hearts are attached. In a somewhat similar way, the liberal preacher says that Jesus is God. He does not mean at all to say that Jesus is identical in nature with a Maker and Ruler of the universe, of whom an idea could be obtained apart from Jesus. In such a Being he no longer believes. All that he means is that the man Jesus—a man here in the midst of us, and of the same nature as ours—is the highest thing we know. It is obvious that such a way of thinking is far more widely removed from Christian belief than is Unitarianism, at least the earlier forms of Unitarianism. For the early Unitarianism no doubt at least believed in God. The modern liberals, on the other hand, say that Jesus is God not because they think high of Jesus, but because they think desperately low of God.

In another way also, liberalism within the "evangelical" churches is inferior to Unitarianism. It is inferior to Unitarianism in the matter of honesty. In order to maintain themselves in the evangelical churches and quiet the fears of their conservative associates, the liberals resort constantly to a double use of language. A young man, for example, has received disquieting reports of the unorthodoxy of a prominent preacher. Interrogating the preacher as to his belief, he receives a reassuring reply. "You may tell everyone," says the liberal preacher in effect, "that I believe that Jesus is God." The inquirer goes away much impressed.

It may well be doubted, however, whether the assertion, "I believe that Jesus is God," or the like, on the lips of liberal preachers, is strictly truthful. The liberal preacher attaches indeed a real meaning to the words, and that meaning is very dear to his heart. He really does believe that "Jesus is God." But the trouble is that he attaches to the words a different meaning from that which is attached to them by the simple-minded person to whom he is speaking. He offends, therefore, against the fundamental principle of truthfulness in language. According to that fundamental principle, language is truthful, not when the meaning attached to the words by the speaker, but when the meaning intended to be produced in the mind of the particular person addressed, is in accordance with the facts. Thus the truthfulness of the assertion, "I believe that Jesus is God," depends upon the audience that is addressed. If the audience is composed of theologically trained persons, who will attach the same meaning to the word "God" as that which the speaker attaches to it, then the language is truthful. But if the audience is composed of old-fashioned Christians, who have never attached anything but the old meaning to the word "God" (the meaning which appears in the first verse of Genesis), then the language is untruthful. And in the latter case, not all the pious motives in the world will make the utterance right. Christian ethics do not abrogate common honesty; no possible desire of edifying the Church and of avoiding offence can excuse a lie.

At any rate, the deity of our Lord, in any real sense of the word "deity," is of course denied by modern liberalism. According to the modern liberal Church, Jesus differs from the rest of men only in degree and not in kind; He can be divine only if all men are divine. But if the liberal conception of the deity of Christ thus becomes meaningless, what is the Christian conception? What does the Christian man mean when he confesses that "Jesus is God"?

The answer has been given in what has already been said. It has already been observed that the New Testament represents Jesus as a supernatural Person. But if Jesus is a supernatural Person He is either divine or else He is an intermediate Being, higher indeed than man, but lower than God. The latter view has been abandoned for many centuries in the Christian Church, and there is not much likelihood that it will be revived; Arianism certainly is dead. The thought of Christ as a super-angelic Being, like God but not God, belongs evidently to pagan mythology, and not to the Bible or to Christian faith. It will usually be admitted, if the theistic conception of the separateness between man and God be held, that Christ is either God or else simply man; He is certainly not a Being intermediate between God and man. If, then, He is not merely man, but a supernatural Person, the conclusion is that He is God.

In the second place, it has already been observed that in the New Testament and in all true Christianity, Jesus is no mere example for faith, but the object of faith. And the faith of which Jesus is the object is clearly religious faith; the Christian man reposes confidence in Jesus in a way that would be out of place in the case of any other than God. It is no lesser thing that is committed to Jesus, but the eternal welfare of the soul. The entire Christian attitude toward Jesus as it is found throughout the New Testament presupposes clearly, then, the deity of our Lord.

It is in the light of this central presupposition that the individual assertions ought to be approached. The individual passages which attest the deity of Christ are not excrescences in the New Testament, but natural fruits of a fundamental conception which is everywhere the same. Those individual passages are not confined to any one book or group of books. In the Pauline Epistles, of course, the passages are particularly plain; the Christ of the Epistles appears again and again as associated only with the Father and with His Spirit. In the Gospel of John, also, one does not have to seek very long; the deity of Christ is almost the theme of the book. But the testimony of the Synoptic Gospels is not really different from that which appears everywhere else. The way in which Jesus speaks of *my* Father and *the* Son—for example, in the famous passage in Matt. 11:27 (Lk. 10:22): "All things have been delivered unto me of my Father, and no man knoweth the Son but the Father, neither knoweth any man the Father save the Son and He to whomsoever the Son will reveal Him"—this manner of presenting Jesus' relation to the Father, absolutely fundamental in the Synoptic Gospels, involves the assertion of the deity of our Lord. The Person who so speaks is represented as being in mysterious union with the eternal God.

Yet the New Testament with equal clearness presents Jesus as a man. The Gospel of John, which contains at the beginning the stupendous utterance, "The Word was God," and dwells constantly upon the deity of the Lord, also represents Jesus as weary at the well and as thirsty in the hour of agony on the Cross. Scarcely in the Synoptic Gospels can one discover such drastic touches attesting the humanity of our Saviour as those which appear again and again in the Gospel of John. With regard to the Synoptic Gospels, of course there can be no debate; the Synoptists clearly present a Person who lived a genuine human life and was Himself true man.

The truth is, the witness of the New Testament is everywhere the same; the New Testament everywhere presents One who was both God and man. And it is interesting to observe how unsuccessful have been all the efforts to reject one part of this witness and retain the rest. The Apollinarians rejected the full humanity of the Lord, but in doing so they obtained a Person who was very different from the Jesus of the New Testament. The Jesus of the New Testament was clearly, in the full sense, a man. Others seem to have supposed that the divine and the human were so blended in Jesus that there was produced a nature neither purely divine nor purely human, but a *tertium quid*. But nothing could be more remote from the New Testament teaching than that. According to the New Testament the divine and human natures were clearly distinct; the divine nature was pure divinity, and the human nature was pure humanity; Jesus was God and man in two *distinct* natures. The Nestorians, on the other hand, so emphasized the distinctness of divine and human in Jesus as to suppose that there were in Jesus two separate persons. But such a Gnosticizing view is plainly contrary to the record; the New Testament plainly teaches the unity of the Person of our Lord.

By elimination of these errors the Church arrived at the New Testament doctrine of two natures in one Person; the Jesus of the New Testament is "God and man, in two distinct natures, and one Person forever." That doctrine is sometimes regarded as speculative. But nothing could be further from the fact. Whether the doctrine of the two natures is true or false, it was certainly produced not by speculation, but by an attempt to summarize, succinctly and exactly, the Scriptural teaching.

This doctrine is of course rejected by modern liberalism. And it is rejected in a very simple way—by the elimination of the whole higher nature of our Lord. But such radicalism is not a bit more successful than the heresies of the past. The Jesus who is supposed to be left after the elimination of the supernatural element is at best a very shadowy figure; for the elimination of the supernatural logically involves the elimination of much that remains, and the historian constantly approaches the absurd view which effaces Jesus altogether from the pages of history. But even after such dangers have been avoided, even after the historian, by setting arbitrary limits to his process of elimination, has succeeded in reconstructing a purely human Jesus, the Jesus thus constructed is found to be entirely unreal. He has a moral contradiction at the very centre of His being—a contradiction due to His Messianic consciousness. He was pure and humble and strong and sane, yet He supposed, without basis in fact, that He was to be the final Judge of all the earth! The liberal Jesus, despite all the efforts of modern psychological reconstruction to galvanize Him into life, remains a manufactured figure of the stage. Very different is the Jesus of the New Testament and of the great Scriptural creeds. That Jesus is indeed mysterious. Who can fathom the mystery of His Person? But the mystery is a mystery in which a man can rest. The Jesus of the New Testament has at least one advantage over the Jesus of modern reconstruction—He is real. He is not a manufactured figure suitable as a point of support for ethical maxims, but a genuine Person whom a man can love. Men have loved Him through all the Christian centuries. And the strange thing is that despite all the efforts to remove Him from the pages of history, there are those who love Him still.

6

Salvation

It has been observed thus far that liberalism differs from Christianity with regard to the presuppositions of the gospel (the view of God and the view of man), with regard to the Book in which the gospel is contained, and with regard to the Person whose work the gospel sets forth. It is not surprising then that it differs from Christianity in its account of the gospel itself; it is not surprising that it presents an entirely different account of the way of salvation. Liberalism finds salvation (so far as it is willing to speak at all of "salvation") in man; Christianity finds it in an act of God.

The difference with regard to the way of salvation concerns, in the first place, the basis of salvation in the redeeming work of Christ. According to Christian belief, Jesus is our Saviour, not by virtue of what He said, not even by virtue of what He was, but by what He did. He is our Saviour, not because He has inspired us to live the same kind of life that He lived, but because He took upon Himself the dreadful guilt of our sins and bore it instead of us on the cross. Such is the Christian conception of the Cross of Christ. It is ridiculed as being a "subtle theory of the atonement." In reality, it is the plain teaching of the word of God; we know absolutely nothing about an atonement that is not a vicarious atonement, for that is the only atonement of which the

New Testament speaks. And this Bible doctrine is not intricate or subtle. On the contrary, though it involves mysteries, it is itself so simple that a child can understand it. "We deserved eternal death, but the Lord Jesus, because He loved us, died instead of us on the cross"—surely there is nothing so very intricate about that. It is not the Bible doctrine of the atonement which is difficult to understand—what are really incomprehensible are the elaborate modern efforts to get rid of the Bible doctrine in the interests of human pride.[1]

Modern liberal preachers do indeed sometimes speak of the "atonement." But they speak of it just as seldom as they possibly can, and one can see plainly that their hearts are elsewhere than at the foot of the Cross. Indeed, at this point, as at many others, one has the feeling that traditional language is being strained to become the expression of totally alien ideas. And when the traditional phraseology has been stripped away, the essence of the modern conception of the death of Christ, though that conception appears in many forms, is fairly plain. The essence of it is that the death of Christ had an effect not upon God but only upon man. Sometimes the effect upon man is conceived of in a very simple way, Christ's death being regarded merely as an example of self-sacrifice for us to emulate. The uniqueness of this particular example, then, can be found only in the fact that Christian sentiment, gathering around it, has made it a convenient symbol for all self-sacrifice; it puts in concrete form what would otherwise have to be expressed in colder general terms. Sometimes, again, the effect of Christ's death upon us is conceived of in subtler ways; the death of Christ, it is said, shows

1. See "The Second Declaration of the Council on Organic Union," in *The Presbyterian,* for March 17, 1921, p. 8.

how much God hates sin—since sin brought even the Holy One to the dreadful Cross—and we too, therefore, ought to hate sin, as God hates it, and repent. Sometimes, still again, the death of Christ is thought of as displaying the love of God; it exhibits God's own Son as given up for us all. These modern "theories of the atonement" are not all to be placed upon the same plane; the last of them, in particular, may be joined with a high view of Jesus' Person. But they err in that they ignore the dreadful reality of guilt, and make a mere persuasion of the human will all that is needed for salvation. They do indeed all contain an element of truth: it is true that the death of Christ is an example of self-sacrifice which may inspire self-sacrifice in others; it is true that the death of Christ shows how much God hates sin; it is true that the death of Christ displays the love of God. All of these truths are found plainly in the New Testament. But they are swallowed up in a far greater truth—that Christ died instead of us to present us faultless before the throne of God. Without that central truth, all the rest is devoid of real meaning: an example of self-sacrifice is useless to those who are under both the guilt and thralldom of sin; the knowledge of God's hatred of sin can in itself bring only despair; an exhibition of the love of God is a mere display unless there was some underlying reason for the sacrifice. If the Cross is to be restored to its rightful place in Christian life, we shall have to penetrate far beneath the modern theories to Him who loved us and gave Himself for us.

Upon the Christian doctrine of the Cross, modern liberals are never weary of pouring out the vials of their hatred and their scorn. Even at this point, it is true, the hope of avoiding offence is not always abandoned; the words "vicarious atonement" and the like—of course in a sense totally at variance from their Christian meaning—are still sometimes used. But despite such occasional employment of traditional language the liberal preachers reveal only too clearly what is in their minds. They speak with disgust of those who believe "that the blood of our Lord, shed in a substitutionary death, placates an alienated Deity and makes possible welcome for the returning sinner."[2] Against the doctrine of the Cross they use every weapon of caricature and vilification. Thus they pour out their scorn upon a thing so holy and so precious that in the presence of it the Christian heart melts in gratitude too deep for words. It never seems to occur to modern liberals that in deriding the Christian doctrine of the Cross, they are trampling upon human hearts. But the modern liberal attacks upon the Christian doctrine of the Cross may at least serve the purpose of showing what that doctrine is, and from this point of view they may be examined briefly now.

In the first place, then, the Christian way of salvation through the Cross of Christ is criticized because it is dependent upon history. This criticism is sometimes evaded; it is sometimes said that as Christians we may attend to what Christ does now for every Christian rather than to what He did long ago in Palestine. But the evasion involves a total abandonment of the Christian faith. If the saving work of Christ were confined to what He does now for every Christian, there would be no such thing as a Christian gospel—an account of an event which put a new face on life. What we should have left would be simply mysticism, and mysticism is quite different from Christianity. It is the connection of the present experience of the believer with an actual historic ap-

---

2. Fosdick, *Shall the Fundamentalists Win?*, stenographically reported by Margaret Renton, 1922, p. 5.

pearance of Jesus in the world which prevents our religion from being mysticism and causes it to be Christianity.

It must certainly be admitted, then, that Christianity does depend upon something that happened; our religion must be abandoned altogether unless at a definite point in history Jesus died as a propitiation for the sins of men. Christianity is certainly dependent upon history.

But if so, the objection lies very near. Must we really depend for the welfare of our souls upon what happened long ago? Must we really wait until historians have finished disputing about the value of sources and the like before we can have peace with God? Would it not be better to have a salvation which is with us here and now, and which depends only upon what we can see or feel?

With regard to this objection it should be observed that if religion be made independent of history there is no such thing as a gospel. For "gospel" means "good news," tidings, information about something that has happened. A gospel independent of history is a contradiction in terms. The Christian gospel means, not a presentation of what always has been true, but a report of something new—something that imparts a totally different aspect to the situation of mankind. The situation of mankind was desperate because of sin; but God has changed the situation by the atoning death of Christ—that is no mere reflection upon the old, but an account of something new. We are shut up in this world as in a beleaguered camp. To maintain our courage, the liberal preacher offers us exhortation. Make the best of the situation, he says, look on the bright side of life. But unfortunately, such exhortation cannot change the facts. In particular it cannot

remove the dreadful fact of sin. Very different is the message of
the Christian evangelist. He offers not reflection on the old but
tidings of something new, not exhortation but a gospel.[3]

It is true that the Christian gospel is an account, not of something that happened yesterday, but of something that happened
long ago; but the important thing is that it really happened. If
it really happened, then it makes little difference when it happened. No matter when it happened, whether yesterday or in the
first century, it remains a real gospel, a real piece of news.

The happening of long ago, moreover, is in this case confirmed by present experience. The Christian man receives first
the account which the New Testament gives of the atoning death
of Christ. That account is history. But if true it has effects in the
present, and it can be tested by its effects. The Christian man
makes trial of the Christian message, and making trial of it he
finds it to be true. Experience does not provide a substitute for
the documentary evidence, but it does confirm that evidence.
The word of the Cross no longer seems to the Christian to be
merely a far-off thing, merely a matter to be disputed about
by trained theologians. On the contrary, it is received into the
Christian's inmost soul, and every day and hour of the Christian's life brings new confirmation of its truth.

In the second place, the Christian doctrine of salvation
through the death of Christ is criticized on the ground that it
is narrow. It binds salvation to the name of Jesus, and there are
many men in the world who have never in any effective way
heard of the name of Jesus. What is really needed, we are told,
is a salvation which will save all men everywhere, whether they

3. Compare *History and Faith*, 1915, pp. 1–3.

J. Gresham Machen

The original Westminster Theological Seminary student body.
The seminary's first home was here, at 1528 Pine Street, Philadelphia.

Westminster Theological Seminary faculty, March 17, 1931.
Standing (L to R): John Murray and Allan A. MacRae.
Seated (L to R): Paul Woolley, Cornelius Van Til,
J. Gresham Machen, Oswald T. Allis, Ned B. Stonehouse.

The library at the Pine Street campus.

The dining club at the Pine Street campus.

A Session of the Checker Club, 1928 or 1929.

Mountain climbing. Summer, 1936.

The last known photograph of J. Gresham Machen (L),
with his brother, Arthur (R), and Arthur's brother-in-law (C).
1936. Photograph courtesy of the OPC.

have heard of Jesus or not, and whatever may be the type of life to which they have been reared. Not a new creed, it is said, will meet the universal need of the world, but some means of making effective in right living whatever creed men may chance to have.

This second objection, as well as the first, is sometimes evaded. It is sometimes said that although one way of salvation is by means of acceptance of the gospel there may be other ways. But this method of meeting the objection relinquishes one of the things that are most obviously characteristic of the Christian message—namely, its exclusiveness. What struck the early observers of Christianity most forcibly was not merely that salvation was offered by means of the Christian gospel, but that all other means were resolutely rejected. The early Christian missionaries demanded an absolutely exclusive devotion to Christ. Such exclusiveness ran directly counter to the prevailing syncretism of the Hellenistic age. In that day, many saviours were offered by many religions to the attention of men, but the various pagan religions could live together in perfect harmony; when a man became a devotee of one god, he did not have to give up the others. But Christianity would have nothing to do with these "courtly polygamies of the soul";[4] it demanded an absolutely exclusive devotion; all other Saviours, it insisted, must be deserted for the one Lord. Salvation, in other words, was not merely through Christ, but it was only through Christ. In that little word "only" lay all the offence. Without that word there would have been no persecutions; the cultured men of the day would probably have been willing to give Jesus a place, and an honorable place, among the saviours of mankind. Without its exclusiveness, the Christian

4. Phillimore, in the Introduction to his translation of Philostratus, *In Honour of Apollonius of Tyana*, 1912, vol. 1, p. iii.

message would have seemed perfectly inoffensive to the men of that day. So modern liberalism, placing Jesus alongside other benefactors of mankind, is perfectly inoffensive in the modern world. All men speak well of it. It is entirely inoffensive. But it is also entirely futile. The offence of the Cross is done away, but so is the glory and the power.

Thus it must fairly be admitted that Christianity does bind salvation to the name of Christ. The question need not here be discussed whether the benefits of Christ's death are ever applied to those who, though they have come to years of discretion, have not heard or accepted the gospel message. Certainly the New Testament holds out with regard to this matter no clear hope. At the very basis of the work of the apostolic Church is the consciousness of a terrible responsibility. The sole message of life and salvation had been committed to men; that message was at all hazards to be proclaimed while yet there was time. The objection as to the exclusiveness of the Christian way of salvation, therefore, cannot be evaded, but must be met.

In answer to the objection, it may be said simply that the Christian way of salvation is narrow only so long as the Church chooses to let it remain narrow. The name of Jesus is discovered to be strangely adapted to men of every race and of every kind of previous education. And the Church has ample means, with promise of God's Spirit, to bring the name of Jesus to all. If, therefore, this way of salvation is not offered to all, it is not the fault of the way of salvation itself, but the fault of those who fail to use the means that God has placed in their hands.

But, it may be said, is that not a stupendous responsibility to be placed in the hands of weak and sinful men; is it not more natural that God should offer salvation to all without requiring them to accept a new message and thus to be dependent upon the faithfulness of the messengers? The answer to this objection is plain. It is certainly true that the Christian way of salvation places a stupendous responsibility upon men. But that responsibility is like the responsibility which, as ordinary observation shows, God does, as a matter of fact, commit to men. It is like the responsibility, for example, of the parent for the child. The parent has full power to mar the soul as well as the body of the child. The responsibility is terrible; but it is a responsibility which unquestionably exists. Similar is the responsibility of the Church for making the name of Jesus known to all mankind. It is a terrible responsibility; but it exists, and it is just like the other known dealings of God.

But modern liberalism has still more specific objections to the Christian doctrine of the Cross. How can one person, it is asked, suffer for the sins of another? The thing, we are told, is absurd. Guilt, it is said, is personal; if I allow another man to suffer for my fault, my guilt is not thereby one whit diminished.

An answer to this objection is sometimes found in the plain instances in ordinary human life where one person does suffer for another person's sin. In the war, for example, many men died freely for the welfare of others. Here, it is said, we have something analogous to the sacrifice of Christ.

It must be confessed, however, that the analogy is very faint; for it does not touch the specific point at issue. The death of a volunteer soldier in the war was like the death of Christ in that it was a supreme example of self-sacrifice. But the thing to be accomplished by the self-sacrifice was entirely different from the thing which was accomplished on Calvary. The death of those who sacrificed themselves in the war brought peace and protection to the loved ones at home, but it could never avail to wipe out the guilt of sin.

The real answer to the objection is to be found not in the similarity between the death of Christ and other examples of self-sacrifice, but in the profound difference.[5] Why is it that men are no longer willing to trust for their own salvation and for the hope of the world to one act that was done by one Man of long ago? Why is it that they prefer to trust to millions of acts of self-sacrifice wrought by millions of men all through the centuries and in our own day? The answer is plain. It is because men have lost sight of the majesty of Jesus' Person. They think of Him as a man like themselves; and if He was a man like themselves, His death becomes simply an example of self-sacrifice. But there have been millions of examples of self-sacrifice. Why then should we pay such exclusive attention to this one Palestinian example of long ago? Men used to say with reference to Jesus, "There was no other good enough to pay the price of sin." They say so now no longer. On the contrary, every man is now regarded as plenty good enough to pay the price of sin if, whether in peace or in war, he will only go bravely over the top in some noble cause.

It is perfectly true that no mere man can pay the penalty of another man's sin. But it does not follow that Jesus could not do it; for Jesus was no mere man but the eternal Son of God. Jesus is master of the innermost secrets of the moral world. He has done what none other could possibly do; He has borne our sin.

The Christian doctrine of the atonement, therefore, is altogether rooted in the Christian doctrine of the deity of Christ. The reality of an atonement for sin depends altogether upon the

---

5. For what follows, compare "The Church in the War," in *The Presbyterian*, for May 29, 1919, pp. 10f.

New Testament presentation of the Person of Christ. And even the hymns dealing with the Cross which we sing in Church can be placed in an ascending scale, according as they are based upon a lower or a higher view of Jesus' Person. At the very bottom of the scale is that familiar hymn:

> Nearer, my God, to thee,
>   Nearer to thee!
> E'en though it be a cross
>   That raiseth me.

That is a perfectly good hymn. It means that our trials may be a discipline to bring us nearer to God. The thought is not opposed to Christianity; it is found in the New Testament. But many persons have the impression, because the word "cross" is found in the hymn, that there is something specifically Christian about it, and that it has something to do with the gospel. This impression is entirely false. In reality, the cross that is spoken of is not the Cross of Christ, but our own cross; the verse simply means that our own crosses or trials may be a means to bring us nearer to God. It is a perfectly good thought, but certainly it is not the gospel. One can only be sorry that the people on the *Titanic* could not find a better hymn to use in the last solemn hour of their lives.

But there is another hymn in the hymn-book:

> In the cross of Christ I glory,
>   Towering o'er the wrecks of time;
> All the light of sacred story
>   Gathers round its head sublime.

That is certainly better. It is here not our own crosses but the Cross of Christ, the actual event that took place on Calvary, that is spoken of, and that event is celebrated as the centre of all history. Certainly the Christian man can sing that hymn. But one misses even there the full Christian sense of the meaning of the Cross; the Cross is celebrated, but it is not understood.

It is well, therefore, that there is another hymn in our hymn-book:

> When I survey the wondrous cross
>   On which the Prince of glory died,
> My richest gain I count but loss,
>   And pour contempt on all my pride.

There at length are heard the accents of true Christian feeling—"the wondrous cross on which the Prince of glory died." When we come to see that it was no mere man who suffered on Calvary but the Lord of Glory, then we shall be willing to say that one drop of the precious blood of Jesus is of more value, for our own salvation and for the hope of society, than all the rivers of blood that have flowed upon the battlefields of history.

Thus the objection to the vicarious sacrifice of Christ disappears altogether before the tremendous Christian sense of the majesty of Jesus' Person. It is perfectly true that the Christ of modern naturalistic reconstruction never could have suffered for the sins of others; but it is very different in the case of the Lord of Glory. And if the notion of vicarious atonement be so absurd as modern opposition would lead us to believe, what shall be said of the Christian experience that has been based upon it? The modern liberal Church is fond of appealing to experience.

But where shall true Christian experience be found if not in the blessed peace which comes from Calvary? That peace comes only when a man recognizes that all his striving to be right with God, all his feverish endeavor to keep the Law before he can be saved, is unnecessary, and that the Lord Jesus has wiped out the hand-writing that was against him by dying instead of him on the Cross. Who can measure the depth of the peace and joy that comes from this blessed knowledge? Is it a "theory of the atonement," a delusion of man's fancy? Or is it the very truth of God?

But still another objection remains against the Christian doctrine of the Cross. The objection concerns the character of God. What a degraded view of God it is, the modern liberal exclaims, when God is represented as being "alienated" from man, and as waiting coldly until a price be paid before He grants salvation! In reality, we are told, God is more willing to forgive sin than we are willing to be forgiven; reconciliation, therefore, can have to do only with man; it all depends upon us; God will receive us any time we choose.

The objection depends of course upon the liberal view of sin. If sin is so trifling a matter as the liberal Church supposes, then indeed the curse of God's law can be taken very lightly, and God can easily let by-gones be by-gones.

This business of letting by-gones be by-gones has a pleasant sound. But in reality it is the most heartless thing in the world. It will not do at all even in the case of sins committed against our fellow-men. To say nothing of sin against God, what shall be done about the harm that we have wrought to our neighbor? Sometimes, no doubt, the harm can be repaired. If we have de-frauded our neighbor of a sum of money, we can pay the sum back with interest. But in the case of the more serious wrongs such repayment is usually quite impossible. The more serious wrongs are those that are done, not to the bodies, but to the souls of men. And who can think with complacency of wrongs of that kind which he has committed? Who can bear to think, for example, of the harm that he has done to those younger than himself by a bad example? And what of those sad words, spoken to those we love, that have left scars never to be obliterated by the hand of time? In the presence of such memories, we are told by the modern preacher simply to repent and to let by-gones be by-gones. But what a heartless thing is such repentance! *We* escape into some higher, happier, respectable life. But what of those whom we by our example and by our words have helped to drag down to the brink of hell? We forget them and let by-gones be by-gones!

Such repentance will never wipe out the guilt of sin—not even sin committed against our fellow-men, to say nothing of sin against our God. The truly penitent man longs to wipe out the effects of sin, not merely to forget sin. But who can wipe out the effects of sin? Others are suffering because of our past sins; and we can attain no real peace until we suffer in their stead. We long to go back into the tangle of our life, and make right the things that are wrong—at least to suffer where we have caused others to suffer. And something like that Christ did for us when He died instead of us on the cross; He atoned for all our sins.

The sorrow for sins committed against one's fellowmen does indeed remain in the Christian's heart. And he will seek by every means that is within his power to repair the damage that he has done. But atonement at least has been made—made as truly as if the sinner himself had suffered with and for those whom he has wronged. And the sinner himself, by a mystery of grace, becomes right with God. All sin at bottom is a sin against God. "Against thee, thee only have I sinned" is the cry of a true penitent. How terrible is the sin against God! Who can recall the wasted moments and years? Gone they are, never to return; gone the little allotted span of life; gone the little day in which a man must work. Who can measure the irrevocable guilt of a wasted life? Yet even for such guilt God has provided a fountain of cleansing in the precious blood of Christ. God has clothed us with Christ's righteousness as with a garment; in Christ we stand spotless before the judgment throne.

Thus to deny the necessity of atonement is to deny the existence of a real moral order. And it is strange how those who venture upon such denial can regard themselves as disciples of Jesus; for if one thing is clear in the record of Jesus' life it is that Jesus recognized the justice, as distinguished from the love, of God. God is love, according to Jesus, but He is not only love; Jesus spoke, in terrible words, of the sin that shall never be forgiven either in this world or in that which is to come. Clearly Jesus recognized the existence of retributive justice; Jesus was far from accepting the light modern view of sin.

But what, then, it will be objected, becomes of God's love? Even if it be admitted that justice demands punishment for sin, the modern liberal theologian will say, what becomes of the Christian doctrine that justice is swallowed up by grace? If God is represented as waiting for a price to be paid before sin shall be forgiven, perhaps His justice may be rescued, but what becomes of His love?

Modern liberal teachers are never tired of ringing the changes upon this objection. They speak with horror of the doctrine of an "alienated" or an "angry" God. In answer, of course it would be easy to point to the New Testament. The New Testament clearly speaks of the wrath of God and the wrath of Jesus Himself; and all the teaching of Jesus presupposes a divine indignation against sin. With what possible right, then, can those who reject this vital element in Jesus' teaching and example regard themselves as true disciples of His? The truth is that the modern rejection of the doctrine of God's wrath proceeds from a light view of sin which is totally at variance with the teaching of the whole New Testament and of Jesus Himself. If a man has once come under a true conviction of sin, he will have little difficulty with the doctrine of the Cross.

But as a matter of fact the modern objection to the doctrine of the atonement on the ground that that doctrine is contrary to the love of God, is based upon the most abysmal misunderstanding of the doctrine itself. The modern liberal teachers persist in speaking of the sacrifice of Christ as though it were a sacrifice made by some one other than God. They speak of it as though it meant that God waits coldly until a price is paid to Him before He forgives sin. As a matter of fact, it means nothing of the kind; the objection ignores that which is absolutely fundamental in the Christian doctrine of the Cross. The fundamental thing is that God Himself, and not another, makes the sacrifice for sin— God Himself in the person of the Son who assumed our nature and died for us, God Himself in the Person of the Father who spared not His own Son but offered Him up for us all. Salvation is as free *for us* as the air we breathe; God's the dreadful cost, ours the gain. "God so loved the world that He gave His only begotten Son." Such love is very different from the complacency found in the God of modern preaching; this love is love that did not count the cost; it is love that is love indeed.

This love and this love alone brings true joy to men. Joy is indeed being sought by the modern liberal Church. But it is being sought in ways that are false. How may communion with God be made joyful? Obviously, we are told, by emphasizing the comforting attributes of God—His long-suffering, His love. Let us, it is urged, regard Him not as a moody Despot, not as a sternly righteous Judge, but simply as a loving Father. Away with the horrors of the old theology! Let us worship a God in whom we can rejoice.

Two questions arise with regard to this method of making religion joyful—in the first place, Does it work? and in the second place, Is it true?

Does it work? It certainly ought to work. How can anyone be unhappy when the ruler of the universe is declared to be the loving Father of all men who will never permanently inflict pain upon His children? Where is the sting of remorse if all sin will necessarily be forgiven? Yet men are strangely ungrateful. After the modern preacher has done his part with all diligence—after everything unpleasant has carefully been eliminated from the conception of God, after His unlimited love has been celebrated with the eloquence that it deserves—the congregation somehow persistently refuses to burst into the old ecstasies of joy. The truth is, the God of modern preaching, though He may perhaps be very good, is rather uninteresting. Nothing is so insipid as indiscriminate good humor. Is that really love that costs so little? If God will necessarily forgive, no matter what we do, why trouble ourselves about Him at all? Such a God may deliver us from the fear of hell. But His heaven, if He has any, is full of sin.

The other objection to the modern encouraging idea of God is that it is not true. How do you know that God is all love and kindness? Surely not through nature, for it is full of horrors. Human suffering may be unpleasant, but it is real, and God must have something to do with it. Just as surely not through the Bible. For it was from the Bible that the old theologians derived that conception of God which you would reject as gloomy. "The Lord thy God," the Bible says, "is a consuming fire." Or is Jesus alone your authority? You are no better off. For it was Jesus who spoke of the outer darkness and the everlasting fire, of the sin that shall not be forgiven either in this age or in that which is to come. Or do you appeal, for your comforting idea of God, to a twentieth-century revelation granted immediately to you? It is to be feared that you will convince no one but yourself.

Religion cannot be made joyful simply by looking on the bright side of God. For a one-sided God is not a real God, and it is the real God alone who can satisfy the longing of our soul. God is love, but is He only love? God is love, but is love God? Seek joy alone, then, seek joy at any cost, and you will not find it. How then may it be attained?

The search for joy in religion seems to have ended in disaster. God is found to be enveloped in impenetrable mystery, and in awful righteousness; man is confined in the prison of the world, trying to make the best of his condition, beautifying the prison with tinsel, yet secretly dissatisfied with his bondage, dissatisfied with a merely relative goodness which is no goodness at all, dissatisfied with the companionship of his sinful fellows, unable to forget his heavenly destiny and his heavenly duty, longing for communion with the Holy One. There seems to be no hope; God is separate from sinners; there is no room for joy, but only a certain fearful looking for of judgment and fiery indignation.

Yet such a God has at least one advantage over the comforting God of modern preaching—He is alive, He is sovereign, He is not bound by His creation or by His creatures, He can perform wonders. Could He even save us if He would? He has saved us—in that message the gospel consists. It could not have been foretold; still less could the manner of it have been foretold. That Birth, that Life, that Death—why was it done just thus and then and there? It all seems so very local, so very particular, so very unphilosophical, so very unlike what might have been expected. Are not our own methods of salvation, men say, better than that? "Are not Abana and Pharpar, rivers of Damascus, better than all the waters of Israel?" Yet what if it were true? "So, the All-Great were the All-Loving too"—God's own Son delivered up for us all, freedom from the world, sought by philosophers of all the ages, offered now freely to every simple soul, things hidden from the wise and prudent revealed unto babes, the long striving over, the impossible accomplished, sin conquered by mysterious grace, communion at length with the holy God, our Father which art in heaven!

Surely this and this alone is joy. But it is a joy that is akin to fear. It is a fearful thing to fall into the hands of the living God. Were we not safer with a God of our own devising—love and only love, a Father and nothing else, one before whom we could stand in our own merit without fear? He who will may be satisfied with such a God. But we, God help us—sinful as we are, we would see Jehovah. Despairing, hoping, trembling, half-doubting and half-believing, trusting all to Jesus, we venture into the presence of the very God. And in His presence we live.

The atoning death of Christ, and that alone, has presented sinners as righteous in God's sight; the Lord Jesus has paid the full penalty of their sins, and clothed them with His perfect righteousness before the judgment seat of God. But Christ has done for Christians even far more than that. He has given to them not only a new and right relation to God, but a new life in God's presence for evermore. He has saved them from the power as well as from the guilt of sin. The New Testament does not end with the death of Christ; it does not end with the triumphant words of Jesus on the Cross, "It is finished." The death was followed by the resurrection, and the resurrection like the death was for our sakes. Jesus rose from the dead into a new life of glory and power, and into that life He brings those for whom He died. The Christian, on the basis of Christ's redeeming work, not only has died unto sin, but also lives unto God.

Thus was completed the redeeming work of Christ—the work for which He entered into the world. The account of that work is the "gospel," the "good news." It never could have been predicted, for sin deserves naught but eternal death. But God triumphed over sin through the grace of our Lord Jesus Christ.

But how is the redeeming work of Christ applied to the individual Christian man? The answer of the New Testament is plain. According to the New Testament the work of Christ is applied to the individual Christian man by the Holy Spirit. And this work of the Holy Spirit is part of the creative work of God. It is not accomplished by the ordinary use of means; it is not accomplished merely by using the good that is already in man. On the contrary, it is something new. It is not an influence upon the life, but the beginning of a new life; it is not development of what we had already, but a new birth. At the very centre of Christianity are the words, "Ye must be born again."

These words are despised to-day. They involve supernaturalism, and the modern man is opposed to supernaturalism in the experience of the individual as much as in the realm of history. A cardinal doctrine of modern liberalism is that the world's evil may be overcome by the world's good; no help is thought to be needed from outside the world.

This doctrine is propagated in various ways. It runs all through the popular literature of our time. It dominates religious literature, and it appears even upon the stage. Some years ago great popularity was attained by a play which taught the doctrine in powerful fashion. The play began with a scene in a London boarding-house. And it was a very discouraging scene. The persons in that boarding-house were not by any means desperate criminals, but one could almost have wished that they had been—they would have been so much more interesting. As it was, they were simply sordid, selfish persons, snapping and snarling about things to eat and about creature comforts—the sort of persons about whom one is tempted to say that they have no souls. The scene was a powerful picture of the hideousness of the commonplace. But presently the mysterious stranger of "the third floor back" entered upon the scene, and all was changed. He had no creed to offer, and no religion. But he simply engaged in conversation with everyone in that boardinghouse, and discovered the one good point in every individual life. Somewhere in every life there was some one good thing—some one true human affection, some one noble ambition. It had long been hidden by a thick coating of sordidness and selfishness; its very existence had been forgotten. But it was there, and when it was brought to the light the whole life was transformed. Thus the evil that was in man was overcome by the good that was already there.

The same thing is taught in more immediately practical

ways. For example, there are those who would apply it to the prisoners in our jails. The inmates of jails and penitentiaries constitute no doubt unpromising material. But it is a great mistake, it is said, to tell them that they are bad, to discourage them by insisting upon their sin. On the contrary, we are told, what ought to be done is to find the good that is already in them and build upon that; we ought to appeal to some latent sense of honor which shows that even criminals possess the remnants of our common human nature. Thus again the evil that is in man is to be overcome not by a foreign good but by a good which man himself possesses.

Certainly there is a large element of truth in this modern principle. That element of truth is found in the Bible. The Bible does certainly teach that the good that is already in man ought to be fostered in order to check the evil. Whatsoever things are true and pure and of good report—we ought to think on those things. Certainly the principle of overcoming the world's evil by the good already in the world is a great principle. The old theologians recognized it to the full in their doctrine of "common grace." There is something in the world even apart from Christianity which restrains the worst manifestations of evil. And that something ought to be used. Without the use of it, this world could not be lived in for a day. The use of it is certainly a great principle; it will certainly accomplish many useful things.

But there is one thing which it will not accomplish. It will not remove the disease of sin, it will indeed palliate the symptoms of the disease; it will change the form of the disease. Sometimes the disease is hidden, and there are those who think that it is cured. But then it bursts forth in some new way, as in 1914, and startles the world. What is really needed is not a salve to palliate the symptoms of sin, but a remedy that attacks the root of the disease.

In reality, however, the figure of disease is misleading. The only true figure—if indeed it can be called merely a figure—is the one which is used in the Bible. Man is not merely ill, but he is dead, in trespasses and sins, and what is really needed is a new life. That life is given by the Holy Spirit in "regeneration" or the new birth.

Many are the passages and many are the ways in which the central doctrine of the new birth is taught in the Word of God. One of the most stupendous passages is Gal. 2:20: "I have been crucified with Christ; and it is no longer I that live but Christ liveth in me." That passage was called by Bengel the marrow of Christianity. And it was rightly so called. It refers to the objective basis of Christianity in the redeeming work of Christ, and it contains also the supernaturalism of Christian experience. "It is no longer I that live, but Christ liveth in me"—these are extraordinary words. "If you look upon Christians," Paul says in effect, "you see so many manifestations of the life of Christ." Undoubtedly if the words of Gal. 2:20 stood alone they might be taken in a mystical or pantheistic sense; they might be taken to involve the merging of the personality of the Christian in the personality of Christ. But Paul had no reason to fear such a misinterpretation, for he had fortified himself against it by the whole of his teaching. The new relation of the Christian to Christ, according to Paul, involves no loss of the separate personality of the Christian; on the contrary, it is everywhere intensely personal; it is not a merely mystical relationship to the All or the Absolute, but a relationship of love existing between one person and another. Just because Paul had fortified himself against misunderstanding, he was not afraid of an extreme boldness of language. "It is no longer I that live, but Christ liveth in me"—these words involve a tremendous conception of the break that comes in a man's life when he becomes a Christian. It is almost as though he became a new person—so stupendous is the change. These words were not written by a man who believed that Christianity means merely the entrance of a new motive into the life; Paul believed with all his mind and heart in the doctrine of the new creation or the new birth.

That doctrine represents one aspect of the salvation which was wrought by Christ and is applied by His Spirit. But there is another aspect of the same salvation. Regeneration means a new life; but there is also a new relation in which the believer stands toward God. That new relation is instituted by "justification"— the act of God by which a sinner is pronounced righteous in His sight because of the atoning death of Christ. It is not necessary to ask whether justification comes before regeneration or *vice versa*; in reality they are two aspects of one salvation. And they both stand at the very beginning of the Christian life. The Christian has not merely the promise of a new life, but he has already a new life. And he has not merely the promise of being pronounced righteous in God's sight (though the blessed pronouncement will be confirmed on the judgment day), but he is already pronounced righteous here and now. At the beginning of every Christian life there stands, not a process, but a definite act of God.

That does not mean that every Christian can tell exactly at what moment he was justified and born again. Some Christians, indeed, are really able to give day and hour of their conversion. It is a grievous sin to ridicule the experience of such men. Sometimes, indeed, they are inclined to ignore the steps in the providence of God which prepared for the great change. But they are right on the main point. They know that when on such and such a day they kneeled in prayer they were still in their sins, and when they rose from their knees they were children of God never to be separated from Him. Such experience is a very holy thing. But on the other hand it is a mistake to demand that it should be universal. There are Christians who can give day and hour of their conversion, but the great majority do not know exactly at what moment they were saved. The effects of the act are plain, but the act itself was done in the quietness of God. Such, very often, is the experience of children brought up by Christian parents. It is not necessary that all should pass through agonies of soul before being saved; there are those to whom faith comes peacefully and easily through the nurture of Christian homes.

But however it be manifested, the beginning of the Christian life is an act of God. It is an act of God and not an act of man.

That does not mean, however, that in the beginning of the Christian life God deals with us as with sticks or stones, unable to understand what is being done. On the contrary He deals with us as with persons; salvation has a place in the conscious life of man; God uses in our salvation a conscious act of the human soul—an act which though it is itself the work of God's Spirit, is at the same time an act of man. That act of man which God produces and employs in salvation is faith. At the centre of Christianity is the doctrine of "justification by faith."

In exalting faith, we are not immediately putting ourselves in contradiction to modern thought. Indeed faith is being exalted very high by men of the most modern type. But what kind of faith? There emerges the difference of opinion.

Faith is being exalted so high to-day that men are being satisfied with any kind of faith, just so it is faith. It makes no difference what is believed, we are told, just so the blessed attitude of faith is there. The undogmatic faith, it is said, is better than the dogmatic, because it is purer faith—faith less weakened by the alloy of knowledge.

Now it is perfectly clear that such employment of faith merely as a beneficent state of the soul is bringing some results. Faith in the most absurd things sometimes produces the most beneficent and far-reaching results. But the disturbing thing is that all faith has an object. The scientific observer may not think that it is the object that does the work; from his vantage point he may see clearly that it is really the faith, considered simply as a psychological phenomenon, that is the important thing, and that any other object would have answered as well. But the one who does the believing is always convinced just exactly that it is not the faith, but the object of the faith, which is helping him. The moment he becomes convinced that it is merely the faith that is helping him, the faith disappears; for faith always involves a conviction of the objective truth or trustworthiness of the object. If the object is not really trustworthy then the faith is a false faith. It is perfectly true that such a false faith will often help a man. Things that are false will accomplish a great many useful things in the world. If I take a counterfeit coin and buy a dinner with it, the dinner is every bit as good as if the coin were a product of the mint. And what a very useful thing a dinner is! But just as I am on my way downtown to buy a dinner for a poor man, an expert tells me that my coin is a counterfeit. The miserable, heartless theorizer! While he is going into uninteresting, learned details about the primitive history of that coin, a poor man is dying for want of bread. So it is with faith. Faith is so very useful, they tell us, that we must not scrutinize its basis in truth. But, the great trouble is, such an avoidance of scrutiny itself involves the destruction of faith. For faith is essentially dogmatic. Despite all you can do, you cannot remove the element of intellectual assent from it. Faith is the opinion that some person will do something for you. If that person really will do that thing for you, then the faith is true. If he will not do it, then the faith is false. In the latter case, not all the benefits in the world will make the faith true. Though it has transformed the world from darkness to light, though it has produced thousands of glorious healthy lives, it remains a pathological phenomenon. It is false, and sooner or later it is sure to be found out.

Such counterfeits should be removed, not out of a love of destruction, but in order to leave room for the pure gold, the existence of which is implied in the presence of the counterfeits. Faith is often based upon error, but there would be no faith at all unless it were sometimes based upon truth. But if Christian faith is based upon truth, then it is not the faith which saves the Christian but the object of the faith. And the object of the faith is Christ. Faith, then, according to the Christian view, means simply receiving a gift. To have faith in Christ means to cease trying to win God's favor by one's own character; the man who believes in Christ simply accepts the sacrifice which Christ offered on Calvary. The result of such faith is a new life and all good works; but the salvation itself is an absolutely free gift of God.

Very different is the conception of faith which prevails in the liberal Church. According to modern liberalism, faith is essentially the same as "making Christ Master" in one's life; at least it is by making Christ Master in the life that the welfare of men is sought. But that simply means that salvation is thought to be obtained by our own obedience to the commands of Christ. Such teaching is just a sublimated form of legalism. Not the sacrifice of Christ, on this view, but our own obedience to God's law, is the ground of hope.

In this way the whole achievement of the Reformation has been given up, and there has been a return to the religion of the Middle Ages. At the beginning of the sixteenth century, God raised up a man who began to read the Epistle to the Galatians with his own eyes. The result was the rediscovery of the doctrine of justification by faith. Upon that rediscovery has been based the whole of our evangelical freedom. As expounded by Luther and Calvin the Epistle to the Galatians became the "Magna Charta of Christian liberty." But modern liberalism has returned to the old interpretation of Galatians which was urged against the Reformers. Thus Professor Burton's elaborate commentary on the Epistle, despite all its extremely valuable modern scholarship, is in one respect a mediæval book; it has returned to an anti-Reformation exegesis, by which Paul is thought to be attacking in the Epistle only the piecemeal morality of the Pharisees. In reality, of course, the object of Paul's attack is the thought that in any way man can earn his acceptance with God. What Paul is primarily interested in is not spiritual religion over against ceremonialism, but the free grace of God over against human merit.

The grace of God is rejected by modern liberalism. And the result is slavery—the slavery of the law, the wretched bondage by which man undertakes the impossible task of establishing his own righteousness as a ground of acceptance with God. It may seem strange at first sight that "liberalism," of which the very name means freedom, should in reality be wretched slavery. But the phenomenon is not really so strange. Emancipation from the blessed will of God always involves bondage to some worse taskmaster.

Thus it may be said of the modern liberal Church, as of the Jerusalem of Paul's day, that "she is in bondage with her children." God grant that she may turn again to the liberty of the gospel of Christ!

The liberty of the gospel depends upon the gift of God by which the Christian life is begun—a gift which involves justification, or the removal of the guilt of sin and the establishment of a right relation between the believer and God, and regeneration or the new birth, which makes of the Christian man a new creature.

But there is one obvious objection to this high doctrine, and the objection leads on to a fuller account of the Christian way of salvation. The obvious objection to the doctrine of the new creation is that it does not seem to be in accord with the observed fact. Are Christians really new creatures? It certainly does not seem so. They are subject to the same old conditions of life to which they were subject before; if you look upon them you cannot notice any very obvious change. They have the same weaknesses, and, unfortunately, they have sometimes the same sins. The new creation, if it be really new, does not seem to be very perfect; God can hardly look upon it and say, as of the first creation, that it is all very good.

This is a very real objection. But Paul meets it gloriously in the very same verse, already considered, in which the doctrine of the new creation is so boldly proclaimed. "It is no longer I that live, but Christ liveth in me"—that is the doctrine of the new creation. But immediately the objection is taken up; "The life which I now live in the flesh," Paul continues, "I live by the faith which is in the Son of God who loved me and gave Himself for me." "The life which I now live in the flesh"—there is the admission. Paul admits that the Christian does live a life in the flesh, subject to the same old earthly conditions and with a continued battle against sin. "But," says Paul (and here the objection is answered), "the life which I now live in the flesh I live by the faith which is in the Son of God who loved me and gave Himself for me." The Christian life is lived by faith and not by sight; the great change has not yet come to full fruition; sin has not yet been fully conquered; the beginning of the Christian life is a new *birth*, not an immediate creation of the full-grown man. But although the new life has not yet come to full fruition, the Christian knows that the fruition will not fail; he is confident that the God who has begun a good work in him will complete it unto the day of Christ; he knows that the Christ who has loved him and given Himself for him will not fail him now, but through the Holy Spirit will build him up unto the perfect man. That is what Paul means by living the Christian life by faith.

Thus the Christian life, though it begins by a momentary act of God, is continued by a process. In other words—to use theological language—justification and regeneration are followed by sanctification. In principle the Christian is already free from the present evil world, but in practice freedom must still be attained. Thus the Christian life is not a life of idleness, but a battle.

That is what Paul means when he speaks of faith working through love (Gal. 5:6). The faith that he makes the means of salvation is not an idle faith, like the faith which is condemned in the Epistle of James, but a faith that works. The work that it performs is love, and what love is Paul explains in the last section of the Epistle to the Galatians. Love, in the Christian sense, is not a mere emotion, but a very practical and a very comprehensive thing. It involves nothing less than the keeping of the whole law of God. "The whole law is fulfilled in one word, even in this: Thou shalt love thy neighbor as thyself." Yet the practical results of faith do not mean that faith itself is a work. It is a significant thing that in that last "practical" section of Galatians Paul does not say that faith produces the life of love; he says that the Spirit of God produces it. The Spirit, then, in that section is represented as doing exactly what in the pregnant words, "faith working through love," is attributed to faith. The apparent contradiction simply leads to the true conception of faith. True faith does not do anything. When it is said to do something (for example, when we say that it can remove mountains), that is only by a very natural shortness of expression. Faith is the exact opposite of works; faith does not give, it receives. So when Paul says that we do something by faith, that is just another way of saying that of ourselves we do nothing; when it is said that faith works through love that means that through faith the necessary basis of all Christian work has been obtained in the removal of guilt and the birth of the new man, and that the Spirit of God has been received—the Spirit who works with and through the Christian man for holy living. The force which enters the Christian life through faith and works itself out through love is the power of the Spirit of God.

But the Christian life is lived not only by faith; it is also lived in hope. The Christian is in the midst of a sore battle. And as for the condition of the world at large—nothing but the coldest heartlessness could be satisfied with that. It is certainly true that the whole creation groaneth and travaileth in pain together until now. Even in the Christian life there are things that we should like to see removed; there are fears within as well as fightings without; even within the Christian life there are sad evidences of sin. But according to the hope which Christ has given us, there will be final victory, and the struggle of this world will be followed by the glories of heaven. That hope runs all through the Christian life; Christianity is not engrossed by this transitory world, but measures all things by the thought of eternity.

But at this point an objection is frequently raised. The "otherworldliness" of Christianity is objected to as a form of selfishness. The Christian, it is said, does what is right because of the hope of heaven, but how much nobler is the man who because of duty walks boldly into the darkness of annihilation!

The objection would have some weight if heaven according to Christian belief were mere enjoyment. But as a matter of fact heaven is communion with God and with His Christ. It can be said reverently that the Christian longs for heaven not only for his own sake, but also for the sake of God. Our present love is so cold, our present service so weak; and we would one day love and serve Him as His love deserves. It is perfectly true that the Christian is dissatisfied with the present world, but it is a holy dissatisfaction; it is that hunger and thirst after righteousness which our Saviour blessed. We are separated from the Saviour now by the veil of sense and by the effects of sin, and it is not selfish to long to see Him face to face. To relinquish such longing is not unselfishness, but is like the cold heartlessness of a man who could part from father or mother or wife or child without a pang. It is not selfish to long for the One whom not having seen we love.

Such is the Christian life—it is a life of conflict, but it is also a life of hope. It views this world under the aspect of eternity; the fashion of this world passeth away, and all must stand before the judgment seat of Christ.

Very different is the "program" of the modern liberal Church. In that program, heaven has little place, and this world is really all in all. The rejection of the Christian hope is not always definite or conscious; sometimes the liberal preacher tries to maintain a belief in the immortality of the soul. But the real basis of the belief in immortality has been given up by the rejection of the New Testament account of the resurrection of Christ. And, practically, the liberal preacher has very little to say about the other world. This world is really the centre of all his thoughts; religion itself, and even God, are made merely a means for the betterment of conditions upon this earth.

Thus religion has become a mere function of the community or of the state. So it is looked upon by the men of the present day. Even hard-headed business men and politicians have become convinced that religion is needed. But it is thought to be needed merely as a means to an end. We have tried to get along without religion, it is said, but the experiment was a failure, and now religion must be called in to help.

For example, there is the problem of the immigrants; great populations have found a place in our country; they do not speak our language or know our customs; and we do not know what to do with them. We have attacked them by oppressive legislation or proposals of legislation, but such measures have not been altogether effective. Somehow these people display a perverse attachment to the language that they learned at their mother's knee. It may be strange that a man should love the language that he learned at his mother's knee, but these people do love it, and we are perplexed in our efforts to produce a unified American people. So religion is called in to help; we are inclined to proceed against the immigrants now with a Bible in one hand and a club in the other offering them the blessings of liberty. That is what is sometimes meant by "Christian Americanization."

Another puzzling problem is the problem of industrial relations. Self-interest has here been appealed to; employers and employees have had pointed out to them the plain commercial advantages of conciliation. But all to no purpose. Class clashes still against class in the destructiveness of industrial warfare. And sometimes false doctrine provides a basis for false practice; the danger of Bolshevism is ever in the air. Here again repressive measures have been tried without avail; the freedom of speech and of the press has been radically curtailed. But repressive legislation seems unable to check the march of ideas. Perhaps, therefore, in these matters also, religion must be invoked.

Still another problem faces the modern world—the problem of international peace. This problem also seemed at one time nearly solved; self-interest seemed likely to be sufficient; there were many who supposed that the bankers would prevent another European war. But all such hopes were cruelly shattered in 1914, and there is not a whit of evidence that they are better founded now than they were then. Here again, therefore, self-interest is insufficient; and religion must be called in to help.

Such considerations have led to a renewed public interest in the subject of religion; religion is discovered after all to be a useful thing. But the trouble is that in being utilized religion is also being degraded and destroyed. Religion is being regarded more and more as a mere means to a higher end.[6] The change can be

---

6. For a penetrating criticism of this tendency, especially as it would result in the control of religious education by the community, and for an eloquent advocacy of the opposite view, which makes Christianity an end in itself, see Harold McA. Robinson, "Democracy and Christianity," in *The Christian Educator*, Vol. V, No. 1, for October, 1920, pp. 3–5.

detected with especial clearness in the way in which missionaries commend their cause. Fifty years ago, missionaries made their appeal in the light of eternity. "Millions of men," they were accustomed to say, "are going down to eternal destruction; Jesus is a Saviour sufficient for all; send us out therefore with the message of salvation while yet there is time." Some missionaries, thank God, still speak in that way. But very many missionaries make quite a different appeal. "We are missionaries to India," they say. "Now India is in ferment; Bolshevism is creeping in; send us out to India that the menace may be checked." Or else they say: "We are missionaries to Japan; Japan will be dominated by militarism unless the principles of Jesus have sway; send us out therefore to prevent the calamity of war."

The same great change appears in community life. A new community, let us say, has been formed. It possesses many things that naturally belong to a well-ordered community; it has a drug-store, and a country club, and a school. "But there is one thing," its inhabitants say to themselves, "that is still lacking; we have no church. But a church is a recognized and necessary part of every healthy community. We must therefore have a church." And so an expert in community church-building is summoned to take the necessary steps. The persons who speak in this way usually have little interest in religion for its own sake; it has never occurred to them to enter into the secret place of communion with the holy God. But religion is thought to be necessary for a healthy community; and therefore for the sake of the community they are willing to have a church.

Whatever may be thought of this attitude toward religion, it is perfectly plain that the *Christian* religion cannot be treated in any such way. The moment it is so treated it ceases to be

Christian. For if one thing is plain it is that Christianity refuses
to be regarded as a mere means to a higher end. Our Lord made
that perfectly clear when He said: "If any man come to me, and
hate not his father and mother ... he cannot be my disciple" (Lk.
14:26). Whatever else those stupendous words may mean, they
certainly mean that the relationship to Christ takes precedence
of all other relationships, even the holiest of relationships like
those that exist between husband and wife and parent and child.
Those other relationships exist for the sake of Christianity and
not Christianity for the sake of them. Christianity will indeed
accomplish many useful things in this world, but if it is accepted
in order to accomplish those useful things it is not Christianity.
Christianity will combat Bolshevism; but if it is accepted in order
to combat Bolshevism, it is not Christianity: Christianity will
produce a unified nation, in a slow but satisfactory way; but if it
is accepted in order to produce a unified nation, it is not Christianity: Christianity will produce a healthy community; but if it
is accepted in order to produce a healthy community, it is not
Christianity: Christianity will promote international peace; but
if it is accepted in order to promote international peace, it is not
Christianity. Our Lord said: "Seek ye first the Kingdom of God
and His righteousness, and all these things shall be added unto
you." But if you seek first the Kingdom of God and His righteousness *in order that* all those other things may be added unto
you, you will miss both those other things and the Kingdom of
God as well.

But if Christianity be directed toward another world, if it
be a way by which individuals can escape from the present evil
age to some better country, what becomes of "the social gospel"? At this point is detected one of the most obvious lines of

cleavage between Christianity and the liberal Church. The older evangelism, says the modern liberal preacher, sought to rescue individuals, while the newer evangelism seeks to transform the whole organism of society: the older evangelism was individual; the newer evangelism is social.

This formulation of the issue is not entirely correct, but it contains an element of truth. It is true that historic Christianity is in conflict at many points with the collectivism of the present day; it does emphasize, against the claims of society, the worth of the individual soul. It provides for the individual a refuge from all the fluctuating currents of human opinion, a secret place of meditation where a man can come alone into the presence of God. It does give a man courage to stand, if need be, against the world; it resolutely refuses to make of the individual a mere means to an end, a mere element in the composition of society. It rejects altogether any means of salvation which deals with men in a mass; it brings the individual face to face with his God. In that sense, it is true that Christianity is individualistic and not social.

But though Christianity is individualistic, it is not only individualistic. It provides fully for the social needs of man.

In the first place, even the communion of the individual man with God is not really individualistic, but social. A man is not isolated when he is in communion with God; he can be regarded as isolated only by one who has forgotten the real existence of the supreme Person. Here again, as at many other places, the line of cleavage between liberalism and Christianity really reduces to a profound difference in the conception of God. Christianity is earnestly theistic; liberalism is at best but halfheartedly so. If a man once comes to believe in a personal God, then the worship of Him will not be regarded as selfish isolation, but as the chief end of man. That does not mean that on the Christian view the worship of God is ever to be carried on to the neglect of service rendered to one's fellow-men—"he that loveth not his brother whom he hath seen, is not able to love God whom he hath not seen"—but it does mean that the worship of God has a value of its own. Very different is the prevailing doctrine of modern liberalism. According to Christian belief, man exists for the sake of God; according to the liberal Church, in practice if not in theory, God exists for the sake of man.

But the social element in Christianity is found not only in communion between man and God, but also in communion between man and man. Such communion appears even in institutions which are not specifically Christian.

The most important of such institutions, according to Christian teaching, is the family. And that institution is being pushed more and more into the background. It is being pushed into the background by undue encroachments of the community and of the state. Modern life is tending more and more toward the contraction of the sphere of parental control and parental influence. The choice of schools is being placed under the power of the state; the "community" is seizing hold of recreation and of social activities. It may be a question how far these community activities are responsible for the modern breakdown of the home; very possibly they are only trying to fill a void which even apart from them had already appeared. But the result at any rate is plain—the lives of children are no longer surrounded by the loving atmosphere of the Christian home, but by the utilitarianism of the state. A revival of the Christian religion would unquestionably bring a reversal of the process; the family, as over against all other social institutions, would come to its rights again.

But the state, even when reduced to its proper limits, has a large place in human life, and in the possession of that place it is supported by Christianity. The support, moreover, is independent of the Christian or non-Christian character of the state; it was in the Roman Empire under Nero that Paul said, "The powers that be are ordained of God." Christianity assumes no negative attitude, therefore, toward the state, but recognizes, under existing conditions, the necessity of government.

The case is similar with respect to those broad aspects of human life which are associated with industrialism. The "otherworldliness" of Christianity involves no withdrawal from the battle of this world; our Lord Himself, with His stupendous mission, lived in the midst of life's throng and press. Plainly, then, the Christian man may not simplify his problem by withdrawing from the business of the world, but must learn to apply the principles of Jesus even to the complex problems of modern industrial life. At this point Christian teaching is in full accord with the modern liberal Church; the evangelical Christian is not true to his profession if he leaves his Christianity behind him on Monday morning. On the contrary, the whole of life, including business and all of social relations, must be made obedient to the law of love. The Christian man certainly should display no lack of interest in "applied Christianity."

Only—and here emerges the enormous difference of opinion—the Christian man believes that there can be no applied Christianity unless there be "a Christianity to apply."[7] That is where the Christian man differs from the modern liberal. The liberal believes that applied Christianity is all there is of Christianity,

---

7. Francis Shunk Downs, "Christianity and Today," in *Princeton Theological Review*, xx, 1922, p. 287. See also the whole article, *ibid.*, pp. 287–304.

Christianity being merely a way of life; the Christian man believes that applied Christianity is the result of an initial act of God. Thus there is an enormous difference between the modern liberal and the Christian man with reference to human institutions like the community and the state, and with reference to human efforts at applying the Golden Rule in industrial relationships. The modern liberal is optimistic with reference to these institutions; the Christian man is pessimistic unless the institutions be manned by Christian men. The modern liberal believes that human nature as at present constituted can be molded by the principles of Jesus; the Christian man believes that evil can only be held in check and not destroyed by human institutions, and that there must be a transformation of the human materials before any new building can be produced. This difference is not a mere difference in theory, but makes itself felt everywhere in the practical realm. It is particularly evident on the mission field. The missionary of liberalism seeks to spread the blessings of Christian civilization (whatever that may be), and is not particularly interested in leading individuals to relinquish their pagan beliefs. The Christian missionary, on the other hand, regards satisfaction with a mere influence of Christian civilization as a hindrance rather than a help; his chief business, he believes, is the saving of souls, and souls are saved not by the mere ethical principles of Jesus but by His redemptive work. The Christian missionary, in other words, and the Christian worker at home as well as abroad, unlike the apostle of liberalism, says to all men everywhere: "Human goodness will avail nothing for lost souls; ye must be born again."

The Church

I t has just been observed that Christianity, as well as liberalism, is interested in social institutions. But the most important institution has not yet been mentioned—it is the institution of the Church. When, according to Christian belief, lost souls are saved, the saved ones become united in the Christian Church. It is only by a baseless caricature that Christian missionaries are represented as though they had no interest in education or in the maintenance of a social life in this world; it is not true that they are interested only in saving individual souls and when the souls are saved leave them to their own devices. On the contrary true Christians must everywhere be united in the brotherhood of the Christian Church.

Very different is this Christian conception of brotherhood from the liberal doctrine of the "brotherhood of man." The modern liberal doctrine is that all men everywhere, no matter what their race or creed, are brothers. There is a sense in which this doctrine can be accepted by the Christian. The relation in which all men stand to one another is analogous in some important respects to the relation of brotherhood. All men have the same Creator and the same nature. The Christian man can accept all that the modern liberal means by the brotherhood of man. But the Christian knows also of a relationship far more intimate than that general relationship of man to man, and it is for this more intimate relationship that he reserves the term "brother." The true brotherhood, according to Christian teaching, is the brotherhood of the redeemed.

There is nothing narrow about such teaching; for the Christian brotherhood is open without distinction to all; and the Christian man seeks to bring all men in. Christian service, it is true, is not limited to the household of faith; all men, whether Christians or not, are our neighbors if they be in need. But if we really love our fellowmen we shall never be content with binding up their wounds or pouring on oil and wine or rendering them any such lesser service. We shall indeed do such things for them. But the main business of our lives will be to bring them to the Saviour of their souls.

It is upon this brotherhood of twice-born sinners, this brotherhood of the redeemed, that the Christian founds the hope of society. He finds no solid hope in the improvement of earthly conditions, or the molding of human institutions under the influence of the Golden Rule. These things indeed are to be welcomed. They may so palliate the symptoms of sin that there may be time to apply the true remedy; they may serve to produce conditions upon the earth favorable to the propagation of the gospel message; they are even valuable for their own sake. But in themselves their value, to the Christian, is certainly small. A solid building cannot be constructed when all the materials are faulty; a blessed society cannot be formed out of men who are still under the curse of sin. Human institutions are really to be molded, not by Christian principles accepted by the unsaved, but by Christian men; the true transformation of society will come by the influence of those who have themselves been redeemed.

Thus Christianity differs from liberalism in the way in which the transformation of society is conceived. But according to Christian belief, as well as according to liberalism, there is really to be a transformation of society; it is not true that the Christian evangelist is interested in the salvation of individuals without being interested in the salvation of the race. And even before the salvation of all society has been achieved, there is already a society of those who have been saved. That society is the Church. The Church is the highest Christian answer to the social needs of man.

And the Church invisible, the true company of the redeemed, finds expression in the companies of Christians who constitute the visible Church to-day. But what is the trouble with the visible Church? What is the reason for its obvious weakness? There are perhaps many causes of weakness. But one cause is perfectly plain—the Church of to-day has been unfaithful to her Lord by admitting great companies of non-Christian persons, not only into her membership, but into her teaching agencies. It is indeed inevitable that some persons who are not truly Christian shall find their way into the visible Church; fallible men cannot discern the heart, and many a profession of faith which seems to be genuine may really be false. But it is not this kind of error to which we now refer. What is now meant is not the admission of individuals whose confessions of faith may not be sincere, but the admission of great companies of persons who have never made any really adequate confession of faith at all and whose entire attitude toward the gospel is the very reverse of the Christian attitude. Such persons, moreover, have been admitted not merely to the membership, but to the ministry of the Church, and to an increasing extent have been allowed to dominate its councils and determine its teaching. The greatest menace to the Christian Church to-day comes not from the enemies outside, but from the enemies within; it comes from the presence within the Church of a type of faith and practice that is anti-Christian to the core.

We are not dealing here with delicate personal questions; we are not presuming to say whether such and such an individual man is a Christian or not. God only can decide such questions; no man can say with assurance whether the attitude of certain individual "liberals" toward Christ is saving faith or not. But one thing is perfectly plain—whether or no liberals are Christians, it is at any rate perfectly clear that liberalism is not Christianity. And that being the case, it is highly undesirable that liberalism and Christianity should continue to be propagated within the bounds of the same organization. A separation between the two parties in the Church is the crying need of the hour.

Many indeed are seeking to avoid the separation. Why, they say, may not brethren dwell together in unity? The Church, we are told, has room both for liberals and for conservatives. The conservatives may be allowed to remain if they will keep trifling matters in the background and attend chiefly to "the weightier matters of the law." And among the things thus designated as "trifling" is found the Cross of Christ, as a really vicarious atonement for sin.

Such obscuration of the issue attests a really astonishing narrowness on the part of the liberal preacher. Narrowness does not consist in definite devotion to certain convictions or in definite rejection of others. But the narrow man is the man who rejects the other man's convictions without first endeavoring to understand them, the man who makes no effort to look at things from the other man's point of view. For example, it is not narrow to reject the Roman Catholic doctrine that there is no salvation outside the Church. It is not narrow to try to convince Roman Catholics that that doctrine is wrong. But it would be very narrow to say to a Roman Catholic: "You may go on holding your doctrine about the Church and I shall hold mine, but let us unite in our Christian work, since despite such trifling differences we are agreed about the matters that concern the welfare of the soul." For of course such an utterance would simply beg the question; the Roman Catholic could not possibly both hold his doctrine of the Church and at the same time reject it, as would be required by the program of Church unity just suggested. A Protestant who would speak in that way would be narrow, because quite independent of the question whether he or the Roman Catholic is right about the Church he would show plainly that he had not made the slightest effort to understand the Roman Catholic point of view.

The case is similar with the liberal program for unity in the Church. It could never be advocated by anyone who had made the slightest effort to understand the point of view of his opponent in the controversy. The liberal preacher says to the conservative party in the Church: "Let us unite in the same congregation, since of course doctrinal differences are trifles." But it is the very essence of "conservatism" in the Church to regard doctrinal differences as no trifles but as the matters of supreme moment. A man cannot possibly be an "evangelical" or a "conservative" (or, as he himself would say, simply a Christian) and regard the Cross of Christ as a trifle. To suppose that he can is the extreme of narrowness. It is not necessarily "narrow" to reject the vicarious sacrifice of our Lord as the sole means of salvation. It may be very wrong (and we believe that it is), but it is not necessarily narrow. But to suppose that a man can hold to the vicarious sacrifice of Christ and at the same time belittle that doctrine, to suppose that a man can believe that the eternal Son of God really bore the guilt of men's sins on the Cross and at the same time regard that belief as a "trifle" without bearing upon the welfare of men's souls—that is very narrow and very absurd. We shall really get nowhere in this controversy unless we make a sincere effort to understand the other man's point of view.

But for another reason also the effort to sink doctrinal differences and unite the Church on a program of Christian service is unsatisfactory. It is unsatisfactory because, in its usual contemporary form, it is dishonest. Whatever may be thought of Christian doctrine, it can hardly be denied that honesty is one of the "weightier matters of the law." Yet honesty is being relinquished in wholesale fashion by the liberal party in many ecclesiastical bodies to-day.

To recognize that fact one does not need to take sides at all with regard to the doctrinal or historical questions. Suppose it be true that devotion to a creed is a sign of narrowness or intolerance, suppose the Church ought to be founded upon devotion to the ideal of Jesus or upon the desire to put His spirit into operation in the world, and not at all upon a confession of faith with regard to His redeeming work. Even if all this were true, even if a creedal Church were an undesirable thing, it would still remain true that as a matter of fact many (indeed in spirit really all) evangelical churches are creedal churches, and that if a man does not accept their creed he has no right to a place in their teaching ministry. The creedal character of the churches is differently expressed in the different evangelical bodies, but the example of the Presbyterian Church in the United States of America may perhaps serve to illustrate what is meant. It is required of all officers in the Presbyterian Church, including the ministers, that at their ordination they make answer "plainly" to a series of questions which begins with the two following:

> "Do you believe the Scriptures of the Old and New Testaments to be the Word of God, the only infallible rule of faith and practice?"
>
> "Do you sincerely receive and adopt the Confession of Faith of this Church, as containing the system of doctrine taught in the Holy Scriptures?"

If these "constitutional questions" do not fix clearly the creedal basis of the Presbyterian Church, it is difficult to see how any human language could possibly do so. Yet immediately after making such a solemn declaration, immediately after declaring that the Westminster Confession contains the system of doctrine taught in infallible Scriptures, many ministers of the Presbyterian Church will proceed to decry that same Confession and that doctrine of the infallibility of Scripture to which they have just solemnly subscribed!

We are not now speaking of the membership of the Church, but of the ministry, and we are not speaking of the man who is troubled by grave doubts and wonders whether with his doubts he can honestly continue his membership in the Church. For great hosts of such troubled souls the Church offers bountifully its fellowship and its aid; it would be a crime to cast them out.

There are many men of little faith in our troublous times. It is not of them that we speak. God grant that they may obtain comfort and help through the ministrations of the Church!

But we are speaking of men very different from these men of little faith—from these men who are troubled by doubts and are seeking earnestly for the truth. The men whom we mean are seeking not membership in the Church, but a place in the ministry, and they desire not to learn but to teach. They are not men who say, "I believe, help mine unbelief," but men who are proud in the possession of the knowledge of this world, and seek a place in the ministry that they may teach what is directly contrary to the Confession of Faith to which they subscribe. For that course of action various excuses are made—the growth of custom by which the constitutional questions are supposed to have become a dead letter, various mental reservations, various "interpretations" of the declaration (which of course mean a complete reversal of the meaning). But no such excuses can change the essential fact. Whether it be desirable or not, the ordination declaration is part of the constitution of the Church. If a man can stand on that platform he may be an officer in the Presbyterian Church; if he cannot stand on it he has no right to be an officer in the Presbyterian Church. And the case is no doubt essentially similar in other evangelical Churches. Whether we like it or not, these Churches are founded upon a creed; they are organized for the propagation of a message. If a man desires to combat that message instead of propagating it, he has no right, no matter how false the message may be, to gain a vantage ground for combating it by making a declaration of his faith which—be it plainly spoken—is not true.

But if such a course of action is wrong, another course of action is perfectly open to the man who desires to propagate "lib-eral Christianity." Finding the existing "evangelical" churches to be bound up to a creed which he does not accept, he may either unite himself with some other existing body or else found a new body to suit himself. There are of course certain obvious disad-vantages in such a course—the abandonment of church build-ings to which one is attached, the break in family traditions, the injury to sentiment of various kinds. But there is one supreme advantage which far overbalances all such disadvantages. It is the advantage of honesty. The path of honesty in such matters may be rough and thorny, but it can be trod. And it has already been trod—for example, by the Unitarian Church. The Unitarian Church is frankly and honestly just the kind of church that the liberal preacher desires—namely, a church without an authorita-tive Bible, without doctrinal requirements, and without a creed.

Honesty, despite all that can be said and done, is not a trifle, but one of the weightier matters of the law. Certainly it has a value of its own, a value quite independent of consequences. But the consequences of honesty would in the case now under dis-cussion not be unsatisfactory; here as elsewhere honesty would probably prove to be the best policy. By withdrawing from the confessional churches—those churches that are founded upon a creed derived from Scripture—the liberal preacher would in-deed sacrifice the opportunity, almost within his grasp, of so ob-taining control of those confessional churches as to change their fundamental character. The sacrifice of that opportunity would mean that the hope of turning the resources of the evangelical churches into the propagation of liberalism would be gone. But liberalism would certainly not suffer in the end. There would at least be no more need of using equivocal language, no more need of avoiding offence. The liberal preacher would obtain the full personal respect even of his opponents, and the whole discussion would be placed on higher ground. All would be perfectly straightforward and above-board. And if liberalism is true, the mere loss of physical resources would not prevent it from making its way.

At this point a question may arise. If there ought to be a separation between the liberals and the conservatives in the Church, why should not the conservatives be the ones to withdraw? Certainly it may come to that. If the liberal party really obtains full control of the councils of the Church, then no evangelical Christian can continue to support the Church's work. If a man believes that salvation from sin comes only through the atoning death of Jesus, then he cannot honestly support by his gifts and by his presence a propaganda which is intended to produce an exactly opposite impression. To do so would mean the most terrible bloodguiltiness which it is possible to conceive. If the liberal party, therefore, really obtains control of the Church, evangelical Christians must be prepared to withdraw no matter what it costs. Our Lord has died for us, and surely we must not deny Him for favor of men. But up to the present time such a situation has not yet appeared; the creedal basis still stands firm in the constitutions of evangelical churches. And there is a very real reason why it is not the "conservatives" who ought to withdraw. The reason is found in the trust which the churches hold. That trust includes trust funds of the most definite kind. And contrary to what seems to be the prevailing opinion, we venture to regard a trust as a sacred thing. The funds of the evangelical churches are held under a very definite trust; they are committed to the various bodies for the propagation of the gospel as set forth in the Bible and in the confessions of faith. To devote them to any other purpose, even though that other purpose should be in itself far more desirable, would be a violation of trust.

It must be admitted that the present situation is anomalous. Funds dedicated to the propagation of the gospel by godly men and women of previous generations or given by thoroughly evangelical congregations to-day are in nearly all the churches being used *partly* in the propagation of what is diametrically opposed to the evangelical faith. Certainly that situation ought not to continue; it is an offence to every thoughtfully honest man whether he be Christian or not. But in remaining in the existing churches the conservatives are in a fundamentally different position from the liberals; for the conservatives are in agreement with the plain constitutions of the churches, while the liberal party can maintain itself only by an equivocal subscription to declarations which it does not really believe.

But how shall so anomalous a situation be brought to an end? The best way would undoubtedly be the voluntary withdrawal of the liberal ministers from those confessional churches whose confessions they do not, in the plain historical sense, accept. And we have not altogether abandoned hope of such a solution. Our differences with the liberal party in the Church are indeed profound, but with regard to the obligation of simple honesty of speech, some agreement might surely be attained. Certainly the withdrawal of liberal ministers from the creedal churches would be enormously in the interests of harmony and co-operation. Nothing engenders strife so much as a forced unity, within the same organization, of those who disagree fundamentally in aim.

But is not advocacy of such separation a flagrant instance

of intolerance? The objection is often raised. But it ignores altogether the difference between involuntary and voluntary organizations. Involuntary organizations ought to be tolerant, but voluntary organizations, so far as the fundamental purpose of their existence is concerned, must be intolerant or else cease to exist. The state is an involuntary organization; a man is forced to be a member of it whether he will or no. It is therefore an interference with liberty for the state to prescribe any one type of opinion or any one type of education for its citizens. But within the state, individual citizens who desire to unite for some special purpose should be permitted to do so. Especially in the sphere of religion, such permission of individuals to unite is one of the rights which lie at the very foundation of our civil and religious liberty. The state does not scrutinize the rightness or wrongness of the religious purpose for which such voluntary religious associations are formed—if it did undertake such scrutiny all religious liberty would be gone—but it merely protects the right of individuals to unite for any religious purpose which they may choose.

Among such voluntary associations are to be found the evangelical churches. An evangelical church is composed of a number of persons who have come to agreement in a certain message about Christ and who desire to unite in the propagation of that message, as it is set forth in their creed on the basis of the Bible. No one is forced to unite himself with the body thus formed; and because of this total absence of compulsion there can be no interference with liberty in the maintenance of any specific purpose—for example, the propagation of a message—as a fundamental purpose of the association. If other persons desire to form a religious association with some purpose other than the propagation of a message—for example, the purpose of promoting in the world, simply by exhortation and by the inspiration of the example of Jesus, a certain type of life—they are at perfect liberty to do so. But for an organization which is founded with the fundamental purpose of propagating a message to commit its resources and its name to those who are engaged in combating the message is not tolerance but simple dishonesty. Yet it is exactly this course of action that is advocated by those who would allow non-doctrinal religion to be taught in the name of doctrinal churches—churches that are plainly doctrinal both in their constitutions and in the declarations which they require of every candidate for ordination.

The matter may be made plain by an illustration from secular life. Suppose in a political campaign in America there be formed a Democratic club for the purpose of furthering the cause of the Democratic party. Suppose there are certain other citizens who are opposed to the tenets of the Democratic club and in opposition desire to support the Republican party. What is the honest way for them to accomplish their purpose? Plainly it is simply the formation of a Republican club which shall carry on a propaganda in favor of Republican principles. But suppose, instead of pursuing this simple course of action, the advocates of Republican principles should conceive the notion of making a declaration of conformity to Democratic principles, thus gaining an entrance into the Democratic club and finally turning its resources into an anti-Democratic propaganda. That plan might be ingenious. But would it be honest? Yet it is just exactly such a plan which is adopted by advocates of a non-doctrinal religion who by subscription to a creed gain an entrance into the teaching ministry of doctrinal or evangelical churches. Let no one be offended by the illustration taken from ordinary life. We are not for a moment suggesting that the Church is no more than a political club. But the fact that the Church is more than a political club does not mean that in ecclesiastical affairs there is any abrogation of the homely principles of honesty. The Church may possibly be more honest, but certainly it ought not to be less honest, than a political club.

Certainly the essentially creedal character of evangelical churches is firmly fixed. A man may disagree with the Westminster Confession, for example, but he can hardly fail to see what it means; at least he can hardly fail to understand the "system of doctrine" which is taught in it. The Confession, whatever its faults may be, is certainly not lacking in definiteness. And certainly a man who solemnly accepts that system of doctrine as his own cannot at the same time be an advocate of a non-doctrinal religion which regards as a trifling thing that which is the very sum and substance of the Confession and the very centre and core of the Bible upon which it is based. Similar is the case in other evangelical churches. The Protestant Episcopal Church, some of whose members, it is true, might resent the distinctive title of "evangelical," is clearly founded upon a creed, and that creed, including the exultant supernaturalism of the New Testament and the redemption offered by Christ, is plainly involved in the Book of Common Prayer which every priest in his own name and in the name of the congregation must read.

The separation of naturalistic liberalism from the evangelical churches would no doubt greatly diminish the size of the churches. But Gideon's three hundred were more powerful than the thirty-two thousand with which the march against the Midianites began.

Certainly the present situation is fraught with deadly weakness. Christian men have been redeemed from sin, without merit of their own, by the sacrifice of Christ. But every man who has been truly redeemed from sin longs to carry to others the same blessed gospel through which he himself has been saved. The propagation of the gospel is clearly the joy as well as the duty of every Christian man. But how shall the gospel be propagated? The natural answer is that it shall be propagated through the agencies of the Church—boards of missions and the like. An obvious duty, therefore, rests upon the Christian man of contributing to the agencies of the Church. But at this point the perplexity arises. The Christian man discovers to his consternation that the agencies of the Church are propagating not only the gospel as found in the Bible and in the historic creeds, but also a type of religious teaching which is at every conceivable point the diametrical opposite of the gospel. The question naturally arises whether there is any reason for contributing to such agencies at all. Of every dollar contributed to them, perhaps half goes to the support of true missionaries of the Cross, while the other half goes to the support of those who are persuading men that the message of the Cross is unnecessary or wrong. If part of our gifts is to be used to neutralize the other part, is not contribution to mission boards altogether absurd? The question may at least very naturally be raised. It should not indeed be answered hastily in a way hostile to contribution to mission boards. Perhaps it is better that the gospel should be both preached and combated by the same agencies than that it should not be preached at all. At any rate, the true missionaries of the Cross, even though the mission boards which support them should turn out to be very bad, must not be allowed to be in want. But the situation, from the point of view of the evangelical Christian, is unsatisfactory in the extreme. Many Christians seek to relieve the situation by "designating" their gifts, instead of allowing them to be distributed by the mission agencies. But at this point one encounters the centralization of power which is going on in the modern Church. On account of that centralization the designation of gifts is often found to be illusory. If gifts are devoted by the donors to one mission known to be evangelical, that does not always really increase the resources of that mission; for the mission boards can simply cut down the proportion assigned to that mission from the undesignated funds, and the final result is exactly the same as if there had been no designation of the gift at all.

The existence and the necessity of mission boards and the like prevents, in general, one obvious solution of the present difficulty in the Church—the solution offered by local autonomy of the congregation. It might be suggested that each congregation should determine its own confession of faith or its own program of work. Then each congregation might seem to be responsible only for itself, and might seem to be relieved from the odious task of judging others. But the suggestion is impracticable. Aside from the question whether a purely congregational system of church government is desirable in itself, it is impossible where mission agencies are concerned. In the support of such agencies, many congregations obviously must unite; and the question arises whether evangelical congregations can honestly support agencies which are opposed to the evangelical faith.

At any rate, the situation cannot be helped by ignoring facts. The plain fact is that liberalism, whether it be true or false, is no mere "heresy"—no mere divergence at isolated points from Christian teaching. On the contrary it proceeds from a totally different root, and it constitutes, in essentials, a unitary system of its own. That does not mean that all liberals hold all parts of the system, or that Christians who have been affected by liberal teaching at one point have been affected at all points. There is sometimes a salutary lack of logic which prevents the whole of a man's faith being destroyed when he has given up a part. But the true way in which to examine a spiritual movement is in its logical relations; logic is the great dynamic, and the logical implications of any way of thinking are sooner or later certain to be worked out. And taken as a whole, even as it actually exists to-day, naturalistic liberalism is a fairly unitary phenomenon; it is tending more and more to eliminate from itself illogical remnants of Christian belief. It differs from Christianity in its view of God, of man, of the seat of authority and of the way of salvation. And it differs from Christianity not only in theology but in the whole of life. It is indeed sometimes said that there can be communion in feeling where communion in thinking is gone, a communion of the heart as distinguished from a communion of the head. But with respect to the present controversy, such a distinction certainly does not apply. On the contrary, in reading the books and listening to the sermons of recent liberal teachers—so untroubled by the problem of sin, so devoid of all sympathy for guilty humanity, so prone to abuse and ridicule the things dearest to the heart of every Christian man—one can only confess that if liberalism is to return into the Christian communion there must be a change of heart fully as much as a change of mind. God grant that such a change of heart may come! But meanwhile the present situation must not be ignored but faced. Christianity is being attacked from within by a movement which is anti-Christian to the core.

What is the duty of Christian men at such at time? What is the duty, in particular, of Christian officers in the Church?

In the first place, they should encourage those who are engaging in the intellectual and spiritual struggle. They should not say, in the sense in which some laymen say it, that more time should be devoted to the propagation of Christianity, and less to the defence of Christianity. Certainly there should be propagation of Christianity. Believers should certainly not content themselves with warding off attacks, but should also unfold in an orderly and positive way the full riches of the gospel. But far more is usually meant by those who call for less defence and more propagation. What they really intend is the discouragement of the whole intellectual defence of the faith. And their words come as a blow in the face of those who are fighting the great battle. As a matter of fact, not less time, but more time, should be devoted to the defence of the gospel. Indeed, truth cannot be stated clearly at all without being set over against error. Thus a large part of the New Testament is polemic; the enunciation of evangelical truth was occasioned by the errors which had arisen in the churches. So it will always be, on account of the fundamental laws of the human mind. Moreover, the present crisis must be taken into account. There may have been a day when there could be propagation of Christianity without defence. But such a day at any rate is past. At the present time, when the opponents of the gospel are almost in control of our churches, the slightest avoidance of the defence of the gospel is just sheer unfaithfulness to the Lord. There have been previous great crises in the history of the Church, crises almost comparable to this. One appeared in the second century, when the very life of Christendom was threatened by the Gnostics. Another came in the Middle Ages when the gospel of God's grace seemed forgotten. In such times of crisis, God has always saved the Church. But He has always saved it not by theological pacifists, but by sturdy contenders for the truth.

In the second place, Christian officers in the Church should perform their duty in deciding upon the qualifications of candidates for the ministry. The question "For Christ or against Him?" constantly arises in the examination of candidates for ordination. Attempts are often made to obscure the issue. It is often said: "The candidate will no doubt move in the direction of the truth; let him now be sent out to learn as well as to preach." And so another opponent of the gospel enters the councils of the Church, and another false prophet goes forth to encourage sinners to come before the judgment seat of God clad in the miserable rags of their own righteousness. Such action is not really "kind" to the candidate himself. It is never kind to encourage a man to enter into a life of dishonesty. The fact often seems to be forgotten that the evangelical Churches are purely voluntary organizations; no one is required to enter into their service. If a man cannot accept the belief of such churches, there are other ecclesiastical bodies in which he can find a place. The belief of the Presbyterian Church, for example, is plainly set forth in the Confession of Faith, and the Church will never afford any warmth of communion or engage with any real vigor in her work until her ministers are in whole-hearted agreement with that belief. It is strange how in the interests of an utterly false kindness to men, Christians are sometimes willing to relinquish their loyalty to the crucified Lord.

In the third place, Christian officers in the Church should show their loyalty to Christ in their capacity as members of the individual congregations. The issue often arises in connection with the choice of a pastor. Such and such a man, it is said, is a brilliant preacher. But what is the content of his preaching? Is his preaching full of the gospel of Christ? The answer is often evasive. The preacher in question, it is said, is of good standing in the Church, and he has never denied the doctrines or grace. Therefore, it is urged, he should be called to the pastorate. But shall we be satisfied with such negative assurances? Shall we be satisfied with preachers who merely "do not deny" the Cross of Christ? God grant that such satisfaction may be broken down! The people are perishing under the ministrations of those who "do not deny" the Cross of Christ. Surely something more than that is needed. God send us ministers who, instead of merely avoiding denial of the Cross shall be on fire with the Cross, whose whole life shall be one burning sacrifice of gratitude to the blessed Saviour who loved them and gave Himself for them!

In the fourth place—the most important thing of all—there must be a renewal of Christian education. The rejection of Christianity is due to various causes. But a very potent cause is simple ignorance. In countless cases, Christianity is rejected simply because men have not the slightest notion of what Christianity is. An outstanding fact of recent Church history is the appalling growth of ignorance in the Church. Various causes, no doubt, can be assigned for this lamentable development. The development is due partly to the general decline of education—at least so far as literature and history are concerned. The schools of the present day are being ruined by the absurd notion that education should follow the line of least resistance, and that something can be "drawn out" of the mind before anything is put in. They are also being ruined by an exaggerated emphasis on methodology at the expense of content and on what is materially useful at the expense of the high spiritual heritage of mankind. These lamentable tendencies, moreover, are in danger of being made permanent through the sinister extension of state control. But something more than the general decline in education is needed to account for the special growth of ignorance in the Church. The growth of ignorance in the Church is the logical and inevitable result of the false notion that Christianity is a life and not also a doctrine; if Christianity is not a doctrine then of course teaching is not necessary to Christianity. But whatever be the causes for the growth of ignorance in the Church, the evil must be remedied. It must be remedied primarily by the renewal of Christian education in the family, but also by the use of whatever other educational agencies the Church can find. Christian education is the chief business of the hour for every earnest Christian man. Christianity cannot subsist unless men know what Christianity is; and the fair and logical thing is to learn what Christianity is, not from its opponents, but from those who themselves are Christians. That method of procedure would be the only fair method in the case of any movement. But it is still more in place in the case of a movement such as Christianity which has laid the foundation of all that we hold most dear. Men have abundant opportunity to-day to learn what can be said against Christianity, and it is only fair that they should also learn something about the thing that is being attacked.

Such measures are needed to-day. The present is a time not for ease or pleasure, but for earnest and prayerful work. A terrible crisis unquestionably has arisen in the Church. In the ministry of evangelical churches are to be found hosts of those who reject the gospel of Christ. By the equivocal use of traditional phrases, by the representation of differences of opinion as though they were only differences about the interpretation of the Bible, entrance into the Church was secured for those who are hostile to the very foundations of the faith. And now there are some indications that the fiction of conformity to the past is to be thrown off, and the real meaning of what has been taking place is to be allowed to appear. The Church, it is now apparently supposed, has almost been educated up to the point where the shackles of the Bible can openly be cast away and the doctrine of the Cross of Christ can be relegated to the limbo of discarded subtleties.

Yet there is in the Christian life no room for despair. Only, our hopefulness should not be founded on the sand. It should be founded, not upon a blind ignorance of the danger, but solely upon the precious promises of God. Laymen, as well as ministers, should return, in these trying days, with new earnestness, to the study of the Word of God.

If the Word of God be heeded, the Christian battle will be fought both with love and with faithfulness. Party passions and personal animosities will be put away, but on the other hand, even angels from heaven will be rejected if they preach a gospel different from the blessed gospel of the Cross. Every man must decide upon which side he will stand. God grant that we may decide aright!

What the immediate future may bring we cannot presume to say. The final result indeed is clear. God has not deserted His Church; He has brought her through even darker hours than those which try our courage now, yet the darkest hour has always come before the dawn. We have to-day the entrance of paganism into the Church in the name of Christianity. But in the second century a similar battle was fought and won. From another point of view, modern liberalism is like the legalism of the middle ages, with its dependence upon the merit of man. And another Reformation in God's good time will come.

But meanwhile our souls are tried. We can only try to do our duty in humility and in sole reliance upon the Saviour who bought us with His blood. The future is in God's hand, and we do not know the means that He will use in the accomplishment of His will. It may be that the present evangelical churches will face the facts, and regain their integrity while yet there is time. If that solution is to be adopted there is no time to lose, since the forces opposed to the gospel are now almost in control. It is possible that the existing churches may be given over altogether to naturalism, that men may then see that the fundamental needs of the soul are to be satisfied not inside but outside of the existing churches, and that thus new Christian groups may be formed.

But whatever solution there may be, one thing is clear. There must be somewhere groups of redeemed men and women who can gather together humbly in the name of Christ, to give thanks to Him for His unspeakable gift and to worship the Father through Him. Such groups alone can satisfy the needs of the soul. At the present time, there is one longing of the human heart which is often forgotten—it is the deep, pathetic longing of the Christian for fellowship with his brethren. One hears much, it is true, about Christian union and harmony and co-operation. But the union that is meant is often a union with the world against the Lord, or at best a forced union of machinery and tyrannical committees. How different is the true unity of the Spirit in the bond of peace! Sometimes, it is true, the longing for Christian fellowship is satisfied. There are congregations, even in the present age of conflict, that are really gathered around the table of the crucified Lord; there are pastors that are pastors indeed. But such congregations, in many cities, are difficult to find. Weary with the conflicts of the world, one goes into the Church to seek refreshment for the soul. And what does one find? Alas, too often, one finds only the turmoil of the world. The preacher comes forward, not out of a secret place of meditation and power, not with the authority of God's Word permeating his message, not with human wisdom pushed far into the background by the glory of the Cross, but with human opinions about the social problems of the hour or easy solutions of the vast problem of sin. Such is the sermon. And then perhaps the service is closed by one of those hymns breathing out the angry passions of 1861, which are to be found in the back part of the hymnals. Thus the warfare of the world has entered even into the house of God. And sad indeed is the heart of the man who has come seeking peace.

Is there no refuge from strife? Is there no place of refreshing where a man can prepare for the battle of life? Is there no place where two or three can gather in Jesus' name, to forget for the moment all those things that divide nation from nation and race from race, to forget human pride, to forget the passions of war, to forget the puzzling problems of industrial strife, and to unite in overflowing gratitude at the foot of the Cross? If there be such a place, then that is the house of God and that the gate of heaven. And from under the threshold of that house will go forth a river that will revive the weary world.

The Legacy of
Christianity and Liberalism:
Essays by the Faculty of
Westminster Theological Seminary

Machen and History
Chad Van Dixhoorn

Machen's most famous book ought to have experienced the usual expiration date of best-sellers tethered to recent events. *Christianity and Liberalism* was a response to recent history—in particular, a response to a historical record created by New York City editor and stenographer Margaret Renton. It was she who provided the manuscript of Harry Emerson Fosdick's inflammatory sermon, "Shall the Fundamentalists Win?," to which Machen responded with these pages.

That *Christianity and Liberalism* did emerge as a kind of Christian classic, and that it continues to impact the thinking of Christian people after a century of turbulent change, is often attributed to the author's prescience. He saw the road that liberalism was taking and was able to describe the movement so incisively that his book is still relevant almost a century later. That is why evangelistically minded people choose this slim volume when preparing to meet their liberal counterparts at cocktail parties on the mainline or attend a wedding reception populated with parishioners from one of America's grand old Protestant denominations. Despite social conventions dictating that religion should not be discussed, it often is—and Machen's *Christianity and Liberalism* offers many insightful responses to the comments and assumptions typical of our day as well as his. So many insights, in fact, that if Presbyterians were permitted prophets, Machen would be among them.

As much as I'd like to maximize Machen's clear-sightedness,

he was hardly clairvoyant. The real reason why *Christianity and Liberalism* still speaks to us is this: liberalism is fundamentally uncreative. More than two centuries later, its advocates still reduce the Christian religion to morals (courtesy of Kant), human experience (credit Schleiermacher), philosophical abstractions, or false eschatologies (with a nod to Hegel). Proponents have changed; presuppositions and propositions have stayed the same. This can be seen through a comparison of Christian and pseudo-Christian conceptions of history.

Machen's main point about Christianity and history informs some of the major categories that I apply as a believer when reading the Bible. "Salvation . . . according to the Bible, is not something that was discovered, but something that happened."[1] Again, "without that event, the world, in the Christian view, is altogether dark" for "there can be no salvation by the discovery of eternal truth."[2] Salvation is something accomplished by Christ as an event in history.

In Machen's day, New Testament scholarship isolated, and then emphasized, ideas that Christianity enjoyed in common with other religions. This project continues today but is mainstreamed outside the academy with the hope that reducing religion to the lowest common denominator will lead the enlightened world to find religious grounds for peace. The problem with this project, as Machen pointed out, is that "Christianity depends, not upon a complex of ideas, but upon the narration of an event."[3] The very concept of a "gospel" or "good news" assumes there is a significant occurrence that calls for an an-

---

1. Page 72 of this present volume.
2. Ibid.
3. Ibid.

nouncement. Much of the Bible does address the interpretation and meaning of facts—but there must be facts to interpret.

If some reduce Christianity to clusters of generically religious ideas, others reduce Christianity to experience. They do not want to be held to the historicity of biblical accounts; they wish to be free to follow their hearts, or their feelings, wherever they might lead. Here, too, *Christianity and Liberalism* is helpful. Experience is important for Christians—it even carries importance as a Christian evidence of sorts. The experience of the disciples following the resurrection of Christ offers one example of this kind of evidence. The experiences of transformed Christians in our own day, who have encountered the ascended Christ and his gospel, offers another example of the importance of experience. But religious experience in the abstract is not to be confused with Christian experience, and even Christian experience cannot stand alone. As Machen explains, "Christian experience . . . is useful as confirming the gospel message. But because it is necessary, many men have jumped to the conclusion that it is all that is necessary."[4]

The truth is that Christian experience is only Christian if it participates in historic events. Indeed, however we are to understand that participation, we must insist upon the historical nature of those events—events of long ago, such as the virgin birth, death, resurrection, and ascension of our Savior and, we might add, a future historical event: the return of Christ. If our experience is based on something other than real events, our experience is vain and, indeed, the whole Christian faith is in vain (1 Cor. 15).

---

4. Page 73 of this present volume.

Machen's insistence that Christianity is both a set of facts and a set of interpretations of facts has profoundly shaped my task as someone who teaches church history. Martin Luther once declared that every Christian must be a theologian. In effect, Machen insists that every Christian must also be a historian.

The task of the church history department at Westminster Theological Seminary is to make every student a better historian. We have many reasons for this emphasis in our curriculum. Surely a knowledge of our family's history will help us better understand our Father and one another. Surely we have wisdom to glean from Christian history's worst and best moments, and the church's responses to those moments. But arguably, a key reason for honing the tools of a historian may actually be for the student's betterment in other departments, such as biblical studies or homiletics. For, at the end of the day, an abler historian ought to be an abler interpreter of the Bible, that heavenly and historical book that every Christian loves to read.

REV. DR. CHAD VAN DIXHOORN (PhD, University of Cambridge) is professor of church history and the director of the Craig Center for the Study of the Westminster Standards at Westminster Theological Seminary. He also serves as an honorary research fellow at the University of East Anglia, Norwich, UK. An ordained minister in the OPC, he is the editor of the *Minutes and Papers of the Westminster Assembly, 1643-1653* and the author of *Confessing the Faith: A Reader's Guide to the Westminster Confession of Faith.*

J. Gresham Machen, Fundamentalism, and Westminster Seminary

PETER A. LILLBACK

J. Gresham Machen and Westminster Theological Seminary, which he founded in 1929, are connected with what has come to be known as the Fundamentalist Movement in America. However, the exact nature of this connection is not very well understood.

To clarify Machen's theological perspective and that of his seminary regarding Fundamentalism, let me first introduce three sets of popular principles that have broadly shaped conservative Presbyterian churches in America:

1. The Principles of Protestantism: Sola Scriptura, Solus Christus, Sola Fide, Sola Gratia, Soli Deo Gloria, and the Priesthood of the Believer

2. TULIP, or the so-called five points of Calvinism:1 Total Depravity, Unconditional Election, Limited Atonement, Irresistible Grace, and the Perseverance of the Saints

3. The Five Fundamentals of the Faith:2 the Inspiration of the Bible, the Virgin Birth of Christ, the Substitutionary (or Vicarious) Atonement of Christ, the Bodily Resurrection, and the Reality of Miracles Inclusive of the Visible Second Advent of Christ

---

1. The acronym TULIP is derived from the primary theological emphases that emerged at the Synod of Dort, convened in 1618-19 in the Netherlands to critique Arminian theology.

2. These Five Fundamentals of the Faith emerged from the debates between conservative and liberal theologians that raged in the late nineteenth and early twentieth centuries.

As significant as these popular principles were to Machen and the seminary, they are not the theological concerns that primarily shape their legacy. The essential emphases of Machen and Westminster have been the Bible and the documents referenced in Westminster's very name, the Westminster Standards. We find the essence of Westminster's theology as envisioned by Machen in the seminary's motto, taken from Acts 20:27b: "the whole counsel of God." This motto points us to the Bible and the confessional statements that summarize the system of doctrine contained in it. Thus, the essential theology of Westminster is defined first by the Primary Standard (the authority of the Bible), then the Secondary Standards (the Westminster Standards, the Westminster Confession of Faith, and the Larger and Shorter Catechisms). These standards include the Protestant Principles. They express the Five Points of Calvinism, and the theological concerns identified by the Fundamentalist Movement are addressed by them. But neither Machen's nor Westminster's theology can be fully encapsulated by the three general summaries of doctrinal commitments listed above.

The rise of Fundamentalism was precipitated, while Machen was still a young man, with the free, international distribution of *The Fundamentals of the Faith,* published between 1910-15. This collection of articles directly addressed theological issues that were causing debate and deep concern in the church, such as higher criticism of the Scriptures and its impact on the doctrine of inspiration, the deity of Christ, sin and salvation, creation and evolution, the biblical nature of evangelism and missions, the rising cults, and the Roman Catholic impact on American Christianity.

Presbyterians were tied to the *Fundamentals* in that as many as a third of the 64 authors identified themselves as Presbyterian. Professors Charles R. Erdman and B. B. Warfield of Princeton Theological Seminary both contributed articles. In fact, the famous five fundamentals summarized above originated at the Presbyterian General Assembly held in 1910.[3]

The origin of the fundamentalist controversy stemmed from the trend in the Western Protestant church away from Reformed tenets. Novel theological perspectives exchanged a biblical approach to doctrinal and confessional issues for an Enlightenment-based interpretation. This manifested itself in the higher criticism of the Bible, a rejection of Creationism for Darwinian Evolution, and denial of the supernatural elements of Christianity. Key leaders in this liberal side of the theological controversy included Charles A. Briggs, Henry Preserved Smith, Henry Sloan Coffin, and Harry Emerson Fosdick. Leading voices among conservatives from the old Princeton tradition were B. B. Warfield, Robert Dick Wilson, J. Gresham Machen, Clarence Macartney, and Oswald T. Allis.

Machen, for his part, was a dynamic scholar who had studied at Johns Hopkins, Princeton, and Marburg, Germany. He served with YMCA relief efforts as a non-combatant in WWI. He taught Greek and New Testament at Princeton, and in 1923 he completed *Christianity and Liberalism*, a work that, along with the Auburn Affirmation of 1924, would fan the flames of the theological debate between liberals and conservatives. In his

---

3. The 1910 General Assembly responded to the Presbytery of New York's licensing three candidates who had denied the Virgin Birth of Christ. The specific issues affirmed by the General Assembly resolutions were: (1) the inspiration and inerrancy of Scripture in the original languages; (2) Christ's virgin birth; (3) the vicarious atonement; (4) Christ's bodily resurrection; and (5) the reality of miracles as recorded in the Bible.

work, Machen famously declared that Christianity and Liberalism were essentially two different religions; they used the same terminology, but with contradictory meanings. Rejecting liberal Christianity, Machen declared that authentic Christianity held the Gospel to be historical spiritual truth over against the liberal perspective that reduced it to mere myth. By contrast, the Auburn Affirmation defended the acceptance of liberal theology within the Presbyterian Church, deeming it to be a legitimate expression of Christianity.

Machen's book became the leading expression of the concerns of historic Christianity in response to the ascendancy of liberal theology. The opening words of *Christianity and Liberalism* made it clear that that there were fundamental doctrines in the Christian faith that had to be defended:

> Modern liberalism in the Church, whatever judgment may be passed upon it, is at any rate no longer merely an academic matter. It is no longer a matter merely of theological seminaries or universities. On the contrary its attack upon the fundamentals of the Christian faith is being carried on vigorously by Sunday-School "lesson-helps," by the pulpit, and by the religious press.[4]

Yet even in Machen's defense of "the fundamentals of the Christian faith," he did not identify himself as a Fundamentalist or embrace *The Fundamentals of the Faith* as his creed. Rather, holding to the historic Westminster Standards, he saw himself as a Reformed and Presbyterian Christian:

---

4. Page 17 of this present volume.

At any rate, an attack upon Calvin or Turretin or the Westminster divines does not seem to the modern churchgoer to be a dangerous thing. In point of fact, however, the attack upon doctrine is not nearly so innocent a matter as our simple churchgoer supposes; for the things objected to in the theology of the Church are also at the very heart of the New Testament. Ultimately that attack is not against the seventeenth century, but against the Bible and against Jesus Himself.[5]

Machen recognized the inherent rejection of biblical truth by the Auburn Affirmation compelling him to oppose it, not as a Fundamentalist but as a Calvinist, a Reformed theologian who held to the Westminster Standards that upheld the very teachings of Jesus and the Scriptures.

Ultimately, Machen's attempts to redress theological liberalism came to a head when the Presbyterian Church's General Assembly determined to reorganize the Board of Princeton Seminary. The Assembly required that the diverse theological views extant in the denomination be represented on the Board. Recognizing that Princeton's historic defense of classic Reformed orthodoxy was no longer sustainable, Machen led the founding of Westminster Seminary in 1929, to preserve the theology of what became to be known as "the Old Princeton."

Further, to address a concern for biblical and gospel integrity in the Presbyterian denominational mission board, Machen established an Independent Board of Foreign Missions. Machen was concerned for the missionaries' commitment to biblical

---

5. Pages 45-46 of this present volume.

Christianity and the confessional standards of the Presbyterian Church, not merely to an abbreviated list of controverted fundamental doctrines. For his creation of the Independent Board of Foreign Missions, and thus directly competing with the denominational mission program, the General Assembly defrocked Machen. With no other choice, Machen founded the Presbyterian Church of America in 1936.[6] Months later, on January 1, 1937, he died of pneumonia, at the age of 56.

The early faculty at Westminster Theological Seminary were scholarly, conservative, biblical, and confessional, in the tradition of Old Princeton. The new seminary launched the careers of such luminaries as Cornelius Van Til, R. B. Kuiper, Ned Stonehouse, and John Murray. Each identified with the Presbyterian, biblical system of theology in the Westminster Standards, and did not seek to be defined by the Fundamentalist label.

To identify Machen or his Westminster faculty as Fundamentalists is to misrepresent them, and it unjustly truncates their theology, diminishing the theological authority of Scripture that they defended. Westminster's founders held to the *Fundamentals of the Faith* only to the extent that those essays conformed to their belief in the Bible and to their commitment to the confessional theology of the Presbyterian tradition.

Seeking to fulfill Machen's vision for Westminster, the seminary has trained thousands of ministers and missionaries to be specialists in the Bible who proclaim the whole counsel of God for Christ and His global church. Westminster's alumni have served in numerous ecclesiastical settings, including the OPC,

---

6. Later, following a legal challenge to the title of the new denomination, the name was changed to the Orthodox Presbyterian Church.

RPCES, PCA, KAPC, URC, and many other independent and mainline denominations. In fact, the late R.C. Sproul on various occasions observed that nearly every key Reformed thinker that had impacted America in his lifetime had a direct connection with Westminster.

Machen's critique of unbiblical thinking in the church and in culture has remained a hallmark of Westminster's theology, and has developed well beyond Machen's nemesis of liberalism, addressing such varied worldview concerns as secularism, post-modernism, the sexual revolutions, and cultural Marxism. Additionally, Westminster's ethic has supplied biblical content to contemporary debates on cultural issues such as marriage, the sanctity of life, sexuality, faith in the public square, and religious liberty. Such issues continue to be addressed from the vantage point of biblical authority and the Westminster Confession. These substantive positions are developed by biblical exegesis and theological reflection, not merely by a facile appeal to a reduced summary of theological tenets, whether Protestant, Reformed, or Fundamentalist.

Indeed, when one hears the common description of a church or theologian as either conservative or liberal, one hears an echo of Machen's *Christianity and Liberalism* and the abiding significance it retains a century after it was first written. And in so hearing, one is not encountering the bare articulation of the *Fundamentals of the Faith* but rather a deep engagement with biblical revelation. Machen's abiding legacy through Westminster is the proclamation of the whole counsel of God which will preserve biblical Christianity, and thus far more than churches that simply cherish the Protestant Principles, the Reformed distinctives, or the fundamental truths of the Christian faith.

Rev. Dr. Peter A. Lillback (PhD, Westminster Theological Seminary) is president and professor of historical theology and church history at Westminster Theological Seminary. He also serves as the president of The Providence Forum and senior editor of *Unio cum Christo: An International Journal of Reformed Theology and Life.* An ordained teaching elder in the PCA, he is the author of *George Washington's Sacred Fire* and *Saint Peter's Principles: Leadership for Those Who Already Know Their Incompetence.*

Machen and Apologetics

William Edgar

I cannot count the number of times I have read J. G. Machen's *Christianity and Liberalism*. Each time something fresh jumps off the page. In its profound simplicity, it is timeless.

Toward the beginning of his book, Machen asks, "What is the relation between Christianity and modern culture; may Christianity be maintained in a scientific age?"[1] He proceeds to give learned and persuasive answers to the question. Throughout the volume, and in many of his other writings, he asserts that true Christianity is neither against culture nor are its tenets incompatible with true science.

Liberalism, the kind that asserts the Christian faith is incompatible with culture and science, is not the Christian religion. Liberalism attempts to "rescue" the Christian faith by removing from its doctrines anything that would qualify as measurable by scientific means or be otherwise offensive. Worse, it caricatures traditional Christians as believing in a flat earth and other pre-modern ideas. It then affirms a more acceptable kind of Christianity, including a moralistic Bible, a redemption outside of history, a Christ who is not God (though in whom God may be especially present), and a faith without the need for intellectual investigation.

Machen's task was to address the increasingly liberal Christianity of the early twentieth century. Though no doubt chastened, this form of Christianity is still with us today. Liberalism

---

1. Page 5 of this present volume.

redefines all the distinctive elements of the Christian faith to make them palatable to people who do not want to be challenged to repentance by confronting a God who is angry against their sin, or take refuge in a bloody sacrifice. Machen's answers to the way liberalism redefines doctrine, God, the Bible, Christ, etc., I believe, are still convincing. But what is of abiding importance is the recognition that, at the root, we are dealing with two different religions, hence the title of the book. Unbelief is a religious commitment, albeit to a pagan view. The true Christian faith is a religion based upon the reality of a God who is the Creator of the world and who is busy redeeming his people through the atoning work of his Son.

One takeaway for me is that people are never neutral; they are guided by what they love, as Augustine suggested. When the notorious British atheist author Kingsley Amis died, Amis told Yevgeni Yevtushenko that it wasn't simply that he did not believe in God but that he actually hated him.[2] This may be emotional, but it has to qualify as a religious statement. Augustine tells us we are what we love, but he could have said we are what we hate.

Machen's genius was not to contrast fact with fact, though he does that very well—it was to see facts cohering within an entire system. In my own work, I have often found myself referring to the insights in this book when responding to people who have a certain idea of what the Christian faith may be. They might claim that they are not religious. I must gently show them that they are, by virtue of their loves and hates. Or, they might claim a great respect for Jesus but reject his divinity. I presume many

---

2. See Andrew Brown, "God Meets the Old Devil," *Independent*, October 22, 1996, https://www.independent.co.uk/voices/god-meets-the-old-devil-1359631.html.

of us have met the argument that Christ was a great moralist or a first-rate ethical teacher. But, as C. S. Lewis says it so well in a famous paragraph from his radio talks,

> "I am trying here to prevent anyone saying the really foolish thing that people often say about Him: 'I'm ready to accept Jesus as a great moral teacher, but I don't accept his claim to be God.' That is the one thing we must not say. A man who was merely a man and said the sort of things Jesus said would not be a great moral teacher. He would either be a lunatic—on the level with the man who says he is a poached egg—or else he would be the Devil of Hell. You must make your choice. Either this man was, and is, the Son of God, or else a madman or something worse."[3]

Machen would have agreed one hundred percent.

The other takeaway for me is Machen's tone—always gracious, never bitter. While there is plenty of polemic, he never seems to belittle his opponents. This may be one of the reasons why one of the twentieth century's most notorious skeptics, H. L. Mencken, remained an admirer and friend of Machen. Machen says it this way in the volume under consideration: "Many ties—ties of blood, of citizenship, of ethical aims, or humanitarian endeavor—unite us to those who have abandoned the gospel. We trust that those ties may never be weakened, and that ultimately they may serve some purpose in the propagation of the Christian faith."[4] Yet that should not prevent us from proclaiming the Christian faith. We could use this attitude in North

---

3. C. S. Lewis, *Mere Christianity* (San Francisco: HarperOne, 2015), 55–56.
4. Page 52 of this present volume.

America these days! Disagreement is not dislike. We can learn that, and so much else, from J. Gresham Machen.

Rev. Dr. William Edgar (DThéol, Université de Genève) is professor of apologetics at Westminster Theological Seminary, and associate professor at the Faculté Jean Calvin. He is an ordained teaching elder in the PCA, and the author of *Created & Creating: A Biblical Theology of Culture*, and *Francis Schaeffer on the Christian Life: Countercultural Spirituality*.

Machen and Philosophy

K. Scott Oliphint

Jesus was a theist, and rational theism is at the basis of Christianity. Jesus did not, indeed, support His theism by argument; He did not provide in advance answers to the Kantian attack upon the theistic proofs. But that means not that He was indifferent to the belief which is the logical result of those proofs, but that the belief stood so firm, both to Him and to His hearers, that in His teaching it is always presupposed. So to-day it is not necessary for all Christians to analyze the logical basis of their belief in God; the human mind has a wonderful faculty for the condensation of perfectly valid arguments, and what seems like an instinctive belief may turn out to be the result of many logical steps. Or, rather, it may be that the belief in a personal God is the result of a primitive revelation, and that the theistic proofs are only the logical confirmation of what was originally arrived at by a different means. At any rate, the logical confirmation of the belief in God is a vital concern to the Christian; at this point as at many others religion and philosophy are connected in the most intimate possible way. True religion can make no peace with a false philosophy, any more than with a science that is falsely so-called; a thing cannot possibly be true in religion and false in philosophy or in science. All methods of arriving at truth, if they be valid methods, will arrive at a harmonious result.[1]

---

1. Pages 58–59 in this present volume.

For Machen, "religion and philosophy are connected in the most intimate possible way." And because "religion can make no peace with a false philosophy," any philosophy that is a true philosophy will necessarily cohere with Christianity. What this means for philosophy is that, like Christianity, it will presuppose the existence of God and the truth of God in his Word.

For example, one of the typical philosophical proofs for the existence of God is something like the following:

> Everything that comes to be has a cause.
> There cannot be an infinite regress of causes.
> Therefore, there must be something that is uncaused.
> The word "God" refers to an uncaused cause.
> Therefore, God exists.

Most Christians reading this kind of argument would be in hearty agreement with its basic conclusion. Certainly, God is not caused, and he caused everything else to exist that does exist. It must be understood, however, that such agreement flows *from* Christian commitments and truth, and does not automatically move *toward* such commitments.

We could ask, for example, how we could know that there cannot be an infinite regress of causes? For a Christian, we know because we know who God is and that he is altogether uncaused and solely of himself. But what about a non-Christian? What would require a non-Christian to affirm such a thing? The only options he would have to deny an infinite regress of causes would be to appeal to a rational law or an empirical principle. But what rational law available to the non-Christian would serve to explain or otherwise delimit the infinite? What does rationality, on a non-Christian basis, tell us about what infinity is and how it functions? Or how, on an empirical basis alone, can one understand the notion of infinite regress? Certainly, such a thing cannot be experienced or sensed in any way. Our experience tells us nothing about what can and cannot be with regard to infinity.

The natural consequence of the presupposition of Christianity is, as Machen phrased it, "rational theism." Rational theism is theism that, by virtue of its Christian presuppositions, can provide arguments both for God's existence and for the truth of his Word. Without those presuppositions, there can be no such arguments, nor can there be anything that is truly rational. Since God alone is absolute rationality, any rationality deserving of the name must be one that thinks God's thoughts after him.

This radical truth, which acknowledges Christianity as the only basis for rationality, is one reason why Christianity was abandoned for liberalism's religion of feeling. "It is unnecessary, we are told, to have a 'conception' of God; theology, or the knowledge of God, it is said, is the death of religion; we should not seek to know God, but should merely feel His presence."[2] When that which alone can provide the basis of rationality is given up, a religion of feeling becomes the natural option. When the intellect is denied, the emotions will take precedence.

Machen argued that Christianity is a rational religion and thus, by definition, not a religion based on feeling. Not only so, but he argued that Christianity was the only truly rational religion. Because truth has its home in what God has said (both

---

2. Page 55 of this present volume.

in general and special revelation), only a religion—and a philosophy—that finds its source and foundation in God and his Word can be true.

Liberalism's rejection of God's Word, and thus of the God who spoke that Word, locates it squarely within the arena of a false religion. Any philosophy that follows or coheres with such a false religion is itself false. True philosophy can only be set forth when the truth of Christianity grounds, informs, and infuses it.

Rev. Dr. K. Scott Oliphint (PhD, Westminster Theological Seminary) is dean of faculty and professor of apologetics and systematic theology at Westminster Theological Seminary. An ordained minister in the OPC, he is the author of *Know Why You Believe* and *Covenantal Apologetics*.

Christianity and Liberalism
and Preaching

JOHN CURRIE

My first pastoral call was as an associate pastor, to a congregation where the guiding aspiration was to build the biggest following in town by being the most happening church in town. Although I had no idea what Reformed theology was, and even less an idea who J. Gresham Machen was, I had been assigned to read *Christianity and Liberalism* in an undergraduate theology course by a thoughtful professor. Within just a few years, Machen's book would save my fledgling pastoral ministry from being derailed by mystical, quasi-therapeutic pragmatism. In a situation where clarity and conviction about doctrine was considered inconvenient and irritating, I was reading Machen assert just the opposite, with statements like "Nothing in the world can take the place of truth."[1] Needless to say, Machen's convictions won the day.

Christianity and Liberalism repeatedly makes the point that Christianity, unlike liberalism, is founded upon doctrine clearly revealed in Scripture and therefore held and proclaimed by Christian ministers with conviction. Christianity is not a "brotherhood of beneficent vagueness."[2] The Christian faith, and the life that accompanies it, is grounded upon a message: "It was based, not upon mere feeling, not upon a mere program of work,

---

1. Page 48 of this present volume.
2. Page 34 of this present volume.

but upon an account of facts. In other words it was based upon doctrine."[3] Therefore, clarity and conviction about the doctrine revealed in the Word of God is essential not only to Christianity but to the ministry that propagates the Christian faith.

There is no aspect of the ministry in which this clarity of conviction is more necessary than in preaching. As Machen put it, "Vastly more important than all questions with regard to methods of preaching is the root question as to what it is that shall be preached."[4] This foundational conviction about the factual nature of Christianity has formative implications for preaching. In the space available here, I'll mention just four: That Christianity is doctrinally grounded means our preaching should be *expository, Christ-centered, clear,* and *courageous.*

Machen believed that the preacher's job is to "tell the truth, the whole truth and nothing but the truth."[5] Expository preaching is the homiletical discipline that is best suited to keep preaching, and the preacher, within the facts God has sovereignly deposited in the text of Scripture. The pattern of expository preaching is to explain the message of the text according to the words of the text and according to the Holy Spirit's arrangement of that text. The expository preacher sees his job as simply exposing or laying bare what God has already revealed, in the way that God revealed it. Biblical exposition is best suited for promoting and protecting the doctrines that define Christianity because the expository preacher disciplines himself to declare precisely what God has delivered.

The facts upon which Christianity is founded are the facts of

3. Page 21 of this present volume.
4. Page 8 of this present volume.
5. Page 53 of this present volume.

what God promised and accomplished in the person and work of Jesus Christ. Jesus taught his soon-to-be witnesses-to-the-world that the scope and substance of Scripture is the disclosure of who Christ is and what God accomplished for our salvation through him (Luke 24:25–27; 44–48). Paul summarized the apostolic gospel as the proclamation of Christ and his work from the Scriptures (Rom. 1:1–4; 1 Cor. 15:1–4). Machen emphasized the same as he distinguished Christianity from the moralism of liberalism by pointing to the Christ-centeredness of Jesus' own teaching: "A stupendous theology, with Jesus own Person at the center of it, is the presupposition of the whole teaching."[6] Christian preaching takes Christ as the presupposition and point of the doctrine delivered to us—who he is, what he's done, and how he and his work become ours. Therefore, Christian preaching proclaims Christ and his gospel from every text in every sermon. It is the proclamation of Christ from all of Scripture that accomplishes God's redemptive purpose to bring sinners to personally appropriate the objective realities of the Christian faith. "It is the message which makes him ours,"[7] wrote Machen. "It is not enough that [we know] He saved others; we need to know also that He has saved us. That knowledge is given in the story of the Cross."[8]

The liberalism Machen confronted contented itself with a spiritualized, sentimental Jesus and was resistant to the definition and distinction of Christ and his work. Machen styled liberals' objections this way, "May we not cease to ask *how* Jesus saves; may we not simply leave the way to Him? What need is

---

6. Page 37 of this present volume.

7. Page 42 of this present volume.

8. Page 43 of this present volume.

there, then, of defining 'effectual calling,' what need of enumerating 'justification, adoption and sanctification and the several benefits which in this life do either accompany or flow from them'?"[9] In contrast, preaching that truly holds out the Christ of Christianity, the Christ of the Scriptures, will make clear what the Scriptures do (and do not) say about God, his will, and how we are to relate and respond to him. For the glory of God, the Christian preacher is committed to displaying all the riches God has deposited in his revelation. For the eternal good of his hearers, the preacher will contrast the truth, beauty, and blessing of God's message with the distraction, dilution, disbelief, and death preached by the voices of the age.

Machen's cultural moment was not unique in the history of Christ's cause. The period in which the apostles delivered the faith was characterized by compromise and conflict (2 Tim. 4:2–4). But the charge remained to "preach the Word," and even to endure suffering "as a good soldier of Christ Jesus" (2 Tim. 2:3, 8–9). This call has been the lot of the church across nations for many years, and it is increasingly the call of the church in our own nation. In our cultural moment, any attempt at persuasion from an authoritative position is seen as oppression, and principled disagreement with the "orthodoxy" of the cultural narrative is judged as hateful. A faith founded in doctrine and, in truth, revealed by a supreme authority outside ourselves, can expect outraged opposition from those who seek a Jesus more palatable to the sentiments and convictions of their own community.

Like no time in recent memory, preaching driven by the convictions of Scripture will require a compassionate militancy

---

9. Page 39 of this present volume.

(2 Tim. 2:24–26). It will take Spirit-given courage to step into the pulpit week after week and announce all that God has said and *nothing but* what God has said. In the confusion and conflict that is sure to come, we will do well to remember another one of Machen's maxims: "the things that are sometimes thought to be hardest to defend are also the things that are most worth defending."[10]

Rev. Dr. John Currie (DMin, Westminster Theological Seminary) is professor of pastoral theology at Westminster Theological Seminary. He is an ordained minister in the OPC, and a contributor to *Resurrection and Eschatology: Essays in Honor of Richard B. Gaffin, Jr.*

---

10. Page 8 of this present volume.

Christianity and Liberalism
and the Church

ALFRED POIRIER

Christianity and Liberalism concludes with a chapter on the church—what the apostle Paul called "a pillar and buttress of the truth" (1 Tim. 3:15). Though many know J. Gresham Machen, founder of Westminster Theological Seminary, as a great New Testament scholar, defender of the faith, and preacher and teacher of the gospel, we must never forget that he was eminently a churchman.

What is a churchman? A churchman is simply a man or woman who esteems Christ's church and labors within it to preserve and see it mature to the fullness of Christ (Eph. 4:15–16). Yet, today, "churchman" is not a word of praise but one of blame or simple disregard. For if one is to change the culture for good, if we are to look for the institutions that are the true gamechangers of life, we are told to look to the titans of the tech world who reside at Apple, Google, Facebook, or Microsoft. We are not asked to look to the church, and surely not to a so-called churchman. Yet, Machen's voice needs once again to be raised above the fray and heard afresh: "The Church is the highest Christian answer to the social needs of man."[1]

Are you not as amazed as I at Machen's bold confidence in Christ's church? Yet, amazement gives way to reflection once we reexamine the great claims of Christ himself for his church. Was

---

1. Page 163 of this present volume.

it not Christ who, seeking to disciple every people, tribe, tongue, and nation to the end of the age, chose as the means of this endeavor to build only *one* thing—his church (Matt. 16:19)? And are you not amazed, as I am, that Christ, who is humble and gentle of heart, chooses such humble, frail, and sinful people like us believers, and gathers us by equally humble means for the building of his kingdom through his Word, sacrament, and discipline (Matt. 18:15–20; 28:18–20)? And think of the humble agents he chooses: men and women like you and me. He did not choose the mighty or wise or wealthy according to this world. No, whom did he call to himself to build his church? The weary and burdened! The weak and despised of this world (Matt. 11:28–30; 1 Cor. 1:25–31).

To the church alone did our Lord give the keys of the kingdom! To the church alone do those keys open heaven and hell. Heaven to all who believe and repent and turn to Christ as the sole Savior and Lord given among the nations; hell is the destiny for all who reject such a call. Many may agree on principle that these ultimate stakes are true of the invisible church—the company of true believers. But can we say the same for the local and visible church—the concrete expression of Christ's universal body? We can and we must, just as Machen did. This scholar studied the pages of the New Testament and read, with all the color of real people and real churches, the letters of Paul the apostle to local churches, such as Corinth, Rome, Philippi, Thessalonica, Ephesus, and Colossae. In the vast darkness with which sin covers this world, the Lord has appointed an archipelago of visible churches, islands of light, that hold out the hope of the everlasting gospel of God. Bearing this light openly, visibly, and faithfully is God's glorious plan.

Machen knew all of this—and for that reason, he was no idealist when it came to the local church. If Machen contended for the truth of the gospel, he contended for the truth of the gospel in Christ's visible church. Sadly, in his day, in his particular church—the Presbyterian Church of the United States of America (PCUSA)—he witnessed worrying signs of decline and, in some cases, outright denial of the gospel truths. What distressed Machen most, however, were not the church's members, but its ordained yet heterodox ministers. As Machen bemoaned:

> But what is the trouble with the visible Church? What is the reason for its obvious weakness? There are perhaps many causes of weakness. But one cause is perfectly plain—the Church of to-day has been unfaithful to her Lord by admitting great companies of non-Christian persons, not only into her membership, but into her teaching agencies.[2]

Machen anguished over presbyteries that admitted men to the gospel ministry "who have never made any really adequate confession of faith" and instead, whose attitude and practice was inimical to the gospel of Jesus Christ.[3] In biblical language, Machen grieved to see Christ's beloved church receive ministers who were but wolves in sheep's clothing (Acts 20:29–31). *Christianity and Liberalism* makes a clarion call to us to demarcate the radical difference of religion between orthodox Christianity and so-called liberalism, which is paganism by any other name.

In my own day and age, in the Rocky Mountain region, where

---

2. Ibid.
3. Ibid.

I held my last pastorate, we witnessed a PCUSA minister deny the entirety of the Apostles' Creed, the deity of Christ, his atoning death and resurrection, and the infallibility of Scripture; in that same church they preach from the gnostic gospels and affirm the LGBTQ agenda. All of these actions were done without rebuke or discipline by that church body (1 Tim. 5:20–21; Matt. 18:15–17), of which that minister remains a member—the very denomination that seventy years earlier excommunicated Machen.

Nearly one hundred years after its first publication, Machen's chapter titled "On the Church" is necessary reading for us. Now we have the sober witness of history, and it reads like the syncretistic history of Israel under Jeroboam. In the cause of liberalism, we have witnessed rampant idolatry in the form of a counterfeit clergy—men and women who, calling themselves Christian, offer not the light of the true Christ but only the gleam of the golden calves of ancient Bethel and Dan. Let Machen, Christ's faithful churchman, challenge all of us in our local churches, presbyteries, and general assemblies, to renew our labors for Christ, his kingdom, and his church, as we hold fast the Word of truth in our own darkening generation.

Rev. Dr. Alfred Poirier (DMin, Westminster Theological Seminary) is visiting professor of pastoral theology at Westminster Theological Seminary, where he holds the John Boyer Chair of Evangelism and Culture. Dr. Poirier is an ordained minister in the PCA, and author of *The Peacemaking Pastor: A Biblical Guide to Resolving Church Conflict*.

The Value of *Christianity and Liberalism* to World Missions

R. Kent Hughes

In 1811, at the establishment of Princeton Theological Seminary, the framers added a paragraph to the plan of the seminary that set forth a visionary purpose for the school: ". . . to found a nursery for missionaries to the heathen."[1]

Princeton's storied founders, Archibald Alexander and Samuel Miller, passionately embraced the vision. Early in the seminary's history, on the first Monday of each month, a concert for prayer was observed which concluded with a missionary address. Dr. Alexander characteristically "poured out stores of information" on foreign missions.[2] In 1821, newly appointed professor Charles Hodge wrote to his brother about the effect of the preaching of the distinguished missionary William Ward, a colleague of the famed William Carey, saying, "I never felt the importance and grandeur of missionary labors as I did last evening."[3] Dr. Hodge's *Systematic Theology* would later give precise, formative expression to the *pactum salutis* (covenant of redemption), which is the ground for salvation and world mission.[4]

Princeton Seminary would become a great force for world missions in the nineteenth century, as a veritable flood of mis-

---

1. David B. Calhoun, *Princeton Seminary,* vol. 1, *Faith and Learning, 1812–1868* (Edinburgh: Banner of Truth, 1966), 139.
2. Ibid., 141.
3. Ibid., 140.
4. Charles Hodge, *Systematic Theology,* vol. 2, (Grand Rapids, MI: Eerdmans, 1975), 358–361.

sionaries issued from her halls. Many of these missionaries died en route to or upon arrival at their primitive destinations, especially those traveling to Africa. During this time period, nine Princeton grads, including two of their wives, suffered violent deaths in China and India.[5]

Among the Princeton notables was William Thompson, who went to Beirut in 1832, where he helped to found the Syrian Protestant College that eventually became the American University of Beirut. In 1859, Thompson authored the immensely popular *The Land and the Book,* which, until 1900, was outsold only by Harriet Beecher Stowe's *Uncle Tom's Cabin.* In 1854, John Nevius went to China, where he served for more than forty years, establishing schools, traveling extensively, and writing on various topics. He is most famous for a two-month visit to Korea in 1890, where he taught the new missionaries his "Nevius Plan," a strategy for developing self-supporting churches that was wholly adopted and has contributed to the astonishing growth of the Korean church.[6] Ashbel Green Simonton, when challenged by one of Charles Hodge's sermons to embark on foreign missions, went to Brazil in 1859. During the eight remaining years of Simonton's short life, he founded the Presbyterian Church of Brazil as well as the first presbytery and seminary in that country.[7]

These are just a handful of stories that exhibit Princeton Seminary's outreach to the world in the nineteenth century—an influence that shines brightly in the annals of missionary history.

---

5. David B. Calhoun, *Princeton Seminary,* vol. 2, *The Majestic Testimony, 1869–1929* (Edinburgh: Banner of Truth, 1966), 23.

6. Ibid., 108.

7. David B. Calhoun, *Princeton Seminary,* vol. 1, *Faith and Learning, 1812–1868* (Edinburgh: Banner of Truth, 1966), 408.

In 1881, when J. Gresham Machen was born, modernist forces were already well at work in the Northern Presbyterian Church. They increased in power and influence during the turn of the century as young Machen matriculated at John Hopkins University and Princeton Seminary, and even further during his study abroad in Germany. There, Machen himself would come under the temporary thrall of modernist theologian Wilhelm Herrmann. But Machen's interaction with Herrmann and other modernists ultimately caused him to further embrace Reformed theology. Returning to Princeton Seminary in 1906, he joined the faculty as an instructor in New Testament, where his conservative and Reformed commitments deepened.

At Princeton, Machen became known for his ability to scripturally and intellectually defend orthodoxy against the gathering forces of modernism. His book, *The Origin of Paul's Religion*, published in 1921, established his reputation as a front-rank scholar and set the stage in 1923 for his famous volume, *Christianity and Liberalism*—which set forth the withering thesis that Christianity and liberalism were two separate religions, a proposition that continues to have cosmic implications for the gospel and world missions.

In *Christianity and Liberalism*, Machen wrote: "There is a profound difference . . . in the attitude assumed by modern liberalism and by Christianity toward Jesus the Lord. Liberalism regards Him as an example [for faith] . . . Christianity, the object of faith."[8] Therefore, the liberal regards religion as a mere means to a higher end. The liberal missiological change, as Machen saw it, was clearly evidenced in the way that missionaries commended

8. Pages 98–99 of this present volume.

their cause. "Fifty years ago," wrote Machen, "missionaries made their appeal in the light of eternity. 'Millions of men,' they were accustomed to say, 'are going down to eternal destruction; Jesus is a Saviour sufficient for all; send us out therefore with the message of salvation while yet there is time.'"[9] Thus, Machen penned this penetrating contrast between the missionaries of Christianity and those of liberalism:

> The missionary of liberalism seeks to spread the blessings of Christian civilization. . . The Christian missionary, on the other hand, regards . . . a mere influence of Christian civilization as a hindrance rather than a help; his chief business, he believes, is the saving of souls, and souls are not saved by the mere ethical principles of Jesus but by His redemptive work.[10]

Machen's analysis led to his pointing out, in the closing pages of *Christianity and Liberalism,* the folly of funding Presbyterian mission boards that support both kinds of missionaries so that donations are divided between them—in effect, canceling each other out dollar for dollar.[11] He questioned "whether evangelical congregations can honestly support agencies which are opposed to the evangelical faith."[12]

The stage was set for two monumental events. First, the establishment of Westminster Theological Seminary in 1929, when the PCUSA General Assembly voted to reorganize and

---

9. Page 155 of this present volume.
10. Page 160 of this present volume.
11. Pages 175–76 of this present volume.
12. Pages 176 of this present volume.

appointed two signatories of the liberal Auburn Affirmation as Princeton Seminary trustees. Second, the founding of the Independent Board for Presbyterian Foreign missions in 1932, when the Presbyterian Board of Missions failed to renounce the Rockefeller-funded, liberally calibrated volume, *Re-thinking Missions* by William Ernest Hocking.[13]

Machen's brilliant, landmark book, *Christianity and Liberalism,* provided the theological groundwork and rationale for the liberation and energization of Reformed orthodoxy that was needed to continue the divine mission of taking the Gospel to the lost world. As such, it continues to provide the pulsing rationale for Westminster Theological Seminary's ongoing commitment to train and equip men and women to bear the name of Christ to every tongue, tribe, and nation.

REV. DR. R. KENT HUGHES (DMin, Trinity Evangelical Divinity School) is professor of pastoral theology at Westminster Theological Seminary. He has more than 40 years of experience in pastoral ministry and is senior pastor emeritus of College Church in Wheaton, IL. Dr. Hughes is senior editor of the acclaimed Preaching the Word commentary series, and author of *Disciplines of a Godly Man* and *Liberating Ministry from the Success Syndrome.*

---

13. Referenced in D. G. Hart, *Defending the Faith: J. Gresham Machen and the Crisis of Conservative Protestantism in Modern America* (Phillipsburg, NJ: P&R, 2003), 147–51.

Machen and Scholarship

SANDY FINLAYSON

Machen's life was remarkably busy. Along with his regular labors at Westminster Theological Seminary and in the church, he accepted many invitations to speak and teach. One such invitation came to him from the Bible League of Great Britain, where he spoke on multiple occasions. First, in 1927, he presented three lectures that were focused on what the Bible teaches about Jesus. Then, in June of 1932, Machen again spoke at the same organization—this talk was subsequently published in a pamphlet titled, "The Importance of Christian Scholarship."[1] In these lectures, Machen challenged his audience to consider the role that Christian scholarship plays in the growth of the gospel. His message is as relevant today as it was then.

By 1933, Machen had a well-established reputation as a major New Testament scholar who frequently tackled controversial topics, such as the authority of Scripture, the virgin birth of Christ, and the claims of Paul's theology. He was unafraid to speak plainly to those with whom he disagreed, a fact that is strongly evidenced in *Christianity and Liberalism*. But this kind of posture required scholastic credibility. So, what was Machen's approach to scholarship? The addresses he gave at the Bible League provide a number of insights.

In these talks, Machen argued that the spirit of the age encouraged people to be skeptical, to question anything and every-

---

1. These talks have been collected in *What Is Christianity?* ed. Ned B. Stonehouse (Grand Rapids, MI: Eerdmans, 1951) and *Selected Shorter Writings,* ed. D. G. Hart (Phillipsburg, NJ: P&R, 2004).

thing. This phenomenon placed a heavy strain on Christianity, which places a high value on facts, evidence, and truth. No conservative Christian would have argued that truth should not be defended; the question was, how should it be done?

Humility was the first thing evident in Machen's approach. He began by saying, "it is no doubt unfortunate that the person who speaks about this subject should have so limited an experimental acquaintance with the subject, about which he is endeavoring to speak."[2] Of course, Machen could be accused of false modesty here. But it should be noted that while Machen's defense of the faith—in both his writings and interactions with others—could be harsh in tone, a genuinely irenic spirit permeated these lectures.

Given Machen's reputation as a staunch defender of Christian orthodoxy, some might expect him to begin a series of lectures on scholarship by outlining its importance as the key to defending Christianity. Instead, he begins by making the case that scholarship is essential for evangelism. For a man who was renowned as an apologist of Reformed orthodoxy, it is worth noting that his first argument is evangelistic. To be sure, the scholarship he calls for sets forth and defends the good deposit of the faith, but this again is for evangelistic purposes.

In contrast to those who claimed that a religious experience was the central element to Christian belief, Machen argued that the biblical model of evangelism calls for Christians to teach the facts of the gospel so that it may be known and believed. While faith in the person and work of Jesus Christ is at the heart of the gospel message, this faith is not a faith apart from knowledge. As

2. J. Gresham Machen, *The Importance of Christian Scholarship,* (London: The Bible League 1932), 3.

Machen said, the "New Testament gives not one bit of comfort to those who separate faith from knowledge, to those who hold the absurd view that a man can trust a person about whom he knows nothing."[3] Therefore, according to Machen, scholarship is necessary for a correct understanding of the Scriptures so that the truth of the gospel can be embraced. In a world where scholarship can be viewed as an end in itself, this is a helpful reminder.

Only after he had emphasized the outward, evangelical importance of scholarship did Machen turn his attention to the apologetic importance of scholarship. At this point in his life, he had already spent significant time defending the faith. In his these lectures, Machen urged his audience to be willing, trained, and ready to engage those who did not accept the truths of Christianity. To do this, he said, they needed to understand Christianity first and foremost. He stated explicitly that it was for this purpose that Westminster Theological Seminary was founded—to teach the doctrines of the faith. Rather than being merely defensive, a scholarly defense of the Christian faith, according to Machen, can "set the world aflame."[4] True scholarship, Machen said, must be characterized by being "open and above board . . . and always [observing] the Golden Rule."[5] In other words, treating those with whom we are engaging in the same way we would like to be treated.

Lastly, Machen told his audience that Christian scholarship was essential for the establishment and growth of a healthy church. He was quick to point out that sermons should not be lectures but rather shaped so as to build up the saints in their

3. Ibid., 11.
4. Ibid., 30.
5. Ibid., 24.

knowledge of the truth. And what truths should be most empha-sized? According to Machen, the "majesty of the transcendent God . . . the guilt and misery of man in his sin [and] the mystery of salvation."[6]

Machen's legacy—his defense of the virgin birth and the teachings of Paul, his classic call for defense of the faith in *Christianity and Liberalism*—is evidence that he took his own advice on scholarship seriously. While his efforts were not always ap-preciated, his passion for defending biblical truth was always present.

Machen's lectures on Christian scholarship, written more than eighty-five years ago, still ring true today. As Westminster Theological Seminary trains experts in the Bible, we must heed Machen's advice that scholarship is to be done so that the lost may be won for Christ, the church built up, and the glory of God revealed—and that all of this be carried out with integrity and humility of spirit.

ALEXANDER (SANDY) FINLAYSON (MLS, University of To-ronto; MTS, Tyndale Seminary) is library director and professor of theological bibliography at Westminster Theological Semi-nary. An ordained ruling elder in the OPC, he is the author of *Unity and Diversity: The Founders of the Free Church of Scotland* and *Thomas Chalmers*.

---

6. Ibid., 39.

Machen and Liberalism

R. Carlton Wynne

In the opening line of his classic work, *Christianity and Liberalism*, J. Gresham Machen declares his aim: to set before his readers "as sharply and clearly as possible"[1] the stark difference between biblical Christianity and the type of religious belief known as "liberalism" or "modernism." Christianity, he points out, relishes the supernaturalism of the God of Scripture and his activity in history, especially the miraculous incarnation and saving work of Jesus Christ, who now reigns over the cosmos as the risen Lord of glory. Theological liberalism, or, as Machen puts it, "modern naturalistic liberalism,"[2] on the other hand, redefines traditional Christian beliefs according to the intellectual and cultural assumptions of modern thought, in particular its unbounded confidence in human reason and its disdain for traditional authorities such as the Bible. As a result, liberalism utterly rejects the supernatural essence of the Christian faith, all the while deceptively deploying Christian terminology. The feature of liberalism that appropriates Christian language but distorts its meaning creates an appearance of godliness while denying its power (2 Tim. 3:5), and this makes it particularly insidious in the church. Indeed, since their rise at the turn of the nineteenth century, liberal ministers have indulged in "mere juggling with words"[3] that leads theologically untrained parishioners into a

---

1. Page 1 of this present volume.
2. Page 2 of this present volume.
3. Page 19 of this present volume.

pseudo-faith that, despite appearances, remains "anti-Christian to the core."[4]

But there is a God who knows (Exod. 2:23), and nearly a century ago he gifted Machen to articulate, in devastatingly clear terms, the internal absurdities that plague the liberal's belief system, anticipating an apologetic approach that would be developed at Westminster, where it is still taught today. Specifically, it was the Spirit of the ascended Christ who enabled Machen to penetrate liberalism's pious veneer and identify its deeply flawed framework and corresponding spiritual pitfalls.

To take but one example, Machen exposed that, at its most basic level, liberalism denies that the absolute, personal, triune God has revealed himself *as he is* to finite man. Instead, in liberalism's view, God freely wills to inhabit man's finite experience in a mode that is indistinguishable from the inviolable laws of nature, onto which modern man projects whatever ethical notions happen to be culturally fashionable. That is, liberalism holds that God does not relate to humans as their Creator and Lord so much as he accommodates his very being to the religious intuitions and values of every age. This was the view of the so-called "father of modern theology," Friedrich Schleiermacher (1763–1834), who could say reverently that God is to be found in everything only after he relegated everything—including God—into categories of modern knowledge and experience.

Machen discerned the root error of this natural religion. By sacrificing the "awful transcendence of God," he writes, "liberalism has lost sight of the very centre and core of the Christian teaching."[5] To be sure, "according to the Bible God is immanent

---

4. Page 164 of this present volume.
5. Page 63 of this present volume.

in the world. Not a sparrow falls to the ground without Him. But He is immanent in the world not because He is identified with the world, but because He is the free Creator and Upholder of it. Between the creature and the Creator a great gulf is fixed."[6] In other words, Machen argued, against liberalism, that the essential difference between the Creator and the creature is preserved in the very midst of God's immanence in creation and redemption. The God who is with those who are contrite and lowly in spirit always lives in a high and holy place (Isa. 57:15). Machen understood that once the "great gulf" between God and man is lost, all of God's activity *as God* in the world—including his judgment against sin, the incarnation of Christ, Jesus' historical death and resurrection, the Spirit's inspiration of the Bible, and his indwelling of the blood-bought church on earth—vanishes with it. Even worse, as liberalism eradicates the distinction between God and man, it redefines the history of redemption as merely symbolic of the deluded notion that "man at his best is one with God"[7]—ultimately because, as Machen saw, in liberalism, God at *his* best has become one with man.

Over against the humanized god of the liberals, *Christianity and Liberalism* spotlights the absolute God revealed in Scripture, particularly as Scripture recounts the divine Son's incarnation and his definite historical work of redemption, together with the one true gospel message that flows from it (cf. 1 Cor. 15:1–4; Rom. 1:1–6; Gal. 1:9). This is a transcendent, supernatural God whom sinners can know through faith in Christ by his Word and in whom they can and should rejoice.

Clearly, Machen's forceful demarcation between Christian-

6. Page 63–64 of this present volume.
7. Page 64 of this present volume.

ity and liberalism was much more than an intellectual exercise. It was an act of spiritual and cruciform devotion to the Lord Jesus Christ and an act of loving service in his kingdom, even at great personal cost to Machen himself. Secular intellectuals marveled at his deconstruction of American idealism but dismissed his religiosity. Fundamentalists cheered his defense of orthodoxy but did not appreciate his ecclesiology. Liberal Protestants assailed him as intolerant and even slanderous. But none could dispute his depiction of their ideas, which were always the focus of Machen's critiques, intent as he was to avoid attacking personally those ministers who espoused them.

Far more significant than any human response to his work, though, was Machen's desire to glorify the true and living God by keeping the Christian faith unsullied from spiritual degradation and doctrinal distortion. For he knew that "there is a river whose streams make glad the city of God, the holy habitation of the Most High" (Ps. 46:4), and those who taste of it are free, indeed. May the Most High God, our Redeemer, grant Westminster Theological Seminary the spiritual mind and gracious will to train pastors who will bring this cup of blessing, and no other, to a dry and needy world.

REV. DR. R. CARLTON WYNNE (PhD, Westminster Theological Seminary) is assistant professor of systematic theology and apologetics. An ordained minister in the PCA, he is co-editor and a contributor to *Zeal for Godliness: Devotional Mediations from Calvin's* Institutes.

Machen on the True Christian Religion

Lane G. Tipton

Machen's *Christianity and Liberalism* represents a milestone of confessional Presbyterian polemics that continues to influence my work in service of the church at Westminster Theological Seminary. Machen's claim is twofold. First, theological liberalism, contained in the works of Schleiermacher, Ritschl, Von Harnack, and Herrmann, advances theories of God, Scripture, man, sin, Christ, salvation, and last things that stand contrary to the teaching of the Word of God in the Scriptures of the Old and New Testaments. Thus, theological liberalism cannot confess with integrity the Ecumenical Creeds and Reformed Confessions of the church. Second, and as a consequence of this doctrinal deviation, theological liberalism is not the Christian religion. It is, in fact, a different religion altogether.

Given Machen's absolute claim that Christianity and liberalism represent different religions, Charles Erdman, a contemporary of Machen, vilified Machen as having a personality disorder that exhibited a morbid obsession with theological truth. Contemporary evangelicals similarly dismiss his Orthodox Presbyterian offspring as sharing in their spiritual father's malady. However, those who follow this line of thinking about Machen miss entirely the way that biblical doctrine led him to the deepest religious concern of the Christian religion—communion with the triune God.

For Machen, in light of the clear doctrinal teaching of Scripture concerning the eschatological kingdom of God, the Christian religion is "directed toward another world,"[1] where Christ is seated at the right hand of God in heaven. This means that Christianity, as a religion, cannot be a means to a higher end of producing a "healthy community"[2] that consists in the social utopia of the "universal fatherhood of God and the universal brotherhood of man."[3] This is the religion of liberalism. The Christian religion, by sharp contrast, offers deliverance "from the present evil age" (Gal. 1:4) to a "better country,"[4] that is, a heavenly country (Heb. 11:16).

In contrast to the "social gospel" of liberalism, Machen observed that "Christianity will produce a healthy community; but if it is accepted in order to produce a healthy community, it is not Christianity: Christianity will promote international peace; but if it is accepted in order to promote international peace, it is not Christianity."[5] The liberal subordination of Christianity to a "higher end" of social justice, cultural transformation, or political influence amounts to a "gospel" that has "little interest in religion for its own sake."[6] It has never occurred to those who follow this "gospel" to "enter into the secret place of communion with the holy God."[7]

Machen made clear the stark antithesis between the two religions. He argued, "According to Christian belief, man exists for

1. Page 156 of this present volume.
2. Ibid.
3. Page 18 of this present volume.
4. Page 156 of this present volume.
5. Page 156 of this present volume
6. Page 155 of this present volume.
7. Ibid.

the sake of God; according to the liberal Church, in practice if not in theory, God exists for the sake of man."[8] The religious conception that flows out of the Christian view is that "as a matter of fact heaven is communion with God and with His Christ. It can be said reverently that the Christian longs for heaven not only for his own sake, but also for the sake of God."[9] The higher end toward which Christianity directs us is the worship of the triune God in "union and communion" with the ascended Christ "in grace and glory" (Westminster Larger Catechism Q. 65). It is this precious truth that liberalism replaced with its naturalistic theories of doctrine and social action.

Machen argued that since liberalism is not the Christian religion but a different religion altogether, it should not be tolerated in the PCUSA or at Princeton Seminary. Liberalism sought a social utopia rather than the kingdom of God in Christ. Because they held to a different religion, Machen insisted that liberals do not find their lives hidden in heavenly places in union with the ascended Christ (Eph. 2:6), with the worship of the triune God as the central and most vital religious concern. When Machen expressed these points so boldly, it occasioned systematic and vicious opposition from those who loved this different religion. Machen was a witness to the "deeper Protestant conception" of Geerhardus Vos.[10] He suffered the reproach of godless men who denied the true religion and, as such, he

---

8. Page 158 of this present volume.

9. Page 152 of this present volume.

10. "According to our conception, our entire nature should not be free from God at any point; the nature of man must be worship from beginning to end. According to the deeper Protestant conception, the image does not exist only in correspondence with God but in being disposed toward God," Geerhardus Vos, *Reformed Dogmatics*, trans. and ed. Richard B. Gaffin Jr., et al., 5 vols. (Bellingham, WA: Lexham, 2014–2016), 2.13.

followed in the footsteps of his Lord and Savior, Jesus Christ (1 Pet. 2:21–25).

Machen fought so valiantly against liberalism because he walked in union with the ascended Christ of Scripture. Jesus Christ has passed from earth to heaven (1 Cor. 15:47), from condemnation to vindication (1 Tim. 3:16), from death to life (Rom. 6:10), in his redemptive-historical humiliation and exaltation to the right hand of God (Rom. 1:4; Heb. 8:1). It is *this* Christ whom Machen proclaimed and defended. Christ's historical suffering has given way to his consequent historical resurrection and ascension. Now, as ascended to the right hand of God and endowed with the Holy Spirit (Acts 2:33; 1 Cor. 15:45), he indwells his church by his Word and Spirit in a fellowship bond of suffering unto glory (1 Cor. 1:9; Rom. 8:17–18). A supernaturally effected, Spirit-forged communion bond with the glorified Christ conforms the church to his suffering and death (2 Cor. 4:7–11), so that, precisely in such suffering the church finds its "life" to be "hidden with Christ in God" (Col. 3:3). Christ's resurrection power at work in the church in this age consists in the fellowship of his sufferings and conformity to his death (Phil. 3:10).

Machen, knowing such a fellowship of suffering, passed into glory freed from suffering on January 1, 1937. He died of pneumonia that he developed as he was serving his small, wilderness-outpost denomination in the Dakotas. As he neared his death, he spoke of the glory of heaven and the beauty of the Reformed faith and expressed gratitude for the active obedience of Christ, which alone opens the gates of heavenly paradise. "No hope without it."

It is this message we ought to recall each time we think of the religious importance of Machen's *Christianity and Liberalism*. It is his example in Christ Jesus that I seek to emulate in all of my labors as an Orthodox Presbyterian minister of the gospel in my service at Westminster Theological Seminary.

REV. DR. LANE G. TIPTON (PhD, Westminster Theological Seminary) holds the Charles Krahe Chair of Systematic Theology and is associate professor of systematic theology at Westminster Theological Seminary. He is an ordained minister in the OPC, and co-editor of *Revelation and Reason: New Essays in Reformed Apologetics* and *Resurrection and Eschatology: Essays in Honor of Richard B. Gaffin, Jr.*

Salvation's Center:
The Sufferings of Christ
and the Glories that Follow

Iain Duguid

In his chapter titled "Salvation," Machen contrasts the Christian and liberal approach to the atonement. He points out that while modern liberal preachers do indeed sometimes speak of the atonement, "they speak of it just as seldom as they possibly can, and one can see plainly that their hearts are elsewhere than at the foot of the cross."[1] He goes on to point out that when such preachers do speak of the death of Christ, it is primarily in terms of its exemplary value as a model of self-sacrifice rather than as the atoning sacrifice that pays for our sins and reconciles us to God. Sadly, the same could be said of some contemporary evangelical preachers, whose messages are focused more on pressing people to live "morally successful" lives than on proclaiming Christ's atoning death and resurrection. In our day, like Machen's, there is plenty of preaching and teaching from the Bible that seeks to inculcate good behavior and healthy relationships, and that even mentions Jesus as our highest example. But all too often, there is no gospel in any of it.[2]

This is perhaps particularly true when it comes to contemporary reading and preaching from the Old Testament. The Old

---

1. Page 122 of this present volume.
2. See, for example, Michael S. Horton, *Christless Christianity: The Alternative Gospel of the American Church* (Grand Rapids, MI: Baker, 2008).

Testament is plundered for character studies and moral lessons, but, apart from a few messianic prophecies, is not regarded as fertile ground for preaching the gospel. Yet this is not how the New Testament teaches us to read the Old. Repeatedly, the New Testament summarizes the message of the entire Old Testament as "the sufferings of Christ and the glories that will follow." You can hear this on the lips of Jesus (Luke 24:25–27; 44–47), Peter (1 Pet. 1:10–11), and Paul (Acts 26:22–23). According to them, when you interpret the Old Testament correctly, you find that its focus is not primarily stories about moral improvement, or calls for social action, or visions concerning end-times events. The central message is Jesus—specifically, the atoning sufferings of Christ and the glories that will follow.

To be sure, understanding this gospel should lead to a new morality in the life of a believer. Jesus is indeed our example of how we ought to live. But the Christian gospel is not primarily about something we do. As Machen made clear, the gospel is about what God has done for us at a specific moment in history, through the cross of Christ that atones for our sins. What is "new" about the New Testament is not the gospel—for that was proclaimed, the New Testament tells us, from the very beginning. What is new is the complete fulfillment of God's promises, which, partially fulfilled in the Old Testament, now find their ultimate yes and amen in Christ (2 Cor. 1:20). It is from the historical reality of Christ's atoning work that the promised glories of the kingdom flow.

If this is the case, then that reality ought certainly to be reflected in our preaching, both from the Old Testament and the New Testament. The heart of our message must constantly be the proclamation of the atoning sufferings of Christ on the cross and his resurrection from the dead, emphasizing that it is through our faith in this death and resurrection that we become the first-fruits of a glorious new creation. Any message that is meant to merely inspire us to be better human beings—which could be preached equally well in a synagogue or rotary club—is not, at its core, a Christian sermon.

This reality ought also to be reflected in our singing. In *Christianity and Liberalism*, Machen identified "Nearer my God to Thee" as an example of a hymn which, though not opposed to Christianity, was defective. He pointed out that the only cross it mentions is our cross, not that of Christ.[3] What would Machen have to say about modern hymnody and praise music? Some songs, such as Keith Getty and Stuart Townsend's "In Christ Alone,"[4] would probably meet his hearty approval. Others, however, would be swiftly judged and tossed aside as lacking the necessary stamp of gospel-centeredness. We need to be discerning in what we sing as well as what we preach.

Indeed, like the Old Testament writers before him, the apostle Paul was content for his entire ministry to be summarized as the proclamation of Jesus Christ and him crucified (1 Cor. 2:2). Machen judged the same message to be the essential core of true Christianity and what fundamentally separates it from liberal counterfeits. May this gospel be at the center of all our preaching and ministry as well!

---

3. Page 131 of this present volume.
4. Words and music by Stuart Townsend and Keith Getty. © 2001 Thankyou Music.

Rev. Dr. Iain Duguid (PhD, University of Cambridge) is professor of Old Testament at Westminster Theological Seminary. Dr. Duguid is pastor of Christ Presbyterian Church (ARP) in Glenside, PA. He is the author of several books, including *Ezekiel* (NIVAC), *Is Jesus in the Old Testament?* and *Living in the Gap Between Promise and Reality: The Gospel According to Abraham.*

The Historicity of Adam: A Gospel Presupposition

JONATHAN GIBSON

In chapter three of *Christianity and Liberalism*, J. Gresham Machen makes the following statement: "The doctrine of God and the doctrine of man are the two great presuppositions of the gospel. With regard to these presuppositions, as with regard to the gospel itself, modern liberalism is diametrically opposed to Christianity."[1] He goes on to say that "at the very root of the modern liberal movement is the loss of the consciousness of sin."[2] We could extrapolate this and say that at the very root of modern liberalism is a loss of confidence in the historical Adam. For, without Adam, there is no ground for sin or the consciousness thereof. Indeed, without Adam, there is no ground for the gospel or the proclamation thereof.

In light of Machen's categorical statements, this short essay aims to reaffirm the historicity of Adam in the Bible and his significance for one of the great presuppositions of the gospel—namely, the doctrine of man.

Until the rise in popularity of Darwin's theory of evolution in the latter part of the nineteenth century, the Bible's claim that the human race originated in a first man called Adam was hardly questioned. Yet, in the centuries since, the church's confidence in the historical Adam has slowly eroded. The pressure to deny or re-interpret the historicity of Adam has come from both outside and

---

1. Page 55 of this present volume.
2. Page 65 of this present volume.

inside the church. Outside the church, scientific findings seem to call into question the Bible's account of mankind's common, and natural, descent from Adam. Inside the church, some pastors and scholars argue that a literal reading of Genesis 1–2 is misguided and serves only as an unnecessary obstacle to faith for skeptics in a secular age. We are informed that God has given us two books—the book of nature (general revelation) and the book of Scripture (special revelation)—and both must be read together. The Reformed tradition has always believed this to be true, of course, but with the important qualification that the latter has priority over the former. And so, in keeping with the Reformation principle of *sola scriptura*, we must turn to the Bible as our final authority on the historicity of Adam, whatever the claims of modern science.

In this regard, Scripture is both conspicuous and perspicuous. The opening chapters of Genesis—an historical narrative in genre—present Adam as the first man formed from the dust of the earth (2:7), with whom God entered into a covenant of works (2:16–17), and from whom God formed the first woman (2:18–25). Together, this first man and woman, named Adam and Eve, constitute the fountainhead of the human race. Three genealogies in the Bible find their origin in Adam (Gen. 5; 1 Chron. 1–8; Luke 3:23–38). Jude uses Adam as the alpha point of biblical history, describing Enoch as "the seventh from Adam" (v. 14). Jesus refers to Adam and Eve as the first married couple at the beginning of history (Matt. 19:4). The apostle Paul speaks of Adam as the "one man" from whom God made "every nation of mankind" (Acts 17:26), and he employs the order of their creation (Adam first, then Eve) to establish the role relationships of men and women in marriage and in the church (Eph. 5:31–32; 1 Cor. 11:8–9; 1 Tim. 2:11–14).

The historical Adam is also utilized in biblical teaching about sin and salvation. Hosea compares Israel's transgression of the covenant to that of Adam's (6:7), and Paul compares and contrasts the person and work of Adam, pre- and post-Fall, with that of Christ (Rom. 5:12–21; 1 Cor. 15:20–22, 45–49). The several passages of Scripture adduced here, from both Old and New Testaments, make it difficult for evangelicals to accept the suggestion that God intended Adam to be read as a mythical or metaphorical figure. Rather, he is presented, conspicuously and perspicuously, as a real, historical man, created from the dust of the earth and with the breath of God in him—the first living man of the human race.

Throughout *Christianity and Liberalism*, Machen makes the claim that Christianity is founded on the objective fact of an historical event (in contrast to human experience). Yet, he also points out that Christianity is not mere history. Christianity is a message. It is not simply about what happened, but also about the *meaning* of what happened. As he illustrates: "'Christ died'—that is history; 'Christ died for our sins'—that is doctrine."[3] For our purposes, the same could be said in relation to Adam: Adam fell—that is history; Adam fell into sin, as did "all mankind descending from him"[4]—that is doctrine.

In other words, the biblical presentation of Adam as the root of humanity is not a fact of mere historical interest. Rather, the historical Adam comprises one of the foundational *doctrines* of Christianity. This is because the Bible presents Adam as "a public

---

3. Page 27 of this present volume. On a related note, Machen continues: "Without these two elements, joined in an absolutely indissoluble union, there is no Christianity."

4. Westminster Shorter Catechism (A. 16).

person,"[5] upon whose shoulders rested the potential of eternal life or eternal death for all humanity. Paul speaks in no uncertain terms about the profound consequences of Adam's performance in the covenant of works:

> Therefore, just as sin came into the world through one man, and death through sin, and so death spread to all men because all sinned . . . many died through one man's trespass . . . one trespass brought condemnation . . . death reigned through that one man . . . one trespass led to condemnation for all men . . . so one act of righteousness leads to justification and life for all men. (Rom. 5:12, 15–18)

And elsewhere: "[B]y a man came death . . . in Adam all die" (1 Cor. 15:21–22).

These statements reveal that any denial or reinterpretation of Adam is like a seismic earthquake in the theological foundation of the gospel. No Adam? No sin, no guilt, no death. No sin, no guilt, no death? No Christ. No Christ? No gospel. No gospel? No salvation. No salvation? No hope. No hope? Then Christians, of all people, are to be most pitied (1 Cor. 15:19).[6] But Adam did exist in history, and he did fall in a garden, and, as a result, he brought sin, guilt, and death into the human race.

It is against the backdrop of this dark and depressing history

---

5. Westminster Larger Catechism (A. 22).

6. See Richard B. Gaffin, Jr., *No Adam, No Gospel: Adam and the History of Redemption* (Philadelphia, PA: Westminster Seminary Press, 2015), 10. Gaffin's helpful booklet presents similar themes reflected here.

of humanity that the light of the gospel of Jesus Christ shines most brightly. Adam was the first man, but Jesus Christ is the second and last man, the one whose work was so much more effective than Adam's:

> For if many died through one man's trespass, much more have the grace of God and the free gift by the grace of that one man Jesus Christ abounded for many… For if, because of one man's trespass, death reigned through that one man, much more will those who receive the abundance of grace and the free gift of righteousness reign in life through the one man Jesus Christ… Therefore, as one trespass led to condemnation for all men, so one act of righteousness leads to justification and life for all men. For as by the one man's disobedience the many were made sinners, so by the one man's obedience the many will be made righteous… as sin reigned in death, grace also might reign through righteousness leading to eternal life through Jesus Christ our Lord. (Rom. 5:15, 17–19, 21)

And elsewhere: "For as by a man came death, by a man has come also the resurrection of the dead. For as in Adam all die, so also in Christ shall all be made alive" (1 Cor. 15:21–22).

In short, where Adam brought sin, guilt, and death, Jesus Christ brought grace, justification, and resurrection life.

The contrast between Adam and Jesus Christ, as the two great Adamic figures of redemptive history (the alpha and omega points, respectively),[7] sheds light on Machen's claim that one of

---

7. "As Christ is the omega point of redemptive history, Adam is its alpha point" (Gaffin, *No Adam, No Gospel*, 10).

the great presuppositions of the gospel is the doctrine of man. As noted above, the doctrine of man necessarily entails a doctrine of Adam. Put differently, the gospel we defend and proclaim in the twenty-first century, as Machen did in the last century, does not make sense without the historical Adam. While the issues pertinent to Machen's day concerned liberal perspectives on the doctrine of God, the doctrine of man, the Bible, Christ, salvation, and the church, in our day the issue of Adam's historicity has become another touchstone of orthodoxy.

In his introduction to *Christianity and Liberalism*, Machen argues that the liberal attempt to reconcile Christianity with modern science "has really relinquished everything distinctive of Christianity." He goes on:

> In trying to remove from Christianity everything that could possibly be objected to in the name of science, in trying to bribe off the enemy by those concessions which the enemy most desires, the apologist has really abandoned what he started out to defend. Here as in many other departments of life it appears that the things that are sometimes thought to be hardest to defend are also the things that are most worth defending.[8]

This is no truer than when it comes to defending the historicity of Adam as one of the distinctive elements of the Christian gospel. If Machen was correct that Christianity "begins with the consciousness of sin"—that it is "the starting-point of all preaching"[9]—then Christian ministers must return Adam to the pulpit.

---

8. Pages 7–8 of this present volume.
9. Pages 67 and 65 of this present volume.

For, without Adam, there is no sin. And if there is no sin, then there is no Savior. As the first man, Adam is the point of comparison and contrast for the second and last man, Jesus Christ—not metaphorically, but metaphysically. Adam is one of the great presuppositions of the gospel; indeed, he is what makes Christ the great proposition of the gospel—a Savior worth proclaiming.

Rev. Dr. Jonathan Gibson (PhD, University of Cambridge) is assistant professor of Old Testament at Westminster Theological Seminary. An ordained teaching elder in the International Presbyterian Church, UK, he is the author of *Covenant Continuity and Fidelity: A Study of Inner-Biblical Allusion and Exegesis in Malachi* and co-editor of *Reformation Worship: Liturgies from the Past for the Present,* and *From Heaven He Came and Sought Her: Definite Atonement in Historical, Biblical, Theological, and Pastoral Perspective.*

Christianity and Liberalism and the Old Testament as History

ELIZABETH W. D. GROVES

In his book *Christianity and Liberalism*, J. G. Machen repeatedly emphasizes that Christianity cannot float in a vague, ethereal sea of timeless principles. Rather, it is and must always be tethered to the historical events that founded it—namely, the life, death, and resurrection of Jesus.

Historicity is similarly critical for the Hebrew Bible, which Christians call the Old Testament. It tells about a God who created the world, chose Abraham, and rescued his people from slavery in Egypt, among hundreds of other things. If these events did not really happen, if they are just legends or embellishments, then the Old Testament is no more than the musings of an ancient people about what sort of god they longed for. Both the legends and the god featured in them are, for people of other times and places, just a passing curiosity or a subject of scholastic research.

However, if the events that the Old Testament narrates really did happen in time and space as it records, then we see a God who exists independent of man's imaginings, who acted on his own initiative and according to his own plan, who is, in fact, *real*! That is something that is relevant to all people of all times.

Mercifully, gloriously, this God of the Bible is eager to be known, and is generous in his self-disclosure. Each time God acted in human history, he revealed something about himself to those who witnessed it or heard about it—just ask Rahab

(Josh. 2:9–11). But each revelation would have benefitted only the people of that time if God had not preserved a record for people of later generations. Yet he went beyond merely recording his deeds. As Machen says of New Testament history,[1] the biblical documents provide more than just the bare facts. In the Old Testament as well as the New, God also supplied his own explanation of the meaning of his actions, lest his people misapprehend him based on faulty interpretation of the events. For instance, God let Israel know that he sent the plagues on Egypt and parted the Red Sea not because he was grumpy, or bored, or vindictive, but to show them—and Egypt, and all the watching world—that he was mighty beyond imagining, had absolute authority, and was faithful to his people and his promises. In the unfolding show-and-tell throughout the history of the Old Testament, God both demonstrated and explained what he was like and what was on his heart.

Jesus, as Machen notes, held a high view of the truth and authority of the Old Testament as God's Word. When the question arose as to whether or not Jesus was God, the term "God" was not nebulous or pantheistic. For Israelites of the first century, it was filled with all of the rich content God had revealed about himself throughout the Old Testament. Because God recorded both his deeds and their interpretation, we today can know that rich content too, and can better understand what it means that Jesus is God.

Machen says that Jesus "was conscious of standing at the turning-point of the ages, when what had never been was now to come to be."[2] Throughout the Old Testament, God is presented as reigning over the affairs of men and the unfolding of history.

---

1. Page 29 of this present volume.
2. Page 32 of this present volume.

God was taking history somewhere, and that somewhere was the incarnation, life, death, and resurrection of his Son. Because God knew every detail of his unfolding plan of salvation in advance, he could embed symbols, types, and shadows of Jesus in every aspect of the Old Testament—not just in prophecy, but also in the very events of history and the structures of Israelite society. The signposts are present in God promising Adam and Eve a descendant who would defeat the serpent; in God providing a ram to die in Isaac's place; in the Passover; in the sacrificial system; in the judges, kings, prophets, and priests; in a boy from Bethlehem defeating the Lord's giant enemy; and in every other event in Old Testament history. All of it points forward to Jesus, as Jesus himself explained to his traveling companions *en route* to Emmaus.

As Machen emphasizes, it matters that Jesus really rose from the dead, and it also matters that God acted in human history leading up to that event, recording and interpreting his own actions in his Word. Thankfully, God continues to be involved with humanity in this broken world today as we look forward to Christ's second coming. To that end, Westminster aims to train men and women to love God and his Word—both Old and New Testaments—and to be instruments of his continued involvement in human history by sharing his incomparably good news.

ELIZABETH (LIBBIE) W. D. GROVES (MAR, Westminster Theological Seminary) is lecturer in biblical Hebrew at Westminster Theological Seminary. A member of the PCA, she is a contributor to the *ESV Women's Devotional Bible* and the author of *Grief Undone: A Journey with God and Cancer*.

Christianity and Liberalism
and Biblical Prophecy

STEPHEN M. COLEMAN

Perhaps more than any other portion of the Old Testament, the prophets were a favorite of the theological liberals of Machen's day. The reason for this is simple: Liberals saw in the prophets a mirror image of themselves—preachers whose great burden, they believed, was not so much to promulgate orthodox doctrine or to maintain precision in worship, but rather to cultivate a deep, religious sentiment toward God and a practical social justice toward neighbor. They looked to passages like Hosea 6:6 as paradigmatic for the entire prophetic enterprise: "For I desire steadfast love and not sacrifice, the knowledge of God rather than burnt offerings."

With little modification, this view of the biblical prophets is still alive and well today. Contemporary Marxist and liberation theologies interpret the prophets as essentially counter-cultural (if not revolutionary) figures, speaking for the marginalized and oppressed. According to this view, the prophets exposed and denounced the religious, political, and economic abuses in their day and in so doing offer us a model for political activism in our own. Unsurprisingly, this interpretation of the prophets as social reformers has made its way from the academy to the pulpit. Today, as in Machen's day, preachers continue to conscript the prophets in support of various social and political agendas, almost all of which seek, through human effort, to establish the kingdom of God in the here and now.

In addition to this old liberal view of the biblical prophets as preachers of religious sentiment and social justice, there is, in contemporary scholarship, a new interest in the cultural context of Israel's prophets and their messages. The chief tool employed in this endeavor is the cache of ancient Near Eastern literature, which shows broad similarities to the biblical material. Scholars have identified what they regard as prophet-like phenomena in texts from ancient Mari, Assyria, Ugarit, Egypt, and Persia, and have interpreted Israel's prophetic tradition in reference to the larger socio-religious landscape of the ancient Near East. The result is that the biblical prophets are now regarded by many as simply one more iteration of a common cross-cultural phenomenon of spiritual mediators and divine spokesmen.

Anyone who has read Machen's *Christianity and Liberalism* knows that he was quick to acknowledge truth in his opponents' arguments as well as areas in which they had genuine agreement. The same should be done here. It is certainly true that the biblical prophets showed great interest in issues of justice and righteousness in the public sphere. Their preaching took aim at the injustice and violence of Israel's political and religious leaders, and there is much that Christians today can and should learn from the prophets about the need to promote and pursue justice in every sphere of society. It is also true that the function of the prophet in Israelite society exhibits broad similarities to the function of similar figures in other cultures. The cross-cultural phenomenon of prophetism no doubt contributed in some way, however general, to ancient Israel's understanding of her own prophets. Consideration of such parallels may, in some instances, prove useful for interpretation.

However, neither the old liberal nor (for lack of a better term)

The

the new liberal understanding of the biblical prophets adequately capture the heart of the prophetic office and message as it is presented in the Bible. In both, the origin of the prophetic office and the content of the prophetic message is irreducibly human. The enduring relevance of Machen's *Christianity and Liberalism* is its sustained criticism of all efforts to reduce the Word of God to the word of man, the divine to the merely human. All attempts to do so, as Machen argued, are fundamentally non-Christian and motivated in many cases by an *a priori* preclusion of the supernatural. The conviction of the earliest Christians is well expressed by the apostle Peter who wrote, "For no prophecy was ever produced by the will of man, but men spoke from God as they were carried along by the Holy Spirit" (2 Pet. 1:21). Christianity is a supernatural religion. For Machen, this isn't an embarrassment to avoid but a necessary truth in which to delight. He writes, "The truly penitent man glories in the supernatural, for he knows that nothing natural would meet his need; the world has been shaken once in his downfall, and shaken again it must be if he is to be saved."[1]

In the final days of the southern kingdom, the prophet Jeremiah declared:

> Thus says the LORD of hosts: "Do not listen to the words of the prophets who prophesy to you, filling you with vain hopes. They speak visions of their own minds, not from the mouth of the LORD. They say continually to those who despise the word of the LORD, 'It shall be well with you'; and to everyone who stubbornly follows his own

---

1. Page 109 of this present volume.

heart, they say, 'No disaster shall come upon you.'" (Jer. 23:16–17)

The desire to hear (or preach) a message that comes from man's imagination and caters to man's longings was a temptation in Jeremiah's day, it was a temptation in Machen's day, and it is a temptation in our day (2 Tim. 4:3–4). However, like the biblical prophets before him, Machen understood that the hope for sinful men and women to be reconciled to a holy God could not be found in an emotional experience from within, but could only be found in a gospel message from without. Machen captures the irreconcilable difference between Christianity and liberalism well when he says, "The real authority, for liberalism, can only be 'the Christian consciousness' or 'Christian experience.' . . . The Christian man, on the other hand, finds in the Bible the very Word of God."[2] The biblical prophets were entrusted with this very thing: a word that has its origin not in the imaginations of man but in the mind and will of God.

The Christian faith, as Machen so powerfully reminds us, is not based on mere sentiment or human opinion, but on the facts of history as interpreted by divine revelation. Israel's prophets cannot be properly understood apart from God's revelation in redemptive history, especially the covenant that established their office and defined the nature of their work (Deut. 17:15–18). The ultimate foundation for our interpretation of the biblical prophets, therefore, is not divination at Mari or shamanism in India, but the peculiar covenant relationship established by God with Israel at Mt. Sinai. The prophetic message of divine judgment

---

2. Page 80 of this present volume.

and mercy is rooted in the terms of this covenant, specifically in the promises of blessings for obedience and curses for disobedience (Deut. 28). Ultimately, however, the prophetic word was a word about the Christ who would come as the second Adam and faithful Israel and who, though perfectly obeying the terms of the covenant, would suffer the covenant curses on behalf of his people when he died on the cross for their sins (Luke 24:27).

Christianity and Liberalism continues to offer the critical reminder that the prophetic word is an utterly unique message about God, man, Christ, and salvation. Israel's hope rested not on their religious sentiment, nor on their own ability to fulfill all righteousness (as the Babylonian exile clearly attests), but on the divine word of promise that God would one day act in history to finally and definitively secure the redemption of his people from the curse of sin and death. Christians today enjoy the even greater privilege of knowing Jesus as the fulfillment of that prophetic word that predicted "the sufferings of Christ and the subsequent glories" (1 Pet. 1:11).

Rev. Dr. Stephen M. Coleman (PhD, The Catholic University of America) is assistant professor of Old Testament at Westminster Theological Seminary, and senior research fellow at the J. Alan Groves Center for Advanced Biblical Research. Dr. Coleman previously served as associate pastor at Wallace Presbyterian Church in College Park, Maryland from 2008–2017. He is an ordained teaching elder in the PCA, and the author of *Haggai, Zechariah, and Malachi: A 12-Week Study*.

Machen and Christ's View of the Old Testament

G. K. BEALE

J. G. Machen perceived that the authorship of the Bible was under attack by the liberalism of his day, as it is in our own day. Liberal theologians were not only critiquing the general authority of the Bible, they were deconstructing its messages and doubting its authors. Are the details of authorship really important to our redemption? In Machen's words, "Must we . . . depend upon what happened so long ago? Does salvation wait upon the examination of musty records?"[1] To such questions, Machen would offer a resounding, "Yes!" But why? One reason is that Jesus and the New Testament authors made assumptions and claims about such authorship. If we are to follow Jesus faithfully and the New Testament authors who witnessed to him, we must take him at his word, even when that word is a reference to the Old Testament author of his quotations.

Machen understood this. In the chapter entitled "The Bible," from *Christianity and Liberalism*, Machen says that "our Lord Himself seems to have held the high view of the Bible which is . . . rejected . . . [by] modern liberalism."[2] In line with that claim, this essay will flesh out one aspect of Christ's view of the Old Testament, which will support Machen's view—a view that not only "liberals" but also several evangelical scholars reject. Jesus

---

1. Page 72 of this present volume.
2. Pages 77–78 of this present volume.

and the New Testament writers attribute numerous quotations from the book of Isaiah to the prophet Isaiah—the real historical *person*. Some believe that Jesus and the New Testament writers refer only to a literary collection of writings known as "Isaiah," so that such allusions do not have to be understood as referring to a personal prophet whose handprint stamps the whole work. Others believe that Jesus' intention was to focus on communicating only the meaning of the prophecy. In either case, some evangelical scholars contend that if Jesus and the gospel writers did not intend to communicate the identity of the human author, they cannot be charged with inaccuracy, even if a real person known as "Isaiah" did not actually write the entire book. Some also argue that the belief of early Judaism and Christianity (including that of Jesus) in the authorship of the whole book of Isaiah was not historically correct but that such a conviction had become part of the socially constructed Jewish tradition. In such a case, Jesus would be either ignorant of the truth that Isaiah did not write all of the book, and so was mistaken, or he knowingly accommodated himself to the false Jewish tradition.

One way to attempt to answer the question of whether or not the personal prophet Isaiah was held to be the author of the quotations of Isaiah in the New Testament is to examine those quotations. The following represents the references to Isaiah mentioned by Jesus or the synoptic gospel writers (Matthew, Mark, and Luke). This list shows that throughout the synoptic Gospels there are references to quotations from all parts of the book of Isaiah that are attributed to the person of Isaiah.[3]

---

3. I have added italics to emphasize the expressions that draw attention to the personal agency attributed to Isaiah.

Matt. 3:3 For this is he who was spoken of *by the prophet Isaiah when he said* . . .

Matt. 4:14 So that what *was spoken by the prophet Isaiah* might be fulfilled . . .

Matt. 8:17 This was to fulfill what *was spoken by the prophet Isaiah* . . .

Matt. 12:17 This was to fulfill what *was spoken by the prophet Isaiah* . . .

Matt. 13:14 In their case the *prophecy of Isaiah* is fulfilled that says . . .

Matt. 15:7 "You hypocrites! *Well did Isaiah prophesy of you* . . ."

Mark 1:2 As it is written *in Isaiah the prophet* . . .

Mark 7:6 And he said to them, "*Well did Isaiah prophesy of you* hypocrites, as it is written . . ."

Luke 3:4 As it is written *in the book of the words of Isaiah the prophet* . . .

Luke 4:17 And the scroll *of the prophet Isaiah* was given to him. He unrolled the scroll and found the place where it was written . . .

The above list does not include significant allusions to Isaiah (e.g., Mark 10:45 and Isa. 53:10–12). There is allusion not typically to the "prophecy" or "prophecies" of Isaiah but to "Isaiah" as a "prophet," as a *person*. These references point to the active, personal role of Isaiah in writing and prophesying in all parts of the book. What is more, these references to Isaiah do not provide sufficient evidence to conclude that they are the insignificant husk that surrounds the real message intended. Rather, they are *part of* the message. In Machen's words, they are part of the purported "musty records" upon which our salvation depends. It is important to Jesus and the New Testament writers that a personal prophet named "Isaiah" actually wrote the prophecies attributed to him, as God inspired him to write those prophesies before they were fulfilled.

Some are persuaded, however, that the above references were part of an understandable stylistic convention, taken from a socially constructed tradition. Consequently, they say, it is only natural that Jesus himself expressed this belief, as he *was* human and accepted the various customs of his Jewish culture, even if they were unbiblical or historically untrue. This is sometimes understood as part of the kenosis theory of Christ's incarnation, whereby he emptied himself or gave up the use of his divine attributes. Accordingly, he was, in part, a typical person of his time and culture, naturally and unconsciously accepting some of the untrue traditions of that culture. This may be referred to as an unconscious accommodation of Jesus to his culture.

Yet any assertion that Christ makes about past, present, or future reality has a truthful force that cannot be blunted.[4] Matthew 24:35 says that no matter how many cultures come and go, Christ's Word remains the same. Cultures with their own idiosyncratic beliefs will rise and fall until Christ comes a final time; this "heaven and earth will pass away, but my [Christ's] words will not pass away." The truth of Christ's words and teachings

---

4. I am grateful to J. I. Packer, *'Fundamentalism' and the Word of God* (Grand Rapids, MI: Eerdmans, 1957), 60–61, for this point about the link between Matt. 24:35 and 24:36. In this connection, note also B. B. Warfield's comment on Christology: "in the case of our Lord's person, the human nature remains truly human while yet it can never fall into sin or error because it can never act out of relation with the Divine nature into conjunction with which it has been brought" (*The Inspiration and Authority of the Bible* [Phillipsburg, NJ: Presbyterian and Reformed, 1948], 162 [cited by Packer, ibid., 83]).

are not culturally bound but transcend all cultures and remain unaltered by cultural beliefs. That is the clear truth that stands in the way of theological liberalism, and there is no way around it—not for Machen's contemporaries, and not for our own.

Others contend that Jesus, as the God-man, may well have known that Isaiah was not the author of the work that went by his name, but that he consciously accommodated himself to the false Jewish view in order to facilitate his communication of the theological message from the book.

There is a common problem with both of these perspectives about Christ's accommodation: it is clear that part of Jesus' mission was to confront and expose the false traditions of Judaism that had grown and were held by the first century.[5] J. I. Packer aptly concluded that Jesus "did not hesitate to challenge and condemn, on His authority, many accepted Jewish ideas which seemed to him false."[6] For instance, the Jews believed that since a well-known Old Testament figure, Moses, was the author of their oral law, their oral laws had equal authority with the written Scripture that had also come from Moses.[7] Jesus says that such traditions did *not* have the authority of Mosaic Scripture. In fact, in Mark 7:1–13, Jesus contrasts Isaiah's prophesying (v. 6, citing Isa. 29:13) and Moses's written word (v. 10), which had divine authority, with "the tradition of the elders," which has

---

5. N. B. Stonehouse, *The Witness of Matthew and Mark to Christ* (Philadelphia: Presbyterian Guardian, 1944; repr. Grand Rapids, MI: Eerdmans, 1958), 195–211, and R. V. G. Tasker, *The Old Testament in the New Testament* (Grand Rapids, MI: Eerdmans, 1954), 32. I am thankful to Packer, *'Fundamentalism,'* p. 56, n. 2, for alerting me to these two sources.

6. *'Fundamentalism,'* 55.

7. J. Neusner, "Rabbinic Literature: Mishnah and Tosefta," in *Dictionary of New Testament Background*, ed. C. A. Evans and S. E. Porter (Downers Grove, IL: IVP, 2000), 895.

no divine authority. Therefore, while Jesus opposed the pseudo-authority of untrue Jewish traditions, he always affirmed the definitive authority of the Old Testament (e.g., John 10:35: "Scripture cannot be broken") and "never qualified the Jewish belief in its absolute authority in the slightest degree."[8]

In light of this, is it possible that Jesus would have gone along with a false Jewish view about the authorship of Isaiah? It is unlikely, especially as the Old Testament was foundational for Jesus' teaching and thought concerning his vocation and identity. Is it likely that he would knowingly or unknowingly be wrong about who was the authoritative author of Isaiah? Again, it is unlikely. And if he were wrong here, why should we have confidence that he was not also wrong in his other important appeals to the Old Testament?[9]

In short, none of the above views are sufficiently compatible with the use of Isaiah in the New Testament except the perspective that understands that these are references to the actual prophet Isaiah, who wrote the entire book that goes by that name.

Following the sentiment of Machen and his reproach of the liberalism he encountered, this essay has shown that the New Testament's repeated affirmation of Isaiah as the personal author of the entire book bearing that name is clear and probable. The obvious New Testament stance on this topic confirms the long-established arguments within the book of Isaiah itself that the prophet Isaiah authored the complete book.

In the spirit of Machen, we must continue to uphold the

---

8. *'Fundamentalism,'* 55.
9. Ibid., 60, though Packer is speaking generally about Christ's view of the authority of the Old Testament.

details of every purported "musty record" of the Bible, including the authorship of particular books. When authorship is threatened, so is the message and the meaning. Only by upholding it can we be faithful to Jesus and the New Testament authors and push back against the liberalism of our own day.[10]

Rev. Dr. Gregory K. Beale (PhD, University of Cambridge) holds the J. Gresham Machen Chair of New Testament and is research professor of New Testament and biblical interpretation at Westminster Theological Seminary. He is an ordained minister in the OPC, and author of *The Temple and the Church's Mission*, and *A New Testament Biblical Theology*.

---

10. This essay is an adapted summary of Beale, Gregory K. *The Erosion of Inerrancy in Evangelicalism: Responding to New Challenges to Biblical Authority*, (Wheaton, IL: Crossway Books, 2008) 123–59.

Christianity and Liberalism
and the Gospels

BRANDON D. CROWE

Central to *Christianity and Liberalism* is the need for a proper understanding of doctrine, not least with respect to the person of Jesus. Machen makes it clear that liberal—or modernistic— approaches to the Gospels are inconsistent and uncompelling. Several aspects of Machen's thought are abidingly relevant for studying the Gospels today.

First, the Gospels are not primarily about grand ideas, but they are about Jesus—about who he *really* is and what he *really* did. This point may seem obvious, but it has not always been taken for granted. It certainly was not in Machen's day. Jesus cannot be understood simply as a great moral teacher, for he claimed much more than that about himself. He came to accomplish the work of salvation.

As Machen avers, a non-historical reading of the Gospels devolves into mysticism. The Christian message—which centers on Christ, the supernatural Son of God—is rooted in history. Though there continue to be studies of the Gospels today that downplay the historicity of the events narrated, we must remember that the message of the Gospels is rooted in what Jesus has actually done. And what has happened in history really matters, as Luke states starkly in his prologue (Luke 1:1–4).

Second, it is not our task to sift the Gospels to identify what the historical Jesus "really" said. A reconstructed and non-supernatural Jesus is not the Jesus of history, nor is it the Jesus of the Gospels. To put one's faith in a reconstructed Jesus is to put one's faith in the subjective principles and methods used by fallible revisionists. The inspired texts must be our authorities, rather than reformatted texts that distort the presentations of the evangelists. Though his point is a bit different, one is reminded of Irenaeus's warning about those who misinterpret the Scriptures and turn a beautiful mosaic of a king into a picture of a dog—they are weaving ropes of sand (*Against Heresies* 1.8.1). So it is with those who cut and paste from the Gospels.

Third, the Gospels are supernatural through and through. Jesus is a supernatural Savior who has come to save sinners. It is clear that he viewed himself as the Messiah throughout his ministry, and he explicitly states that he came to give his life as a ransom (Mark 10:45). Indeed, Machen argues that the atonement only makes sense if Jesus is divine—for what good does the self-sacrifice of a noble man accomplish if that sacrifice is merely an example that cannot save another? There must be something unique about Jesus that enables his sacrifice to be efficacious and salvific. This means the Gospels are good news. Machen argues that the substitutionary death of Christ is predicated upon the uniqueness of Christ himself, and that this anticipates the great miracle of the resurrection. Christ is no mere man, yet he is truly man. He is the divine Son of God, and all four Gospels testify to this. This point is not merely academic. Jesus has come to deal with the real problem of our sin in a way that only he can. He is the answer a sinful world needs. This is the Savior whom we meet in the Gospels, and in whom we must believe.

Brandon D. Crowe (PhD, University of Edinburgh) is associate professor of New Testament at Westminster Theological Seminary, and book review editor for the *Westminster Theological Journal*. He is an ordained teaching elder in the PCA, author of *The Last Adam*, and co-editor of *The Essential Trinity*.

Christianity and Liberalism and Hermeneutical Presuppositions

VERN S. POYTHRESS

"In the sphere of religion, in particular, the present time is a time of conflict; the great redemptive religion which has always been known as Christianity is battling against a totally diverse type of religious belief, which is only the more destructive of the Christian faith because it makes use of traditional Christian terminology."[1]

At the time that J. Gresham Machen wrote his groundbreaking book, *Christianity and Liberalism*, many people had foggy ideas about the nature of Christianity. On the surface, it seemed that liberalism offered merely one more variation on the general theme of Christianity. And indeed, that was how liberals considered themselves. They thought they were working within the framework of Christian faith in order to bring it up to date. They tried to display more clearly and accurately its essential features, while discarding doctrines that modern thinking had shown to be obsolete.

Machen's examination dug down to the religious root. At the root, said Machen, we have two different religions: Christianity and liberalism. The one contradicts the other at many crucial points.

---

1. Page 2 of this present volume.

Machen did not focus his examination primarily on hermeneutics, but his book has implications for the subject. The two
religions produce two distinct sets of hermeneutical presuppositions; this difference in turn produces widespread differences
in interpreting the individual texts of the Bible, and in shaping
overall thinking on any given topic. These differences remain
with us today, which is why Machen's book still has relevance,
specifically for our study of hermeneutics, God, and history.

Christianity, as unfolded in the Bible, is a religion that believes in a God who is continually involved in the world, even
to its minutest detail—including the number of hairs on our
heads (Matt. 10:30). He works in ordinary ways (providence)
and extraordinary ways (miracles), as he chooses. Liberalism,
by contrast, denies miracles—or is at least deeply skeptical of
them. So, before the liberal even opens the Bible to see what it
says, he is committed in principle to explaining away its miracles—either as misunderstandings of natural events, or as exaggerated or mythic representations built upon fluid human
traditions.

The differences affect what we think about the Bible. What
kind of book is it? What kind of communication does it contain? Christianity claims it is the Word of God, written through
human beings inspired by the Holy Spirit. Therefore, herme-
neutically, Christian interpretation treats the Bible as different
from all other books—it is the infallible Word of God. Liberalism, on the other hand, believes in a kind of "inspiration," but
that inspiration is redefined as a mere heightening of human
energies directed toward the divine. Therefore, liberalism views
the Bible as fundamentally equal to all other human endeavors.

The differences affect what we think about divine communication and language as well. Christianity believes that God gives the gift of language to human beings, and that therefore language is a suitable instrument through which God effectively communicates truth. Liberalism believes that language is a purely human product, and that religious language reaches out toward a God who, in the end, escapes linguistic particulars.

Furthermore, the differences affect what we think about Jesus Christ. Is he the divine Son of God? Or is that a dispensable viewpoint theorized by fallible human interpreters? If he is the divine Son of God, we positively expect miracles to come as part of the comprehensive work of salvation that he descended from heaven to accomplish. If he is merely the greatest human teacher of religion and morality, the miracles are dispensable, as are the accounts of his death, resurrection, and ascension.

The differences between Christianity and liberalism continue to propagate in biblical studies, and are, if anything, more pervasively influential than in Machen's day. The hermeneutical presuppositions of liberalism are the presuppositions of modernity and secularity—a vision of a world that consists of matter and human beings without the presence and activity of God. Among the elite thinkers of the West, these presuppositions dominate the hermeneutical project of interpreting the world. Christians who are unaware of these presuppositions may unwittingly swallow corrupting bits of their teaching. While these Christians may try to retain the divine authority of the Bible and its content, their *hermeneutics* gradually become modernist. Over and against this temptation, Machen's antithesis is a useful reminder.

Rev. Dr. Vern S. Poythress (PhD, Harvard; DTh, Stellen-bosch) is distinguished professor of New Testament and biblical interpretation at Westminster Theological Seminary, where he has taught for 42 years. He is an ordained teaching elder in the PCA, and the author of several books, including *Theophany: A Biblical Theology of God's Appearing* and *Knowing and the Trinity: How Perspectives in Human Knowledge Imitate the Trinity.*

Index of Scripture References in *Christianity and Liberalism*

Index of Subjects and Names in *Christianity and Liberalism*